9ᵗʰ Dec 1963

Dear Bill

might ... I th...t you
over ... ... this

Sydney

Spice of
Life

The Author at Clayton Windmills

Henry Longhurst

Spice of
Life

WITH A PREFACE BY

Lord Brabazon of Tara P.C. G.B.E. M.C.

CASSELL · LONDON

CASSELL & COMPANY LTD
35 Red Lion Square · London WC1
and at
MELBOURNE · SYDNEY · TORONTO
JOHANNESBURG · CAPE TOWN · AUCKLAND

———

Printed in Great Britain
by Ebenezer Baylis and Son, Ltd.
The Trinity Press, Worcester, and London
F. 863

Preface

I am one of those, and I find that I am not alone, who, when early on the Sabbath a pile of Sunday papers is thrown upon my bed, thereby rousing me to consciousness, completely ignore the various world crises that arise every week, and start my perusal of these stimulating periodicals by reading Henry Longhurst on golf, after which, there being nothing else to read, I go to sleep again.

That anyone can week after week amuse and entertain us on such a hackneyed theme as golf, is indeed a high tribute to Henry Longhursts' genius, but it also follows that he should be equally entertaining when touching on his experiences in life in other fields. How true this is, and therefore let us indeed welcome this book, in which he has combined in one volume pieces of writing, none of which has anything to do with golf.

This book should be kept by the bedside, and one piece read per night, no more, so that the book really lasts a long time. I know of no pleasanter experience, when endeavouring to pass into the unconsciousness of sleep, than for my mind to be chortling with pleasure at the quaintness and humour of a Longhurst Gem.

And how we dart about! A ride on a fast locomotive—experiences in Parliament—the art of rat-catching—American football—Army experiences—riding the Cresta at St. Moritz—Chicago and Shanghai—flying in a Chinese airliner.

To meet Henry in the flesh is always a stimulating experience; his mere presence makes one purr with friendship and affection, but we can't all have this experience, so the next best thing is to share with him some of his experiences, so deftly and interestingly told in *Spice of Life*.

I know I shall earn the gratitude of everyone whom I can persuade to read this book.

Contents

Foreword

It was comparatively late in my life that a friend crystallized in a single phrase a philosophy by which I realize, on looking back, I have always been influenced. This was 'You don't miss what you've had'.

In other words, what you miss is what you might have had *then*, but didn't, and for one reason or another cannot have now. It is not the fish he caught that the fisherman remembers but the 'ones that got away'.

I have always gone on the principle of what I have come to think of in my own mind as 'gap-filling'—namely doing anything once if you have not done it before and going anywhere once if you have not been there before and, though there have been occasions when it has not been worth the time and the effort, this principle has on the whole paid handsome dividends in the variety of memories and impressions with which it has left me. It is this variety, truly the spice of life, that I modestly hope may entertain the reader.

H.L.

Clayton Windmills
Hassocks, Sussex.

September 1963

TRANSATLANTIC

Nightmare over Niagara

Of all the curious situations in which everyone has at some time imagined himself, such as deep-sea diving, or being hanged, or standing for Parliament, none takes a more universal place than walking Niagara on a tightrope or going over the top in a barrel. For more than a century the place has exercised an uncanny fascination over otherwise sensible people, inspiring them to deeds of useless daring, rewarded, if not by death, by nothing better than the meagre results of taking the hat round afterwards. There is a whole saga of hair-raising episodes by which successive adventurers, women as well as men, chanced or threw away their lives—the barrel enthusiasts over the Horseshoe Falls, under which there is a 190-foot pool, the tightrope merchants over the gorge farther down.

If you tried for a month of Sundays, you would come nowhere near guessing what manner of person first went over Niagara in a barrel. It was a buxom, twelve-stone, middle-aged schoolmistress, Mrs. Anna Taylor. What put the idea into her head, no one knows. Her barrel was little more than an overgrown whisky keg, reinforced with steel hoops and ballasted by a small blacksmith's anvil, which by all the laws of physics should have shot out of the bottom.

Inserting a small kitten she sent it over the Falls on a trial run. When she opened it, the kitten was dead. Next morning, October 4, 1901, sharply reminding would-be dissuaders to mind their own business, the indomitable Mrs. Taylor eased herself into her barrel. Thousands watched as the lid was clamped down and she was cast off, trusting that the middle current would catch her appalling conveyance and toss it into the pool below. Meanwhile her manager retired to a bar and averted his eyes.

Three hours later, bruised, battered, but by no means bewildered, and with the bun on her head still neatly in place, she was hauled alive from her barrel. Having promptly sacked the manager for dereliction of duty in retiring to the bar, she set herself up as the 'Queen of the Mist' and, posing beside a replica of her barrel, cashed in by signing autographs— a tight-waisted, corseted, thoroughly Victorian personage with ground-length skirt and a vast feathered hat—one of the most unlikely figures, perhaps, of all time.

Ten years later, as Mrs. Taylor lay dying, penniless and forgotten, a

3

London cockney, Bobby Leach, took the plunge in a steel barrel. His reward was a smashed jaw, two broken knee-caps, twenty-three weeks in hospital, and the misfortune later to kill himself by slipping on a piece of orange peel in New Zealand.

The next outbreak of Niagara fever erupted in 1930, when another Englishman, Charles Stephens, a man with more children than sense— he had eleven—went over in a crude barrel with an anvil strapped to his feet as ballast. When the apparatus struck the pool, poor Stephens and the anvil shot out of the barrel like a bullet. All they found of him was one arm, wrenched from its socket, still fixed in the harness.

Not long afterwards a Greek waiter, George Stathakis, went over in a rather superior barrel, which survived the drop but remained caught in the swirling cauldron behind the Falls. His oxygen was good for only three hours and, when they retrieved him fourteen hours later, he had died of suffocation.

With the score now two-all, man, in more than one sense, won the rubber. Before the authorities at last put a stop to these adventurous antics (a fellow was forcibly restrained from going over in a barrel only the other day) Jean Laussier beat them all by going over in a six-foot rubber ball. With oxygen for forty hours he shot gracefully over, bobbed his way down the rapids, and was pulled from his harness fifty minutes later without a scratch.

For the succession of men and women who shot the Lower Rapids sealed in canisters, and the manner of their various deaths, I have no space—except, perhaps, to record that our own Captain Webb, having conquered the Channel, poor fellow, but not his own financial affairs, stepped in to swim the Rapids and was swept within a few seconds to extinction.

We come instead to the tightrope walkers and the Awful Moment. The rope was stretched by a horse-drawn winch over the gorge below the present bridge, sagging in the centre, with its ends 200 feet above the seething waters below. The gorge itself is 1,100 feet across— wide enough to make the people look like midgets on the opposite cliff.

Either you can stand heights, or you cannot. Either you can walk a tightrope, or you cannot. If you can, I suppose there is little difference in risking death by dropping from a circus rope or from a rope across Niagara. So we will pass over the various professionals who made the crossing—stopping only to lift our hats to Samuel Dixon, who, on his way home from a photographers' convention at Toronto, noticed the rope, acquired some plimsolls, tights, and a pole, and thereupon walked across as an amateur—and will revert to the first and greatest of them all, Jean François Gravelet, son of one of the heroes of Napoleon's army, otherwise known as Blondin.

A thin cadaverous man with matted hair and beard, Blondin is synonymous with tightrope-walking, and presumably, since none may now simulate his feats, always will be. He first walked Niagara in 1859. A year later he was back, his name a household word all over the world, with the Prince of Wales (later Edward VII) and President Millard Fillmore among the spectators. He put on such a show as made women tear handkerchiefs to shreds and strong men bite their nails to the quick. He ran to and fro, slipping deliberately, in a swirl of legs and arms and recovering himself. He walked across backwards; with baskets on his feet; and on stilts. He lowered a mug, and, hauling it up, drank the waters he defied. He held out his hat at arm's length and the local sharpshooter from the Maid of the Mist put a bullet through it. Finally he took out a portable stove, squatting on the rope, and cooked and ate an omelet. At last it seemed there was nothing more for him to do. At this moment there steps into the picture a man who to me is one of the unsung heroes of all time—Blondin's manager, Harry Colcord, of Chicago.

It was the manager's idea. Somehow they had to go on attracting the crowds. What about taking a man across on his back? Splendid, said Blondin—and we may imagine the scenes that followed. 'What about you, sir? Nice chance to achieve fame and fortune. . . . All over in a few minutes. . . . No? Well, you, sir? Come along, sir. . . . No. . . ?'

At what point the dreadful inspiration entered Colcord's head we do not know. We may surmise, without doing him posthumous injustice, that he had been drinking at the time.

'I suppose,' he said, 'I shall have to do it myself.'

Now Colcord had never in his life stepped on a tightrope. So, while we may never envisage ourselves in Blondin's position, we can without the least stretch of imagination see ourselves in the manager's.

When the great day came, 100,000 people assembled on the banks. Betting was fast and furious. The odds were even money.

The manager, as big a man as Blondin, took off his coat and mounted the maestro's back, and a moment later the pair embarked on their frightful expedition. On the downward journey all went well, but, as they mounted the slope on the other side, their pace was seen gradually to slacken. Amid a muttered rumbling of speculation among the watchers on the cliffs they came to a full stop.

Let us leave the watchers and focus our attention upon the nightmare predicament of the two figures balancing over the abyss. This is the Awful Moment.

'It is no good,' Blondin is saying, 'I am exhausted. *You will have to get down!*'

The reader may be left to imagine for himself what surged through the manager's head; the appeals to the Almighty to spare him but this once, and never again . . .; the urging-on of his exhausted steed; the dread realization; the frantic groping of his shiny shoes for the rope invisible behind and below.

Somehow he made it, and for minutes they stood upon their awful perch, the maestro panting to recover his strength, Colcord clutching his hips from behind, and speculators on the bank advancing the odds to even-money Blondin, six-to-one the manager.

The latter, of course, had no chance of walking up the steeply inclined rope. How was he to remount? A sort of creeping, furtive, one-knee-at-a-time action suggests itself, though whether you can climb on a man's back that way with the remaining foot balanced only on a swaying steel hawser is open to doubt. Yet the full-blooded leap— 'Allez, oop!'—with its attendant probability of the whole ensemble disappearing in a flurry of arms, legs, and twenty-foot pole, gyrating slowly as they fell and vanishing with a scarcely visible splash in the swirling torrent below. . . . No, I cannot think they would have decided on that.

The lonely, desperate conference has never, alas, been recorded, nor the method by which the manager at last climbed back, but get back he did, and at Niagara I found a picture of the pair with ten yards left to go. Colcord's eyes have vanished into their sockets; his mouth is agape; his cheekbones stand out like a skeleton's. And the caption calls him the 'Timorous Manager'!

'I break out into a cold sweat,' he recorded later in life, 'whenever I think of it.'

So, for that matter, do I.

A Memorable Flight

At a quarter to one in the morning we were relieved by the loud-speakers. . . . 'Trans World Airlines announce the departure of their non-stop flight No. 37 to San Francisco. All passengers aboard, please.' And here began a flight which will linger long in the memory.

I was lucky to find myself in the one single seat in the Constellation, back towards the tail. Lucky not so much because the survival rate has long since been proved to be highest in that region, but because, when you are going to spend a night sitting up, a lone seat in which to sprawl and spread yourself is like finding an empty first-class compartment in a British train—and furthermore, there was in this case a window for my exclusive use, from which to gaze with thoughts uninterrupted at the fantastic pageant which the dawn was in a few hours to illuminate below.

(Talking of survival rates, I have always relished the tale of my friend Douglas Bader, D.S.O., D.F.C., the 'legless ace', who flew with such distinction in the war. Seating himself hastily in the rear of some aero-plane in the United States, he found a man already there. The man turned to him. 'Hey,' he said, 'You bin a pilot too?')

We roared into the night and, as the lights of Chicago swung beneath us and at last faded into the distance, I set about working out the time. This represented defeat in a mild determination I had made before leaving England on my way round the world, namely that, whatever the locals might declare the time to be, Greenwich Mean Time was good enough for me and should remain on my watch till I had duly encircled the globe and it therefore came out right again. Subtracting five hours in New York and Pinehurst was simple enough, including even working out whether the timetable was Eastern Standard Time or Daylight Time, which is one hour different—but when it came to taking another hour off for Mountain Time in Chicago and another three hours for West Coast Time in San Francisco, always assuming one had started with the correct selection of Eastern Standard or Day-light in the first place, and bearing in mind that my watch is one of those fancy affairs which tell you not only the time but the date and day of the week, and that it was now on the point of telling not only a wildly improbable hour but also the wrong day and eventually the wrong month—what with all this I was forced to capitulate at Chicago

7

and, fortified by a magazine item declaring that it was an old wives' tale to suggest that you damaged a watch by putting it back, I retarded it by some ten or eleven hours and hoped that it and the timetable would agree upon eight o'clock next morning as the time of arrival in San Francisco.

Aided by one of those small pink pills so indispensable to long-distance travel, I slept the sleep of the righteous for six or seven hours and woke just before dawn, to find a full moon riding high on my side and the lights of Salt Lake City passing slowly alongside on the other. On the right the symmetrical lights of a little town called Ogden, all in regular rows except for one long transverse avenue, glowed like a diamond brooch and clasp. Then the dawn came up and the pageant began to unfold. With the world below bathed only in the soft moon-light the sun rose from behind and, if one may adapt the poet Omar to more prosaic days—Morning in the bowl of night had flung the stone that puts the stars to flight and Lo! the Hunter of the East had caught the vast tail fin of the Constellation in a noose of light. Dawn is always a humbling experience, and never more so than when flying, a mere speck in the firmament, at some 20,000 feet, when the new day reaches you long before it reaches the rest of the world. The tail fin blazed with silver and bronze and then at last the sun's rays caught some distant snow peaks, suspending them like pink lampshades in the sky and sending my mind back to the days when, crouching in the dark beside the lake at Killarney and waiting for the geese, I had turned to find the topmost peak of Carrantouil glowing silently behind my back.

Gradually the sun caught the nearer mountains, first brown, then a vivid orange slashed with deep purple shadows, and the whole scene unfolded itself in all the violent colours of the early days of coloured postcards. These were the amazing wastes of Nevada, comparable with Sinai and the deserted lost-world of Baluchistan on the way down to Karachi. For a full hour we flew on, 300 miles or more, without a vestige of the hand of man showing in the wilderness below. At last a road appeared and the first habitation of man in the shape of a mining camp, with a trail leading to some great excavation in the hillside. Then the desert closed in again and for hundreds of miles only a yellowish waste was to be seen, like the appalling plains between the Persian oilfields and the Gulf. Then another trail and a long brown valley, which might have been central India, with little square patches of cultivation dividing the desert from the sown. Over a good deal of these deserted lands a railway pierced its solitary way and I thought for the hundredth time of the pioneers who pushed out the original feelers, the veins through which the blood now courses across a whole continent, all in a short century and a half; and the difference between their lot and the ridiculous luxury with which my own generation now soars over the 1,800 rugged miles from Chicago to San Francisco between midnight and breakfast.

For much of the night we had been flying over a waste of desert which gleamed faintly white in the moonlight and might have been snow but was, I take it, salt. To a lifelong student of Sherlock Holmes this had a singular appeal which would hardly manifest itself to one's fellow passengers, for here down below, surely, was the stage on which began the *Study in Scarlet*—the 'arid and repulsive desert . . . in winter white with snow and in summer grey with the saline alkali dust', in which on the fourth of May, 1847, the lone figure of John Ferrier was rescued on the point of death by the migrating Mormons, thus setting into motion the chain of events that led to the untimely decease of Enoch Drebber in the Brixton Road, London, at the hands of Jefferson Hope.

I fell to talking with the stewardess, who, noticing my B.O.A.C. bag, made the familiar opening gambit, 'You from England?' You can tell Irish girls by their eyes, of course, though I cannot for the life of me describe how, and there was no doubting where this one came from. The precise location turned out to be Limerick. After three years with B.O.A.C. at Shannon she had been rewarded with a 'ticket to anywhere you like' and had chosen to go to some friends at New York. Here, she took a job at Idlewild, but, what with having to handle twenty planes in eight hours, and irregular meals, and oh my poor feet, had had to quit and was now flying with T.W.A. They sent her for four weeks to their school at Kansas City and then gave her the 'plum' posting to San Francisco. 'The loveliest place in the world,' she said. 'Yesterday I was swimming at 77°'—this being November. Two days on, five days off, sixteen hours flying a week, pay and allowances £90 a month. A happy girl, whose delight in her job radiated itself to at least one of her passengers.

This refreshing interlude over, I looked out to find that Switzerland had now replaced the desert below, with mountains, lakes and pines reaching up to the snowline. We followed a valley where the river dashed along the bottom, and the road and the railway criss-crossed each other in competition for the slopes above. In some tiny town an engine warming up for the day's work had shot a plume of white smoke which hung motionless several hundred feet high in the crisp morning air. A mile or two later the line dived under some snowsheds on the lakeside. Though I had never seen them before, they seemed to strike a chord and when I got back I took down the bound volumes of 'Railway Wonders of the World', which I collected so assiduously nearly forty years ago, and found a picture of them.

Miss Limerick brought up a tray of eggs, bacon and coffee and by the time this was dealt with the earth had turned soft and green again and we were descending to a land of neat white farmsteads, plough-patterns on rich dark earth, and poplars casting black shadows twice as long as themselves. Soaring down over the bay, we came straight in to the runway and touched down as the clock struck eight—a memorable flight indeed and one which set me wondering how many Americans had had the luck to see so much of their country as this roving and grateful stranger.

'Top of the Mark'

Let me confess to be unshamedly 'tourist'. It seems ridiculous, on visiting, say, Cairo for the first time, not to make an expedition to the Pyramids, or in New York to the top of the Empire State building or Rocke-feller Plaza, whence the *Queen Elizabeth*, lying in her dock below, looks like a boat to be played with in the bath. So likewise the first-time traveller to San Francisco must ascend to the bar of the Mark Hopkins, more particularly at night, and gaze down from all four of its outer walls to the whole vast panorama of the city and the Bay and the Bay Bridge, the Golden Gate Bridge and indeed the Golden Gate itself, past which even Drake sailed without guessing that here was the link be-tween the Pacific and one of the greatest harbours in the world. I never thought to see anything to equal the view from the Peak at Hong Kong. With a certain patriotic reluctance I have to admit that this prospect from the 'Top of the Mark' does so.

And what of San Francisco? 'You're going to San Francisco?' people had said. 'Lucky devil . . . wonderful place . . . wonderful people . . . you'll love San Francisco. . . . I must say I envy you going to San Francisco . . . only been there once, always wanted to go back . . . you'll never leave, once you get there. . . .' Everyone in the States had the same thing to say. After all this, San Francisco had better be good.

It was. Perhaps it is the climate. Far from shining eternally, as in the travel brochures, the sun is frequently obscured for days at a time by the sea mists sweeping in from the Pacific and thus is the more appreciated when it returns to shine on the amazing natural loveliness of the city and its landlocked, whale-shaped bay. Perhaps it is the air, which, un-polluted by the grime and soot of factories, is indeed like the proverbial champagne. Perhaps it is that the sense of adventure which brought the Spanish and the Mexicans and the Russians, South Americans, Japanese, Polynesians, Chinese, and Italians, to say nothing of a good many 'founder-members' of Botany Bay, all surging into San Francisco, still pervades the now prosperous and law-abiding city. After all it is only one hundred and six years since an army of sixty-two men turfed out the Mexicans and claimed San Francisco as American.

What tremendous times they must have been! It was in the summer of 1848 that John Sutter discovered the gold in 'them thar hills', thus emptying the town and indeed the harbour, where ships lay abandoned on their sides as every inhabitant made a wild rush to stake his claim. The news reached the East in the autumn and from all over America every trail led to the West. San Francisco sprang to life again. A room cost 300 dollars a month, an egg cost a dollar, and a loaf of bread 75 cents. Up in the gold-fields, where men were men, the sight of a woman walking down the streets was enough to empty the saloons. This was the real thing. Six shooters, rough liquor, and the Barbary Coast; flashing knives, opium, and bodies pitched over the wharf at dead of night. Those were the days.

The sensible ones were those who stayed behind and assisted the miners to dispose of their gold. Mark Hopkins himself was one. He ran an ironmongery store and finished with a castle. Another was Leland Stanford, who gave his name to one of California's principal Universities. He was a wholesale grocer and finished with a palatial establishment on Nob Hill where the Grace Cathedral now stands. From this inaccessible eyrie he constructed a cable car, forerunner of the antiquated cable cars for whose preservation every good San Franciscan is prepared to fight to the death.

Ever since the days when the sailors rushed from the clippers to the old Bella Melodeon, the people of San Francisco have been patrons of music and the arts. Early one morning in 1906 those who happened to be in Union Square were treated to the remarkable spectacle of Caruso rushing out of the St. Francis Hotel in his nightshirt. The earthquake had begun. Doubtless the St. Francis was not the same magnificent building in which I myself had the good fortune to stay. Nor perhaps would Union Square be recognizable to the citizens of those days. It is now nothing less than the roof over the largest underground car park in the world, holding some 2,000 cars, some of which, they will tell you maliciously, get lost for as long as two days.

Two San Francisco scenes, however, must be as near as no matter the same—the Chinese quarter, indistinguishable, with its narrow streets and the coloured banners hanging from the shops, from Hong Kong; and that haunt of resident and tourist alike, Fishermen's Wharf. The latter is sheer delight, mainly perhaps because it is alive, authentic, and in full working order, in no sense a museum piece. As many as 2,000 fishing boats put out from the various wharves, mostly manned by Italians. You can watch them landing their catch, and can pick out the lobsters, crabs, or whatever you fancy, and have them cooked there and then in the great copper cauldrons that line the wharf. Alternatively you can dine, as we did, on the wharf itself, looking out through the glass at the closely packed boats and feasting yourself on what we should call Dublin Bay prawns, of an excellence far beyond my poor powers to describe. They remain, I am ashamed to confess, one of the half-dozen outstanding memories of a journey all round the world and my mouth waters as I write of them.

Fisticuffs in Philadelphia

Soon after the 1936 Walker Cup match, Joe Louis, who rhymes with the town of Lewes and not with Louis Quatorze, was to fight one Al Ettore, who rhymed with 'ashore', in Philadelphia. One did not need to be a boxing fan to be intrigued by this drawling, slow-witted negro who had for years defied challengers from all over the world. I was happy to have a chance of seeing him in person.

Local enthusiasts were in a frenzy of excitement, and on the day before the fight the gate had already reached 130,000 dollars. Ettore, who hailed from Philadelphia, was not ranked in Louis's class as a boxer, but he had a great reputation for stolidity and courage. He was out-reached, too, but against that, as one scribe recorded, he could 'move those arms of his quicker than a lunch counter-man in a rush hour'. He had won his last ten fights and had only once been knocked out—when he was caught napping by a certain Charley Retzlaff. They reckoned he had a three to one chance against Louis.

In order that my 'prospects' story for a London paper should carry conviction I talked to one or two of the experts in New York. Frank Jacobs, who I was informed had managed Kid Berg and Nel Tarleton, stated that in his opinion Louis would win, but that he was not so confident as most of the critics. Ettore, he added, was a man who did not know what fear meant.

Paul Damski, Walter Neusel's manager, confirmed with an engagingly atrocious accent that Louis would win. I then took a cab to a down-town gymnasium where a number of youths were training under a super-expert, by the name of Whitey Bimstein. Mr. Bimstein, apparently, had trained Paolino Uzcudum. He had the traditional black cigar stub, unlit, and would have been ruled out of the average Hollywood film as a caricature. He shook me cordially by the hand, conducted me proudly round the establishment, and told me blood-curdling stories of what Louis had done to his Paolino.

'He hit Paolino on the side of the jaw', said Mr. Bimstein, 'and drove his teeth through the side of his face. I never seen noth'n like it. I know Ettore can take it. But Louis aint like the others. When he hits 'em, they usually stays hit.'

Meanwhile the 'Brown Bomber' himself, having been severely beaten up by Max Schmeling in the recent past—I believe he was in rather poor condition at the time—was taking no chances and was in magnificent shape. But it was significant that, contrary to his usual practice, he refused to nominate the exact round in which he reckoned to render 'Philadelphia's fistic pride and joy' unconscious.

'Some likes one round, some likes another,' was his final comment. 'Me, ah jest ketches him on the fly and brings him down first chance I gets.'

Philadelphia is a city of black and white millions. On the night of 22nd September, 1936, the whites, to a man, were thinking: 'Can the local lad make good and knock hell out of this nigger?' and the blacks were thinking: 'To hell with Philadelphia and local pride. Let's go and watch a black man knock hell out of a white man.'

Broad Street, Philadelphia, they will tell you, is the widest street in the world. They had made it 'one-way' for the first time in its history and cars made for the stadium seven, eight, sometimes nine abreast at terrifying speed. We arrived to find a great open-air horseshoe bowl filled already with sixty thousand people. Nearly half of them were black.

Overhead, enterprising gentlemen were displaying a form of advertising which we have mercifully been spared over here. The beauty of the full moon and the stars, a romantic ceiling for the vast assembly, was obscured by banners floating in the night sky and illuminated by searchlights. I made a mental note of protest never to sample the various beverages, chewing gum, and whatnot that they advertised, just as at home I have never used any product whose manufacturers have made the sky hideous by trailing banners behind aeroplanes.

We enjoyed a bloodthirsty appetizer between Purple Pants and Black Pants—whose names I have forgotten—in which Purple Pants staggered drunkenly round the ring until he was battered unconscious; and then the mayor climbed into the ring and invited us to stand in silence, in memory of one of the joint promoters of the fight, who had died on the previous Sunday. 'Neither race nor colour nor creed will enter into the hearts of any one of us watching the fight tonight,' he added. The blacks licked their lips in anticipation.

Cheers rose in a mighty roar as Philadelphia's hero clambered into the ring and waved his hands clasped over his head. He was a great, beefy, blond young man, obviously with the strength of a bullock.

A moment later a thunder of cheering greeted the arrival of a dark figure at the far end of the stadium. He was clad in a dazzling black and scarlet silk dressing-gown and escorted by a dozen mounted policemen and perhaps a hundred clamouring hangers-on. He looked, when he came near, as if he were not quite fully awake.

An extraordinary fellow. The proceedings seemed to arouse in him none of the emotional tension without which the champions in all walks of life will tell you they cannot give of their best. Here was none of the animal savagery of Jack Dempsey, nor that handsome, manly air of determination that characterized the ambitious Tunney. Was Louis nervous? Was he confident, or apprehensive? Did victory mean everything to him, or didn't he care very much one way or the other? No onlooker could tell. His eyelids drooped, his huge lips hung relaxed.

Out went the lights and the battle was on. Physically, if you did not object to the colour, Louis was the answer to the maiden's prayer. Rippling, sinewy muscle, and not an ounce of surplus. He looked like a sleek, gleaming panther beside his paler opponent. The bell seemed to bring his body, if not his mind, to life. Agile as a cat, with the poise of a ballet dancer, he provoked Ettore very much as a matador provokes the bull. I retain the impression of a long dusky left arm darting back and forth like a piston of a railway engine—jab, jab, jab on its white target.

Still, Ettore kept up his reputation as a sticker that night, if nothing else. After a tremendous battering in the second round, he came out in fine style for the third and set about Louis as if to murder him. But Louis weathered the storm with the balance of a tightrope walker. Apart from a frown or two his facial expression might have been a mask. I presume he must have been thinking about something or other. If so, his face did not show it.

To the student of psychology in sport the fourth round held a richly entertaining moment. Ettore came fresh from his corner and squarely and solidly landed two gigantic thumps, perfectly timed, to Louis's body. They might have felled an elephant, and certainly would have killed the average untrained mortal. On Louis they had no effect at all. A bewildered, frightened look came into Ettore's eye. 'Well, if that's no good,' it seemed to say, 'what the devil else can I do?' From that moment you could see that he knew he was done. He had played his ace, and it had been nonchalantly trumped.

A moment later a copper-coloured whirlwind had swept him up and was pummelling him against the ropes, while twenty thousand blacks stood on seats and roared 'He's got him! He's got him!' He staggered till the end of the round, but in the fifth a tremendous right-handed punch sent 189 pounds of Ettore flying six inches into the air, and he fell prostrate on his back. He tottered to his feet, but his limbs had turned to water and he sank slowly into insensibility. The winner retired to his corner expressionless and unmoved by the babel and was led away.

News travels fast, and as we drove home along Broad Street the whole coloured population lined the pavements for public exultation. Men and women danced grotesquely in their glee, and the children turned cartwheels in the gutter, while the whites drove sullenly home, looking steadfastly to the front and muttering: 'After all, it's only a game!'

The Lotus Eater

On the last night of the voyage I joined a party in what may be termed the *Queen Mary*'s night-club, known as the Veranda Grill—an establishment endowed with all the attributes of the modern bottle party; tiny, over-crowded, unbelievably stuffy, and opaque with the smoke of cigars. The band stopped nominally at two, but were willing to continue so long as any of the patrons had any spare dollars. At the time in question it was about four in the morning.

A man sitting at the table I had joined, and whose name I didn't know, was quietly intoxicated—so quietly, indeed, that nothing would induce him to speak. In the centre of the table was a vase of gladioli. Waking from his torpor, my neighbour stretched out a listless hand and drew forth a large bloom. He then broke off the spiky green piece at the end, popped the rest of the flowers into his mouth, and solemnly munched and swallowed them. Without uttering a syllable, he ate three whole gladioli.

We then adjourned to someone's cabin, where my eye at once fell upon a bowl of chrysanthemums—great big white ones, seven or eight inches in diameter. Our friend sat silently on the table and ate two of them. He was starting on his third when I left for bed.

I have never met any one able to account for this strange phenomenon. Lotus-eaters, yes: gladiolus- and chrysanthemum-eaters, no. Next morning, as we edged our way slowly up Southampton Water, I saw the fellow walking silently round the deck. He seemed as fit as a fiddle.

Some years later, having read the above, he reintroduced himself when our paths happened to cross again. He said he still enjoyed an occasional bowl of flowers—and he still looked as fit as a fiddle.

To Hell with Tennessee!

For presumably the first time in its history the 1951 Ryder Cup golf match between Britain and the United States was played on a Friday and Sunday, to enable the company to adjourn for a football match on the Saturday. This took place some seventy miles away, between the Universities of North Carolina and Tennessee, and was, of course, the college football with which in England we are familiar, if bewildered, on the screen.

The University of North Carolina, in the little town of Chapel Hill, left on all of us a deep impression. We were entertained to lunch by the Faculty in a building of noble design, with a round entrance hall whose alcoves framed among other pictures a Gainsborough, and we later had time to gaze open-mouthed at the sun, the earth, and the stars with their various moons circulating gravely round the planetarium upstairs. The rest of the buildings, the fraternity houses and laboratories, to say nothing of a most magnificent swimming pool, had clearly been planned on the same generous and expansive lines. The alumni, it struck us, might well be proud of their Alma Mater.

One glance at the stadium, to which we trooped up with 50,000 others after lunch, showed it to be in keeping with the rest of the institution, though this time man had been helped generously by nature. It is a vast, almost natural bowl and, crowned all round its upper fringe by tall trees in vivid 'fall' colours, it made on that sunny November afternoon as fine a sporting arena as any of us had set eyes on.

The rugby football enthusiast (I am a soccer man myself), brought up on the Oxford and Cambridge match at Twickenham, might at first be affronted by the strangeness of the spectacle and inclined even to scoff mildly at some of the more artificial manifestations of zeal. On the other hand he might well go away with grudging reflections that we could improve our own rather sombre occasions with a little more spectacle—without, as it were, going the whole hog. The first change to strike him would be the block of 2,000-odd undergraduates who do the official cheering. Led by white clad young men and girls with feathered fans who cartwheel and gesticulate and dance up and down like dervishes, the students not only roar to order but also put on at half time, by holding up squares of coloured paper, a series of 'pictures' and slogans whose precision would do no discredit to the Brigade of Guards. How these are rehearsed I do not know. I should have thought it to take many weeks of meticulous preparation, since one man with the wrong coloured square can ruin the lot. Yet the whole exhibition was flawless.

As the stadium filled up, we were entertained by the student band of some sixty-three performers, in uniforms, I was glad to see, of good Cambridge light blue, led by a Ruritanian character with a white busby and cockade. If one cannot quite see the boys from Cambridge putting on this show without a good many disconcerting observations from the sidelines, let me say that it does greatly enliven the proceedings.

We are familiar over here with the menacing Men-from-Mars aspect of the American footballer with his space helmet, padded shoulders and tight breeches. What I had not been prepared for was their number. A stream of yellow Martians—the all-conquering Tennessee—poured into the stadium like wasps from a nest. The game is eleven a side but here were not eleven and one or two spares, but twenty, forty, fifty, sixty.

They certainly knew their drill. In a moment they had formed up in six ranks, laid down their white helmets, and begun P.T. exercises under the direction of the coach. After a while they got down to a quarter of an hour or more of practice with twenty or thirty balls flying about the arena at the same time. These balls, incidentally, are rather smaller than a rugger ball and very pointed, and it seemed somehow odd to see a fellow with one in each hand, holding them by the end. An expert can throw one forty yards or so with extraordinary accuracy, making it screw through the air, point forward, as though fired from some rifled projector.

As to the game itself, it struck me as a mixture of all-in wrestling and leapfrog, with occasional flashes of rugby. The field is marked in ten yard spaces and the game consists not of open, flowing movement, but a sort of closed slogging to gain ground—the first war in Flanders, in fact, as compared with the second. Without launching into too many technicalities the game, broadly, is this. Each team in turn has four 'Downs'—i.e. it passes the ball out behind, a general mêlée ensues, and this goes on till the man with the ball is 'downed'. If he has gained ten yards his side has four more 'Downs'. If, in four, the side has not gained ten yards, the 'defence' side goes into 'offence' and in turn has four 'Downs'. The object, of course, is to gain ground until such time as you can score a touchdown—for which, unlike rugger, you have only to carry the ball over the line. For this you score six points, with a bonus of one if you convert.

The supreme difference between this and all other forms of football, so far as I could judge, lies in the fact that it consists not of a theoretically continuous game, but a series of innumerable separate games or 'Plays'—one 'Play' for each 'Down'—and these, instead of being left to chance, improvisation, and providence, are worked out in advance with the coach, rehearsed, debated, learnt by heart, and protected by vows of secrecy akin to, and rather more effective than, those imposed upon workers in atomic research. Thus before each Play the offence side retire out of earshot, lean down with their heads together, and hold a sort of mothers' meeting (though their conduct in a few seconds is to be far from matronly) to decide which gambit they will next employ.

The teams then crouch opposite one another till the ball is passed back, whereupon they assault each other with unparalleled ferocity, irrespective of where the ball may be. This personal obstruction, or blocking, is an integral theme, alien to other forms of football, and must, I think, be put on the 'anti' side of an impartial observer's summing-up—quite apart from the personal antagonisms created by hand-to-hand combat between two husky, steak-fed gladiators neither of whom has either the ball or any idea of its whereabouts. (Some moving-picture stills in *Life* magazine recently showed *A* on two occasions making a bee-line for *B*—no pun intended—and, without so much as looking for the ball, clocking him on the jaw, till eventually *B* retired with it broken.)

The normal span of one play is a matter of seconds, by which time the player with the ball is downed, together with others who, deceiving the spectators as well as their opponents, had run in such a manner as to convey the impression that they had got it, and many who had made no pretence of being connected with the play at all. The usual end is a pile of writhing, kicking, and no doubt swearing bodies, from underneath which the ball is later unearthed.

Sometimes, however, the mothers' meeting has decided on a forward pass and this is a spectacle of wonderful grace and suspense as the ball soars through the air—comparable with those sweeping passes of Alex James to his wing forwards in the golden days of the Arsenal. To me they 'made' the game as a spectacle. Furthermore, since one successful forward pass might make as much ground as ten or twenty furiously contested 'Downs', they seemed a good business proposition. For some reason, though, they appeared to be frowned upon.

Comparing the game, naturally, with rugger and striking a balance when all was over, I found a good deal to put both to credit and debit. To a lover of a fast, open game there is a rather depressing artificiality about the advanced planning of each play and the limited ambition to gain a few yards instead of starting a movement which might with luck sweep the ball from one end of the field to the other.

Heaven knows, the rugby football man cannot in these days complain about stoppages of play in other games. Last time I saw a rugger match —it was Cambridge versus Richmond—play was stopped so incessantly that I began keeping a record. From that moment the whistle went eighty-five times in the first half and ninety-seven in the second. In American football these constant halts are an accepted feature of the play and, what with the whispered consultations and the measuring up of the yards gained, by a sort of chain gang who dash on from the side-lines with a pair of uprights and a ten-yard string, a game consisting of four quarter-hour periods of actual play took in fact two hours and ten minutes. Perhaps because most of us were untuned to it, this struck us as rather too long for sustained enthusiasm.

On the debit side, too, I should unhesitatingly put the eternal sub-stitutions of players. There is much to be said, even if rugger fans turn apoplectic at the mere suggestion, in favour of allowing substitutes in the case of serious injury. But when you have a constant stream of players to and from the discard pile on the sideline, it is almost impos-sible to tell who is playing and who is just being yanked off by the coach for fumbling a pass. And when, furthermore, you have two completely separate elevens for offence and defence chopping and changing throughout, the game brings to mind a sort of glorified musical chairs. Nor, of course, on account of the grotesque defensive armament they all wear, even their faces being enclosed in leather cages, can you tell one man from another except by the number on his back.

On the other hand some aspects of the play, and particularly of its presentation to the spectator, struck me as infinitely superior and I am sure that anyone responsible for staging rugby football in Britain who observed it with an open mind, if such a one may be assumed to exist, would come home with ideas that might revolutionize rugger as a spectacle.

As to the play, most of us were intrigued by their different method of converting a touchdown. It loses something by virtue of the fact that, since there is no actual touching-down, the kick is always taken from dead centre—even those who see little point in rugger as a whole will concede a try converted in a high wind from the sideline to be one of the classic thrills of sport—but it gains from the fact that the converting side do have to do something more than merely kick it over the bar. Three of them are concerned in the manœuvre. One passes the ball backwards between his legs, a second, on one knee, catches it and holds it by the tip, poised for the kick, and the third kicks it. In the meantime the defenders are poised menacingly beside the passer-back and are on top of the kicker and his assistant in a flash. The slightest hesitation or fumble and they have had it. Mostly the conversions seemed to go, like the executions, 'without a hitch'. The three men concerned had presumably practised at this alone night and day for some months and may even have been admitted to the university largely on account of their prowess at it, but still it did seem to give the defenders one last chance and personally I liked it.

From the spectators' point of view, and not only the uninitiated like ourselves but the experts too, this particular game had Twickenham knocked into a cocked hat. I hold the revolutionary view that the spectator, having paid his money—or for that matter having been entertained to a free ticket by the management—is entitled to know what is going on; and if there is one indisputable fact about rugger as a spectacle it is that the spectator does not know what is going on. He knows the whistle has blown, he knows there is a scrum, but at least half the time that is all he does know. Even the radio and television commentators have to descend to evasions that 'So-and-so probably knocked-on', or 'looks as though it may have been a forward pass by Such-and-such'. Now Americans may from time to time, according to our lights, overdo the showmanship but at least they must be right in assuming that the watcher wishes to be informed of what is happening. So they give you a fine electric scoreboard, like the Tote, telling you how long remains in each quarter, how many downs are left, and such like, and a man on the loudspeaker, while not giving a running commentary, tells you which man is now running on to the field as substitute for which; what the foul is given for; what is the penalty— 'fifteen yards penalty against Tennessee for offside' or whatever it may be—and generally keeps you in touch in a manner which in rugger is exasperating by its absence. The referee also makes an unmistakable sign, whenever he blows his whistle, as to why he has done so.

Anyway there was no doubting it to be a great spectacle and, while I could not see myself, if posted to the United States, becoming wildly enamoured of that brand of football, I would not have missed this exhibition.

Acting under instructions, as the police witnesses say, I spent the afternoon yelling, 'To hell with Tennessee!' Alas, they won by 27–0.

Raucous Voice in Brooklyn

From Philadelphia I turned my thoughts to the presidential election. From New York to San Francisco, from Hollywood to New Orleans, an outsider was stealing the limelight from the four candidates.

He was Father Charles Coughlin, first and greatest of the 'Radio Priests'. A plumpish, bespectacled pedagogue in the middle forties, with a magic turn of phrase and an infectious, friendly smile. Prophet or parasite? Saviour-deliverer or common mountebank? Coughlin (pronounced 'Coglin') was widely ridiculed by his enemies—though often a hint of nervous apprehension could be detected behind their derision—but he claimed eight million active disciples. His radio audiences may have amounted to thirty or forty millions. His followers believed him destined to lead the United States back to a glorious prosperity, to find work with his Sixteen Points of Social Justice for ten million idle hands. His detractors looked forward to the time for him to fade back into obscurity and dismissed him with a nervous shrug of the shoulders as another of what Mr. H. G. Wells termed America's 'raucous voices', but at least his enemies thought highly enough of him to descend to the most desperate, if unavailing, attempts to bar him from the medium by which he rose to fame—the radio. They indulged in every kind of unscrupulous manœuvre to keep him off the air—but still the millions listened.

'Father Coughlin,' declared Chicago's Bishop Gallagher, 'speaks with the voice of God.' The Pope sent a cardinal all the way to the United States to declare that this was by no means the official view.

I went one night to hear Coughlin speak at Ebbet's Field, a baseball park down in Brooklyn. It was a stifling evening and the subway stank to high heaven as it disgorged thirty thousand perspiring units of humanity to make up his audience.

It might have been a cup final, from the noise that was going on. Hoarse gentlemen, for the most part tie-less and unshaven, endeavoured to uplift the spirit by the sale of tracts on social justice, life stories of Father Coughlin, and the coat-badges of his supporters. Vendors of peanuts, Coca Cola, and ice cream administered to the needs of the flesh. Both parties were continuously sniped at by members of organizations hostile to the hero of the evening.

Inside the ground the first hour was spent in the process of stimulating our minds into an appropriately receptive mood for the arrival of the priest, and a very remarkable and well-staged process it was, though I doubt whether it would have had quite the same reception at the White City.

In the centre of the arena rose a tall, white-draped, floodlit tower; at the side a band was playing; around the fringe was a cordon of five hundred armed police. Inside this ring three hundred of Coughlin's 'Branch Leaders' waited, uniformly dressed in dark coat and white trousers. Some were negroes, many were Jews. Most of them seemed substantial, middle-class citizens.

Soon a second band appeared, forty-eight strong and impossibly attired in brass helmets, white capes, blue bell-boy jackets, and white trousers—as remarkable a force as ever paraded out of Hollywood.

At the head of a procession of the district leaders, the rear brought up by the original band, they trumpeted their way round the ground to a thunder of cheers. It wasn't long before the two bands passed within twenty yards of each other, playing two different tunes in two different times. I knew it would happen. Nobody seemed to mind.

The chairman of the meeting then ascended the tower—quite a young fellow—and the audience stood up and recited the oath of allegiance to the flag, before submitting to a final 'pep talk'. The chairman recited 'My country, 'tis of thee,' and exhorted us to make some 'financial sacrifice to see that the magic voice of the air shall not be stifled for lack of funds.'

A few more exhortations, a community rendering of the Coughlin theme song ('Now there came a righteous man, with a real constructive plan. . . .'), and stage and audience were set to receive the star of the evening.

I have witnessed a jubilee and a coronation and have heard the Arsenal score the winning goal in a cup-tie, but never have I heard anything to touch the ovation they gave to Coughlin as he marched into the stadium in the midst of his bodyguard, a battery of cameras recording his smile, his careless Fascist-like salute, the glint of his rimless spectacles in the floodlight.

'I've a bad leg and a bad heart but I hobbled here just the same,' said a little woman in black on my right. 'They shot Huey Long. Every night I pray to God that nothing will happen to Father Coughlin. If it does, I shall give up hope. He is America's only salvation.' There was no doubting the old lady's sincerity. I was much impressed.

Coughlin is the showman *par excellence*. He takes the stage alone,

with a microphone strapped to his chest to give him liberty of movement and gesture. As a priest he may be dabbling outside his proper
sphere; as an economist he may be, almost certainly is, unsound; as a
politician he may be crazy; but as a public spellbinder he is the master
of them all.

He speaks with an attractive Irish brogue, which his enemies will tell
you has been studiously acquired. His lapses in moments of stress seem
to bear out the theory, as when in maligning Roosevelt he cried: 'Did
he dew it? . . . NAW!' His microphone technique is a treat to watch.
He will shield his mouth with the back of his hand, suggesting to each
individual in the audience: 'I'm telling you this in confidence. Don't
let the others hear.'

He mixes straight politics, frenzied appeal, vivid similes from every-
day life, quotations from the Bible, satire and jest in studied proportions. I never knew a preacher in church who could keep his audience
spellbound, not noticing the time, for an hour and a half.

On the night I am recalling he was soon well into his stride, deep in
the old controversy of machine versus man: the steam engine, the
dynamo, Edison, Arkwright. 'We have won the war over want,' he
cried, 'and still there is want in the midst of plenty. . . . *Whatsoever thou
doest unto my little ones thou doest unto Me.* . . .'

Workers in the Chrysler factory were still paid seventy-five cents an
hour 'as if God had never enlightened the minds of our engineers. That
system must pass, it *shall* pass; and until it does pass no man shall stand
up and talk of a NOO DEAL . . . *a little crib in Bethlehem.* . . .

'You remember the National Recovery Act—the Act that did not
recover?' ('Oh, my! That's a home run,' said the little woman in black.)
'The noble experiment of ploughing under cotton, sacrificing pigs?
You cannot *destroy* yourself into prosperity—the Cromwellian path of
destruction. It is immoral to throw God's gift back in His face . . . *the
blood of Jesus Christ.* . . .'

And the Big Bad Wolves of Banking—'The bankers created the
money—pardon me, I missed a word—the *busted* bankers created the
money. . . . Usury? What is usury? Not only lending money at too big
interest, but lending bogus money at any interest . . . until the last sun
shall set in its crimson settings. . . .'

The sweat was pouring off his brow as he flung himself dramatically
from side to side of his flood-lit tower, for all the world like a black-
jacketed monkey on a vast, illuminated barrel organ.

As for Roosevelt—'He's sold you up the river at six per cent. He's put the money changers back in the Temple and given the key to the people—fashioned in the shape of a double cross.

'Landon? Well, you can't afford the time to monkey around with a good honest man who happens to be ignorant.

'And Browder? I love the Communists, but I hate Communism. There's not a child born who wants to share his mother with every other child in the street!'

So he told us to vote for Lemke.

At the end of an hour and a half he left the stage as he had entered it, a solitary figure in an army of jostled and jostling police, waving his hand in a farewell salute. When she had done cheering, the little woman turned to me and asked where I was from.

'England,' I said.

She took off her blue-ribbon badge, emblem of her faith in Coughlin, and pinned it to my coat. 'Then go back to England,' she exclaimed, 'and tell them the truth.' Tears were streaming down her cheeks.

NEARER HOME

The Engine and the Fly

With a little ingenuity I have generally found it possible to introduce alien subjects into articles allegedly about golf. For instance, after a few lines of introduction concerning the speed with which the club-head met the ball and what happened thereon, I was able once to slip in the problem of the Railway Engine and the Fly.

The fly is buzzing merrily along the railway line, when he meets the Flying Scotsman coming along at sixty miles an hour in the other direction. The contest is unequal, and the fly retires whence he came, squashed on the front of the engine. *Was the fly at any point in this operation stationary?*

Surely the fly must stop for a split second? How else could he be going in one direction one moment and in the reverse direction the next? But if, for a split second, he was stationary, it must have been when he was in contact with the engine. Therefore the engine, too, must have been stationary. *Quod est absurdum.*

Letters and solutions poured in, from mathematical wranglers down-wards. One man, with a string of impressive letters after his name, wrote in patronizing terms to state that people of only normal intelli-gence assumed that a body must be either at rest or in movement, whereas if only their brains were capable of grasping it, there was a third state midway between the two. I forget what he called it. Any-how, it was all very learned and technical.

For myself, I still do not know the answer—though I suspect that maybe the fly becomes stationary *before* he strikes the engine, on account of air pressure. All I know is that the argument lasted me for three weeks.

Of course, there were other diversions, too. The coronation of George VI, for instance. I was one of a series of 'trained observers' with which my employers covered the route, in case any misguided gentle-man should heave a bomb. Our instructions were to send nothing at all unless there was an 'incident'.

My own perch—I believe it cost ten guineas—was the most pre-carious contraption you could imagine. Just a plank balanced across two girders on the top of Grand Buildings, Trafalgar Square. I shared it with a number of others, mostly office boys who worked in the buildings and therefore got in for nothing. The plank was not attached to the girders in any way and we sat with our feet dangling over the roofs, between which we could see the crowd like ants in the square below. The more the boys wriggled, the more parlous our position became; the plank jumped about on the girders, and several times I thought that its end would become disconnected altogether. My particular perch was at the far end, and by leaning over a few inches I looked directly down on the heads of the swarm below. Under my right elbow the minute hand of a vast clock—I should say it was twenty feet long—heaved its way spasmodically round, jerking nearly a foot at a time. Extraordinary how these things move when you get close to them.

Many is the time that I have recounted a little human tragedy that was enacted on that plank midway through the morning. We had arrived there, according to instructions, at some ungodly hour in the morning, most of the company bringing their own rations with them. One of the boys on the plank had brought an orange.

Every so many minutes he would produce this orange from his pocket and eye it fondly. He would inspect it from all angles and polish its skin till it glowed. It was the pride of his life, the orange of his eye. Often, as the hours passed, I thought he was going to eat it, but always he managed to get it back into his pocket.

This went on from about six in the morning almost until the procession was due to pass. I suppose he must have had this orange out of his pocket a dozen times. Then at last came the Moment. The irrevocable decision was made, and the boy dug his thumb into the peel.

Casually he cast the pieces of peel down into the abyss below, peering over to watch them bounce merrily down among the rooftops and with luck fall through into the square. He was coming to the end of this operation when there was some sort of hullabaloo on the other side of the square, over by the National Gallery. It was a welcome distraction and at once claimed all attention, the boy's included.

Meanwhile he went on peeling his orange. Suddenly there was a choked cry of anguish. I turned to see the boy clutching a small piece of peel in his hand. In his excitement he had chucked away the orange and kept the peel!

Nine Hours to Live

One thing about newspaper life—you never know what's going to turn up. 'There's a man downstairs wanting to see the news editor,' said one of the women secretaries. 'I didn't catch his name. Will you see him instead?'

'All right. Ask them to send him up.'

Into the waiting-room there stepped a virile-looking man in his early forties, with glittering blue eyes and a pleasant smile, attired in a camel-hair coat and 'Anthony Eden' black hat. I inquired politely of what service I could be.

'Oh,' he said, rather sheepishly, 'it's about my case. I'm trying to reopen it.'

I felt I ought to know all about his case, but in fact, of course, I didn't know him from Adam.

'Let me see. I didn't quite get your name.'

He lowered his voice cautiously.

'I'm Donovan,' he replied, as if that settled it. I'm afraid I must still have looked puzzled.

'Dartmoor,' he whispered.

'Ah, yes. Of course, of course,' I replied. 'I am so sorry.' I didn't want him to realize that even then the name meant nothing to me. I drew up a chair for him at my desk and we started talking.

George Thomas Donovan, it turned out, was the 'hero' of the Dartmoor mutiny of 1932. He had been released a short time before and had come to sell the 'inside story'. I promised to put his offer to the management and we arranged to meet in a day or two. Meanwhile I hastened to the cuttings library to look into the man's history.

With two other men he had been sentenced to death in 1926 for the murder of an old man who had died a month after being beaten up on the Brighton Downs, where he had been lured for a, shall I say, not wholly moral purpose. Donovan, it is fair to add, had not ceased in the past twelve years to protest that he was not present at the time of the murder. That in itself is not unusual, but he produced evidence purporting to show who was the third man present for whom he was mistaken and so nearly hanged. That evidence is unprintable, being highly libellous of an individual still living, so I will say only that it convinced me that there were at least good grounds for reopening his case.

He had come to sell his story of the Dartmoor mutiny. What he did not realize was that stored away in his mind were the still vivid impressions of an experience that every man, woman, and child among the rest of us have at some time or another imagined happening to ourselves—namely sitting in the condemned cell waiting to be hanged in the morning.

'Gallows Cheated of its Prey.' No novelette could beat the drama of Donovan's tale of his last hours in Wandsworth as he recounted it over the fireside in my flat. The story needed no emotional embellishment, no fancy writing. The bare facts were enough. The story, headed 'Nine Hours to Live', ran as follows:

I suppose there is hardly a man in the world who has not at some time in his life imagined himself sitting in the condemned cell, due for execution in the morning. A good many have done it in real life.

I am one of the very, very few who have lived to tell the tale.

In March 1928, Ernest Friend Smith, a retired chemist, was murdered near Brighton by three men in a motor car. On Friday, 13th July, Percival Leonard Taylor, James Weaver, and myself were sentenced to death.

If I tell you that I was not present on the night when the deed was done, and that I had not seen these two men for several months, it is unlikely that you will believe me. Anyway, that evening I found myself sitting in the condemned cell at Wandsworth, with six officers (we don't call them warders) to be with me, two at a time, night and day till I was executed. The cell was really two cells knocked into one, and quite bare except for a table, a small bed, and a chair or two. The only decoration was a crucifix.

The officers were very good fellows—one of them seemed even more upset than I was; he kept repeating: 'It doesn't seem right. It doesn't seem right'—and if we sometimes got on each other's nerves, it was the situation rather than any fault of theirs.

We talked, laughed very often, played cards and draughts till the early hours of the morning. Sometimes my mind would get completely carried away—but there was always that little voice waiting in the background to say: 'Haven't you forgotten something?'

The officers had to keep an 'Occurrence Book', in which to record everything I did or said. You'd think a new one could be afforded for each victim, but this one had done service for some time. Occasionally I got a glance at it. One of the names I noticed was that of the Frenchman, Vacquier, who had been hanged at Wandsworth four years previously for the murder of Alfred Jones, licensee of the Blue Anchor Hotel at Byfleet. Against it was the comment: 'Docile. Refused to play games.'

The officers used to bring in small luxuries for me, and the wife of one of them sent me in a bunch of flowers every day. I lived on the prison diet. People seem to think a condemned man can have anything he likes: that's not so—but I was allowed ten cigarettes and a pint of beer each day. Ten cigarettes don't go far in the condemned cell. I could have smoked a hundred a day.

Very soon the governor came to my cell. The scene, twelve years ago, is planted in my memory as if it were yesterday, and I remember him word for word. He said: 'I have in my hand a paper which instructs me to inform you that the Sheriff of the County of Sussex has fixed your date of execution on August 15th at eight o'clock.'

It sounds funny now, but I replied: 'Thank you very much.' It was all I could think of to say.

At first the burning resentment put everything else out of my mind. I am not a particularly religious man. Like many others, my religion is confined to believing that there is a God somewhere in heaven and leaving it at that. But for those first few days you could not have convinced me there was a God in heaven or earth.

I was kept going for ten days by hopes of my appeal. It failed.

With a week left I began to count the hours—160, 159, 158. . . . I looked out at the sky and thought: 'Well, I won't be seeing that again very soon.' Resentment passed, and at times I became strangely resigned.

At other times it was all I could do to stop giving way to my feelings. At Wandsworth the execution shed is only a few paces across the passage from the condemned cell. The doors are let in flush with the wall and painted the same colour. Thousands of people must have passed it without knowing it was there.

But I knew it was there, and in the dreary night hours nothing would stop my mind from wandering just across the passage to that shed, trying to imagine what it was like inside.

I petitioned Sir William Joynson Hicks, the Home Secretary. Again the governor came with a paper in his hand: 'I have to inform you that the Home Secretary finds no grounds for interference with your sentence and that you will be executed tomorrow.' Again I could think of nothing better to say than 'Thank you.'

A few minutes later one of the other two men—I won't say which—was also informed that his last hope was gone. He was in the cell above me and the way he carried on, crying and shouting, was about as much as I could stand. I got an officer to go up and tell him to stop.

On the afternoon of that day a bell rang, all the prisoners were locked away (they were not allowed to catch a glimpse of a condemned man), and I was taken to see my father and mother for the last time.

I stood behind a grill with a warder on each side. My father and mother were shown into a room on the far side of the passage, while another officer paced up and down the passage to see that nothing passed between us.

It was a pathetic interview and there wasn't much that we could think of to say. For a while we just stood and stared at each other.

'Never mind, boy,' I remember my father saying. 'I know it will be all right.'

I told my mother to keep smiling—she was sixty-eight at the time—and she did her best to keep cheerful. She was quite brave until the end when, after twenty minutes, we were told that the visit was over.

Then she broke down and sobbed. The last words I heard her speak were: 'I'll meet you there. I'll meet you there.'

I went back to my cell for the last time. It's hard to put my feelings into words. It was like the night you spend in hospital before an operation, intensified a hundred times.

I was sitting there ruminating, when across the passage I heard a sort of thud. A minute later I heard it again.

It was the executioner trying out the drop.

Time and again I tried to picture the scene on the morrow. Was it instantaneous, as people say?—though I don't see how they can tell. What would the executioner look like? Who would be there? What would they do?

Above all, what would *I* do? I think I was as much afraid of letting my feelings get the better of me as I was afraid of being hanged.

Later Canon T. Pym, of Southwark, a friend of long standing, came to visit me. He was to accompany me to the scaffold. He gave me a cigarette and we talked for a while about—football. Then: 'Tomorrow,' he said, 'I want you to walk over like a brave man with your head up. I don't propose to read the burial service—I'll just walk over with you.' His last words were: 'I'll be here early in the morning.'

I sat down to wait for the end, and the hours began to slip by with uncanny speed. I won't say I was happy, but my spirit seemed consoled. I had no time left to waste on resentment.

At eleven o'clock that evening the cell door opened. The governor came in with the sheriff. I was sitting playing cards, I remember, and the object of his visit did not occur to me.

'Well, Donovan, I've got some good news. In my hand I hold a reprieve for you, and I am very pleased.'

'Thank you,' I said for the third time. He shook me by the hand and so did my two officers. Did I jump and shout for joy, as a man might be expected, who had heard the best news the world can offer? No. I remember I walked slowly up and down around the cell, hardly speaking. My mind was numbed.

I was still in a sort of trance five minutes later when they whisked me out of the condemned cell and set me down as an ordinary prisoner to face the prospect of a lifetime in jail.

After a few months at Dartmoor I wondered many a time whether the exchange was worth while. Often I thought it was not. Now, fit, free, and forty-three, I know the answer.

Mutiny on the Moor

Twelve years later Donovan was released from Maidstone. One of the first people he saw was his mother, now aged eighty.

It was after he had been in Dartmoor for four years that Donovan secured five years' remission from his nominally twenty years' sentence. He had become a 'bluecoat' man (in other words, he had earned special privileges) when the mutiny took place. Like every one else in Dartmoor, he knew it was coming, but he took little or no part in the early stages. When you're in for life anyway, he observed, you let the others do the shouting. No sense in getting yourself a bad name.

His account of the mutiny was a stirring narrative, all the more entertaining for the matter-of-fact, detached, objective way in which he told it. He would have made a good reporter.

No one in the prison, it appears, slept a wink on the Friday night when it began. Men were shouting and rampaging in their cells all night. 'Let's get a rope and hang him to the clock tower'—referring to Mr. S. N. Roberts, the governor—was among the few printable remarks that Donovan could recall eight years later.

Mr. Roberts, according to the convicts' way of thinking, was responsible for the abolition of the privileges that had made life endurable in Dartmoor—especially that of sitting outside and conversing for a couple of hours on a summer evening. And you can imagine what that means when you're locked in a cell for twelve hours at a stretch, and it's three days bread and water for being caught standing on a stool and looking out of the little iron window. The food apparently was so unpalatable that they would throw it on the ground and go hungry rather than eat it—which must be saying something.

On the Saturday in question a pretty scene took place in the chapel when, at the hour when usually the chaplain read the news, the governor got up and said: 'I've come to talk to you about the food.' If he thought to observe the light of hope and encouragement on the homely features of his four hundred listeners, the next few moments must have been something of a shock. With one accord they yelled: 'Get down and get out of it, you——!' A few more pleas for a hearing, and his reception got steadily worse. There was nothing for it but to retire.

The chaplain, Captain Ball, then stepped into the breach. He started to read the news, and was howled down. With commendable optimism he gave out the number of the hymn. The organ started and one or two of the prisoners got up to sing. 'Sit down, you ―― ――s' yelled the gentlemen at the back. The chaplain, noble fellow, went right through the hymn by himself—perhaps one of the most praiseworthy song renderings in history.

Saturday was another bad night.

On Sunday morning shouting and scrimmaging were heard in the passage as a man named Brown was taken off to the punishment cells. 'I saw blood all down the stairs,' said Donovan. The fun began in earnest at half-past ten during the morning exercise. All trace of discipline had gone. Warders shouted 'Stop talking,' and the reply was: 'Stop talking your ―― self.'

Very soon the men from A hall ran round to those of B and D (C was shut) shouting: 'Brownie's been done in!' Those four words, inaccurate as they were, started one of the most sensational stories for years. By telephone, by wire, by aeroplane and hastily hired sports cars, Fleet Street descended on the little town of Princetown. But even now the full story has hardly been told.

I would give a tidy sum to have sat in a bullet-proof glass shelter in Dartmoor and watched the events of those brief two hours. A yelling mob surged up to the governor's office and shouted for Mr. Roberts. It is no reflection on him to record that he failed to appear. If he had, says Donovan, he would have lost his life.

So they shouted for Colonel Turner, an assistant prison commissioner who had been sent by the Home Office to investigate the trouble that was brewing. Colonel Turner came out and stood on the steps. It was the action of a brave man. 'Tell me what's wrong,' he said, 'and I'll straighten it out in the proper way.'

He had misjudged his audience. The mob set on him and pinned him against the wall. 'I'll tell you what's wrong,' said one man, and flung a bowl of Dartmoor porridge into his face. Another deftly purloined his watch, chain, and wallet. Two more had a length of rope and proposed to hang him from the tower.

It was at this point that Donovan stepped in and became the national 'hero' of the day. Shouting 'Don't be bloody fools—you'll only get what I've got,' or words to that effect—he was the only 'lifer' in the prison at the time—he pushed his way into the 'free for all' and, after getting fairly well knocked out, managed to edge Colonel Turner along the wall to where an officer named Webb was able to push him through a door to safety. Incidentally, the same officer saved the governor's life by slipping him out of the back door of the offices and locking him in a cell.

Robbed of their human spoils, the convicts ran completely amuk. A film doing justice to their activities of the next hours might be laughed off the screen as an extravaganza. They seized the large ornamental stone flower pots outside the governor's office and hurled them through the windows. They broke in, heaped documents on the floor, and then set fire to these and, with them, the offices. One fellow emerged with the governor's hat and coat on, with records, documents, and a typewriter under his arm.

Another mob made shrewdly for the officers' mess, where they looted cigars, cigarettes, wine, whisky, beer, and money, and went round offering drinks and free smokes to all and sundry. A good many, states Donovan, were blind drunk inside half an hour. A couple of convicts with homosexual tendencies were found engaged in the potting shed.

What, I asked, were the officers doing all this time? The answer was that most of them, rightly, were standing still and making mental notes of the chief offenders. It was more than their lives were worth to do more. One brave man, perhaps recklessly so, went among the men when the others held back, telling them to go back to their cells. His name was John C. Lewis. He was bashed on the head with a rock and so terribly injured that he never worked again.

The first shot was fired by the engineer from the armoury roof with an old gun like a blunderbuss, aiming at men coming out of the officers' mess. A man named William Mitchell was shot as he was breaking windows on the roof of the twine shed. He fell to the ground shot through the head, neck, and arm, and was carried to hospital, where he nearly died.

A gang of men demanded the keys of the separate cells from two warders, one of whom drew his truncheon. 'Don't be a fool,' said the other—and handed over the keys. Another party raided the boiler-house, hoping to blow it up. A 'red-band', or specially privileged, convict by the name of Jordan, who was in charge of the boiler-house, turned the steam on them and got them out, knowing there was a warder hiding behind the boilers.

Alas, poor Jordan! Another officer arrived at the door, searching for prisoners, and shouted: 'Come out or I fire.' The occasion was too much for his nerves. The gun went off in his hand and Jordan was shot in the arm.

When the riot was at its height there occurred an incident that may never be matched in prison history, even in the United States. The governor's office was blazing like a firework display. Outside, the Dartmoor brass band marched up and down rendering at full blast 'Keep The Home Fires Burning'.

It is significant that hardly an attempt was made to escape from the prison. An exception, however, was one bright spirit who forced an officer to hand over his coat and trousers, got out the prison fire escape, and put it against the outer wall. With a cry of 'Good-bye, boys,' he climbed to the top of the wall. He was met by a volley from the ring of armed officers surrounding the prison and fell off so quickly that he broke his nose on a rung of the ladder.

Things could not go on like this for ever. The damage had reached £3,000 when the big gates opened and police reinforcements dashed in. One charabanc load of thirty-five had covered the sixteen miles from Plymouth, with a rise of fourteen hundred feet from sea level, in twenty-four minutes. A few days later the police gave a dinner in the driver's honour.

The reinforcements asked no questions, but set about them with a will. Shouts by prison officers: 'Not those men. They're not in it,' did not prevent a number of good-conduct men who had stood around and taken no part in the riot from getting stunning cracks on the head. It was just too bad that they happened to be standing near the gates.

Tempers were short. One of the higher police officials, who had better be nameless, lined up a group of prisoners and gave them one minute to empty their pockets. He was wearing plus-fours and carrying a big ash stick. 'What have you got there?' he said to a prisoner after the time limit had ended. 'A bit of bread.' 'Well, make a sandwich of that!' he announced, catching the man a colossal crack over the head with the ash stick.

Gradually the men were herded back to the cells. The hospital looked like a battlefield. One man had the back of his head bashed in, another was shot in the forehead, a third was shouting: 'I'm blind. I'm blind.' Moaning and screaming went on all night. The prison doctor, Dr. Battiscombe, went round extracting pellets from the men. His assistant, aided incidentally by Donovan, followed with needle and stitches.

Later the ringleaders—though the mutiny was never in any sense 'organized'—were sorted out. With the exception, according to my information, of the principal one, who escaped to the cells in time and was never discovered, they received huge, one might almost suggest savage, additions to their sentences.

The official inquiry, whose report I have read with some care, seemed to prove that this mutiny was no one's fault in particular. But, then, that is the way of official inquiries.

Pied Piper, 1940

The rat-catcher lived in a little back street somewhere behind the Elephant and Castle. Small urchins, mocking at the spruceness of the toff's black hat and umbrella, had to be bought off with coppers as I made my way along to his abode. Fat women bawled across the street from their doorways. There were moments when I wished I hadn't come.

William Dalton, doyen of rat-catchers, was sixty-nine, and should have been painted by George Belcher on the lines of 'The Landlord of the Chequers'. He wore a butterfly collar, and overflowed from a blue serge suit. I put him at seventeen stone.

'Come in, sir. Come right in, me boy,' he roared, a nice blend of the respectful and the paternal. I stepped into the little parlour-office. The master rat-catcher was directing operations from a small kitchen chair, of which, as he sat on it, no part was visible. In the window beside the aspidistra sat a girl, by name Moll, tapping out the accounts on a weary typewriter and parrying with a ready sauce the Rabelaisian observations of the old man.

A stuffed ferret labelled 'Old Joe' snarled at the visitor from a glass case over the mantelpiece. Beside him were rows of keys that would have turned a burglar green with envy. They belonged to the banks, business houses, and warehouses that Mr. Dalton numbered among his clients. Pinned to the wall was a charred envelope, bombed by the Irish Republican Army in a pillar-box.

The business, he told me, bellowing genially across the four feet that separated us, was founded by a Dalton in 1710 and has been in the family ever since. He does not do much active work himself these days, but the firm's sixteen 'catchers' are all Daltons or related to Daltons. Young Daltons are trained in the mysteries of the profession the moment they leave school. It says much for the family loyalty that not one of them since 1710 has ever revealed the method by which in the course of a single night they will catch, *and bring home alive*, as many as a thousand rats.

Rats are the canniest, craftiest of man's enemies. A man may have his house infested with them yet never set eyes on one. A couple of Daltons will go out with their Gladstone bags and come back in the morning with every rat in the house tied safely in a sack.

How do they do it? With traps, with their hands, with some magical, invisible bait? Or what is their secret weapon? All they will tell you is that they are not poisoners—for poisoners they have the contempt of the opera singer for the microphone crooner—and they are not Pied Pipers. With high glee 'The Guv'nor' produced, doubtless for the thousandth time, a tattered leaflet advertising a man who styled himself 'The Great Lafini'. He had an accordion and claimed to charm rats from their holes 'with or without music'. It was an unfortunate moment when in a pub one day he tried some sales talk on Dalton senior.

A clatter outside the parlour announced the return of two of the old man's sons who had been engaged in a side-line, catching pigeons in Parliament Square for the Westminster City Council. They had had a tiresome afternoon, harassed by a woman who said she spent a shilling a day in feeding the birds, and generally outwitted by the birds themselves. Only caught thirty. Last time it had been a hundred and forty. 'You couldn't catch a —— pigeon if it was served up in a —— pie,' said the Guv'nor.

Public sentiment prevents their using nets, so they sidle up to the birds, and with a deft snatch thrust them under their macintoshes and wring their necks at the same time. I saw a hamper with a hundred odd corpses neatly on their backs in rows.

'What do you do with them?'

'Sell 'em in the market.'

'What do they taste like?'

'Taste like? They taste of what you'd think they'd taste of—petrol and 'orses.'

We adjourned to the back yard.

The shed in the yard was a mortuary-menagerie. Corpses of rats, mice, beetles, cockroaches laid out in rows: a bushel basket of dried-up rats' tails. How many? The old man consulted his notebook: 1931—47,000 rats. Last year business had improved on account of the war. Rain to drive the rats indoors, sandbags for them to lurk in, and the black-out, all had combined to cause a ratting 'boom'. Total bag, 72,826. 'Let you 'ave thirteen 'undred tails a week, if you want 'em.'

'Now I'm going to show you something you *never* seen before—nor anyone else either for that matter.' Seizing an iron bar, he prodded viciously in the dark end of a long wire cage. A squealing grey mass of rats streamed through the little hole in the partition. (Have you noticed how rats don't seem to run? They *flow*, especially *en masse*: an uneasy spectacle.) The more he prodded, the more rats came out, till they were piled high on each other and clinging upside down to their wire ceiling. I imagined one running up my trouser leg, as the spectator at the flea circus imagines a non-existent itch.

'He's here somewhere. Ah, there he is, the beauty!' A single rat emerged, took a look around—and chucked itself head over heels backwards. Two paces forward, and it did it again. And again. And again. Twelve times in ten seconds.

'Two of my boys and I went to a warehouse down by the docks the other night, and what do we see but two 'undred of 'em turning somer- saults. 'Dalton,' I said, 'you've got 'em coming on. It's time you give up.' But it was true. We caught two hundred and eighty that night and every one of 'em did it. Don't ask me why. No one can tell us. We've 'ad medical gentlemen and university professors to look at 'em—we kept a dozen of these rats—but none of 'em can explain it.'

If I hadn't seen it with my own eyes, sober, in mid-afternoon, I would not have believed it. Perhaps you don't now. If not, I hardly blame you.

More than ever I wondered what was the secret weapon by which seven generations of Daltons have tricked the craftiest wits in the animal kingdom. One night they caught sixteen hundred rats in three hours in a Romford brickfield, while the remainder counter-attacked by gnawing the tyres of their motor car. You or I probably would not have seen a rat all night.

'After fifty years with 'em,' said the Guv'nor, as he drew a big brown rat by the tail from another cage and exhibited it nonchalantly on his sleeve, 'you know what a rat's going to do before he knows it 'imself.'

Perhaps that's the secret.

Episode

I lived for two or three years in a flat in Red Lion Square, conveniently next door to Messrs. Dent & Hellyer, the well-known sanitary specialists, and the Lord's Day Observance Society. Red Lion Square was a relic of old Bloomsbury, and they used to tell me that twenty-five years ago there ought to have been a red light over most of the doors. However, it was quiet enough in my time, except for the occasional bashing of mudguards and the consequent altercations at the narrow corner under my window. On Saturday nights this little backwater was silent as a cemetery.

It was about eleven o'clock one Saturday night that I got home, weary from a week in the north of England. The block of flats was deserted. I carted in my luggage and dumped it in the lift.

Then I noticed a shadowy form fluttering about in the passage. It turned out to be an elderly, grey-haired lady who lived on the top floor.

Could I be of assistance? Well, yes, I could. She was looking for the caretaker. We searched together. Not a sign of a soul. She had to confide her troubles to someone. 'I hate to be a nuisance,' she said, humbly, 'but—well, there's something decidedly queer going on upstairs. It's the young woman who lives next to me. . . .'

'What's she been doing?'

'Well, she's plastered up the windows and door of her flat—and there's a sort of something coming out of the geyser vent in the wall. I don't like it at all.'

Neither did I, but there was nothing for it but to go up and investigate, so up we went to the fifth floor. The flats on each floor had outside passages leading to the front doors, with iron rails to prevent you falling down into the well below—for all the world, as I used to warn visitors, like Sing-Sing.

It was eerie, alone up there in the roof, with the stars shining silently overhead.

'This is the door,' said my neighbour.

There it was, the cracks all plastered up with brown paper as she had said, and the slit for the letter-box too. Above the ventilation chimney leading out from the bathroom geyser the air shuddered almost perceptibly like a summer mirage.

'Well, here goes,' said I. Tearing the paper from the letter-box, I

46

threw aside my cigarette—a dramatic gesture this, as I remember thinking—bent down, thrust my nose inside, and sniffed.

A minute later I tottered back, coughing and spluttering for breath.

'Whoever she is,' I said, 'she can't be alive in that.' So I went down to my flat on the second floor and rang for the police.

Up to now I had been conducting myself in the masterful manner that befits the gentleman aiding a lady in distress. When I sat down alone in the flat to wait for the police, I began to wonder. . . .

That week the papers were full of an 'orrible murder half a mile away in Soho, where a fellow had done a girl in with a hatchet. How were we going to find the girl upstairs? I shivered and felt glad I had not got to go in by myself.

There was a clattering of boots below and I leant over the second floor rail to see that a sergeant and constable had arrived. Together we went up again to the roof.

The sergeant took a sniff at the letter-box and retired wheezing and wiping his eyes with his handkerchief. 'Suicide,' he observed in an impersonal sort of way. 'No doubt about that. We 'ave 'undreds of 'em.'

He turned to the constable. 'Well, come on. We'd better make it the door.' We prepared to charge down the door. In a moment we should know the worst.

Then the sergeant had a better idea. Why not the window? The three of us gave an almighty heave, the window shot up, and we shot in. A moment later we were staggering about the passage, choking and bent grotesquely double.

The woman had gone off for the week-end and was fumigating her flat while she was away.

The whole block of flats in which this episode occurred was blown to smithereens in the war, luckily after I left. Its modern successor by a coincidence houses the publisher of this book, whose office must be within a few feet of my late sitting-room.

'Will I Give Ye the Daylight?'

I have been passing a week in Dublin, a city of strange contrasts, and, to me, poignant memory—for it was here during the worst part of the war that, after much wangling, I arrived on the way to spend a leave with Valentine Castlerosse at Killarney, learnt that he had died that day, and, with a sadness not erased since, took the same boat back to England in the morning.

The contrasts remain. The breath-taking beauty of some of the old Georgian streets glowing in the evening sun with a sort of Italian light that we rarely see in England . . . and the utilitarian drabness of modern Dublin. The tourist lures of Grafton Street, with the visitors in search either of seven-and-sixpenny steaks, or a bottle of E.V.M. ('English Visitors' Mixture'—any Irish chemist knows the formula) after too many of them . . . and the pale woman singing for alms in the gutter, carrying, like the London Communists, a baby in her arms, possibly her own.

To an Englishman, though, Dublin offers 'escape' by means other than the traditional steaks. The devil-may-care attitude towards life and the worries thereof is a happy contrast with the regimented queueing and solemn government posters in England.

A happy instance of this carefree attitude occurred during a broadcast in which I was engaged after the final of the amateur golf championship.

From an upstairs room in the Portmarnock Club we were meant to chip in to a programme run each Saturday evening by Angus McKay, covering the day's sport. An hour previously I had recorded a two-minute talk with Sam McCready, the new champion. On the strength of this and, I suspect, the fact that a good deal of cricket had been washed out, we were to have six minutes.

Eventually the voice from London said, 'Over to Portmarnock . . . .' This was greeted by dead silence—which was not surprising seeing that the only man who could hear London was at that moment making a telephone call.

Eventually 'Another try at Portmarnock. . . .' said the voice, and away we went. In due course on went the record, revolving silently on its plate.

A few seconds later it faded away, leaving four figures gesticulating feverishly to each other over a live microphone and a dead, but still revolving, disc. Complete shambles!

Now whatever you may say of the B.B.C., their outside broadcasts never go wrong. Their organization in this direction is unsurpassed. I imagined the scene in the London studio, the tearing of hair, the subsequent inquests, the search for the culprit.

'Ah, 'tis over now,' said the Irish, packing up their traps, 'I wouldn't be worrying myself about that all.'

That's the spirit!

Irishmen have a great gift for expressing commonplace things in a graphic way. A well-known English friend of mine, for instance, after a thoroughly Irish evening lay slumbering heavily next morning. The elderly hotel valet shook him by both shoulders and, sizing up the situation, asked—not would he like the curtains drawn but: '*Will I give ye the daylight?*'

I am afraid I 'started something' by writing, just after the war, that it seemed to say the least of it peculiar to play the British Amateur Golf Championship in a neighbouring Republic which had been neutral during the war and now declared itself categorically to have 'no connection with the old firm'. Furthermore, that it was an odd prospect to take out a passport and go through the Customs liable to interrogation and possibly search before being permitted to land to play in one's own championship.

This gave considerable offence at Portmarnock and my last memory of that hospitable club is of being penned in against the wall by a ring of outraged Eireans busy celebrating an Ulsterman's success in the championship. Fingers prodded me in the ribs; amber-filled glasses waved before my eyes; a man seized me by the lapel.

'Is this the fellow? . . . Listen to me now. . . . Leave him alone, man. . . . I thought't would be an older man . . . 'tis not the British Championship anyway . . . give him a drink, man.'

It is all very well to say 'keep off politics in Ireland'. You can't! If it is not the republic, it is partition. And if it's not partition, it's the Pope.

'There is no hope for Ireland,' said one of the most renowned citizens of Dublin, 'till they give them bull-fighting!'

Earlier in the week a T.D., which is the Eire equivalent of our M.P., kindly arranged for me to visit the Dail, pronounced Doyle like the Irish boxer. This seemed to hold prospects of entertainment as well as instruction, for the paper that morning contained details of a happy little episode when Mr. Dillon, Minister of Agriculture, had made allegations regarding a Fianna Fail deputy:

Mr. Dillon: 'Stand up like a man. Don't be snivelling there behind your hand!'

Mr. O'Briain (F.F.): 'Can you tell us what a man is at all?'

Mr. Allen (F.F): 'You twisted-nosed cur!'

It was with lively hopes, therefore, that your correspondent passed through the stately portals in Kildare Street, and was ushered into the Strangers' Gallery.

Here the first thing that strikes the eye is the wire caging which prevents the irate visitor from registering displeasure with any missile bigger than, say, a tennis ball. The pattern of this grille, after he has gazed through it for an hour or two, lingers in the visitor's eye long after he re-emerges into the outside world.

The twenty-one deputies in attendance on the day in question, however, did nothing to displease each other or the fifty-six spectators in the gallery.

Mr. Morrissey, Minister of Industry and Commerce, presented the estimates for his department, reading from a typescript in a way that would not have done for the Speaker of the House of Commons, while Mr. Lemass, his opposite number on the other side, deplored that the Ministry had promised so much and done so little.

As I listened to the Minister closing his speech and heard the sonorous, familiar phrases, 'no reason for complacency . . . only by whole-hearted co-operation of all groups . . . enjoy that standard of living to which we all aspire . . . no time, however, to waste . . . much still to be done. . . .' I realized that Ministers do not change much in this world.

Baker Street Revisited

(By Sherlock Holmes in an interview with Henry Longhurst)

I should be obliged if, through the medium of your admirable journal, I might express my appreciation of the St. Marylebone Borough Council's assistance to me in laying open to the public for the Festival of Britain the chambers so long occupied by Dr. John H. Watson and myself in Baker Street.

The rooms, together with my papers, had as usual, through the supervision of my brother Mycroft and the immediate care of Mrs. Hudson, been preserved unchanged during my retirement. Only an unwonted tidiness betrayed my own long absence. How long this absence had indeed lasted was brought home to me on hearing a newspaper photographer inquire which of the items were 'real'—that is, had in fact belonged to me!

The familiar interior, together with the yellow fog swirling outside our windows—almost obscuring the plaque to the actress, Mrs. Sarah Siddons, on the wall opposite, which Watson failed to notice in thirty years—the street cries, the clip-clop of the horses' hooves, and the itinerant musician still repeating the same discordant song almost as though on a gramophone record, all sent my mind racing back to what has well been called 'a world where it is always 1895'.

Those were, we are now assured, the bad old days. That they were more violent days I was reminded as my eye fell again on the harpoon in the corner (I wonder whether Allardyce's would have a whole pig for me to practise upon nowadays?), and knuckle-dusters and handcuffs; Colonel Moran's bullet-mark beside the door, to say nothing of the VR which I so light-heartedly shot in the wall, and all the miscellaneous firearms, including not only Von Herder's celebrated airgun but also the superb gold-damascened Adams muzzle-loading pistol presented by the Duke of Montrose, for my services in a matter which His Grace may yet permit Watson to lay one day before the public.

I have been particularly happy to receive messages of good will from the Baker Street Irregulars in the United States and, as their patron, I return greetings both to them and to such scion societies as the Musgrave Ritualists of New York, the Dancing Men of Providence, the Speckled Band of Boston and the Hounds of the Baskerville in Chicago.

It is always a joy to me to meet an American, as I told Mr. Francis Hay Moulton, and I continue to believe, sir, that the folly of a Monarch and the blundering of a Minister in far gone years will not prevent our children from being some day citizens of the same world-wide country.

As certain members of the public have, during the past week, addressed problems to me at Baker Street, may I add that advancing years—I will not say advanced, for I am only seven years senior to Dean Inge, who preached such an excellent sermon at Oxford only two Sundays ago—advancing years keep me in retirement in Sussex, where, as President of the British Beekeepers' Association, I apply to apiarian problems the same great powers which I so long turned to the detection of crime.

Though I did, it is true, emerge from seclusion during the recent hostilities to assist the department now known as MI5, this was only on occasions when Mycroft had convinced me that continued failure on their part would imperil the entire outcome of the war. In peacetime my retirement remains complete.

I do not, of course, rate as an exception the not unexpected visit of an agitated successor of Lestrade's in connection with the, to him, mysterious episode in Westminster Abbey*—partly because I was able in any case to set him upon the track without leaving my villa and partly because, as I more than once told Lestrade himself, I care only to be associated with those cases which present some little difficulty in their solution.

* The removal of the Stone of Scone by Scottish students.

Done it at Last!

I suppose the small fry of today want to be spacemen when they grow up, but in my day we all wanted to be engine drivers. Recently, some forty-five years late, it fell to my lot to realize this ambition and I found myself, attired in a boiler suit, mounting the footplate of the steam engine 'Robin Hood' to accompany (I will not say assist) Driver Peters—who, like nearly all long distance drivers, looks like a retired Admiral—in hauling the 'Norfolkman' from Liverpool Street to Norwich, 120 miles in 120 minutes with a stop at Ipswich.

I recalled a remark of Lord Brabazon's that it was 'like driving a very powerful sports car—with two big ends gone, *and* a puncture.' We started quietly enough, with 'Robin Hood' puffing and panting in a most human sort of way up the long 1-in-128 'bank' (as we railway-men call it) from Liverpool Street to Brentwood, but it was not long before I realized that his Lordship had understated the case. It is more like driving a very powerful sports car with all the big ends gone, and four punctures.

Thereafter, as Mr. Peters coaxed his iron steed up to ninety miles an hour to make up time, I retain a confused impression of a deafening din, steam, smoke, vibration, blasts of heat as the fireman opened the hatch to feed the inferno blazing within, and a scalding sensation round the ankles as he periodically hosed down the cabin with jets of boiling water.

Above all was the feeling of superiority. This was a surprise. As a passenger, you mount one step and then sit down. On the engine you climb up four steps and then stand up. Both literally and psychologi-cally you look down on the rest of the world. At some little crossing in rural Suffolk a little man was waiting in his little motor car. 'Yes,' I thought, looking contemptuously down at him as we thundered by, '*and* you'd better.'

As for one's own passengers, they scarcely exist. They are coming along behind there somewhere, one supposes, eating, drinking, sleep-ing, reading or whatever it is they are doing, but one thought monopo-lises the mind—to urge this great monster to Norwich on time.

Losing unregainable minutes through work on the new station at Colchester, we nearly did so. As the passengers streamed by without a passing glance for Driver Peters, I felt like rattling a collection box in their faces. I washed my hair in the stationmaster's office, but after the fourth immersion the water still came out like draught stout so I gave it up.

How different was our return in the diesel! Padded armchair; sliding window out of which to lean a nonchalant elbow; uninterrupted, smokeless view of the road and the countryside; everything clean as a new pin and 2,000 horse-power throbbing behind the soundproof door—the Rolls-Royce of the rails.

'Yes,' said Driver Williams, 'but there's no *interest* in 'em. The old steamer's almost human. You've got to *get* something out of her.'

There was another surprise, namely the number of birds that apparently prefer the railway line to the surrounding meadows, heaths and woods. Crows, pigeons, partridges, pheasants and innumerable sparrows. There being no vegetation on the line, one can only suppose them to be in search of grit. The crows, I noticed, are the wariest. They get up at a range of 200 yards. Pigeons step off with an offended air at the last moment—often, indeed, too late.

With merely a couple of levers, one in each hand, and a 'dead man's pedal' which begins to bring the train automatically to a halt if one takes one's foot off it for seven seconds, I formed the impression, doubtless erroneous, that on a clear day I could safely be entrusted with a diesel train myself.

In the open country one felt little impression of speed, but when it came to roaring between the narrow platforms of the suburban stations and over the points at 85 m.p.h. the feeling of superiority and 'Out of my way!' became more insufferable than ever, and the temptation to seize the knob and give the peculiar two-tone diesel tootle to passengers waiting for mere 'stopping' trains proved quite irresistible.

I retired to my bath in the Great Eastern Hotel with a smug satisfaction at having 'done it at last' and the more humble conviction that, whatever the drivers of steam engines are paid, they deserve double.

SOMETHING OF A SOLDIER

Military Characters

I am sure that conditions of peace would never have brought Gunner Merlin and myself together, if only through the fourteen years' difference in our ages. I was brought up with an orthodox and proper respect for authority. Gunner Merlin, now nineteen, was brought up in the back streets of Birmingham with an equally commendable distrust and defiance of it. The rest of us, as newly joined soldiers do, held the officers in considerable awe. To be spoken to by 'the Major' was an event in itself. Merlin, on the other hand, would cheerfully have told a brigadier what he could go and do with his red tabs. 'Crime' is almost unknown among recruits, unfamiliar as yet with the tricks and dodges of the trade, but Merlin took to it like a duck to water.

He was lean, agile, and wiry, and his appearance was remarkable for the fact that he had but a single tooth in the whole of his head—an incredibly long affair, sprouting solitarily from the side of his upper jaw. Nevertheless, his toothless grin had something compelling about it and, if it was difficult to condone some of his activities, it was quite impossible to be cross with him for long. I took a great delight in his company and contrived, whenever possible, to take him with me in my vehicle when detailed, for instance, to go and fetch the rations from Preston. It was an understood thing between us that I supplied the cigarettes which he illicitly smoked in the back and stood the bill for the pies that we consumed at 'Uncle Joe's Good Pull-up for Carmen' on the way home, while he, in turn, worked with a will at his job of loading up the rations. With anyone else he would unaccountably have vanished the first time the vehicle pulled up at the traffic lights.

There never was such a fellow for vanishing. He could have earned a fortune at the Indian rope trick. He vanished in the middle of the afternoon one day, and I remember the mixed awe and astonishment of the rest of us when a chance roll-call at the end brought it to light that Gunner Merlin was no longer with us. He vanished when being transported to the dental centre at Fleetwood and returned refreshed by a pint apiece at the expense of three sailors and two civilians. We coined the definition of an empty cinema as 'Gunner Merlin watching *The Invisible Man*'.

It was only natural that he should be the first of us to appear on a charge—or rather six charges, including arriving home at four in the morning and happening to be absent from certain parades and vanishing during the course of others. His escape with a mere warning earned the admiration of all except the man who had just been awarded twenty-four hours' extra guard for falling asleep at a lecture on carburettors. Our admiration was increased when, grinning amiably, he turned up late for the first parade next morning.

It fell to my lot to instruct this character in the art of driving. He had never sat in the driving seat of a vehicle in his life before, but the business caught his fancy. He was an apt and enthusiastic pupil, and it took him no time to rattle the gears about with a most professional air. Even so, he wanted watching. On one of our convoys over the hills the long line of vehicles had come to one of its innumerable hold-ups, and I was sitting admiring the scenery from the instructor's seat. I turned to find the driving seat vacant and Gunner Merlin hastily pulling carrots in a neighbouring field. In August a number of us volunteered for harvesting duties—Merlin, of course, with an eye to the main chance, among us. On returning to camp he was offering for sale a live rabbit in his respirator haversack and a battledress blouse full of green apples.

Then, again, there was Sergeant Apex, with whom I was, for a time, billeted. He was one of that rich procession of characters that one comes to know intimately only through service life. He came from South Wales, had appealingly large brown eyes, looked about forty, and was, in fact, less than thirty. At the least excuse his mouth would stretch into an enormous grin, revealing his two remaining teeth, hanging down, one on each side. It was perhaps for this reason that he showed such a marked preference for liquid refreshment.

He was taciturn at first—I thought, though probably wrongly, on account of the disparity in our respective ranks—but you cannot be billeted alone with another man and keep that sort of thing up for long. A couple of pints thawed him one evening and gradually I extracted the philosophy and story of his life. In a sing-song Welsh voice he told of the old days at Port Talbot when he had been earning eight pounds a week with an odd five-pound bonus. He spent twenty-seven and six on his lodgings and drank the rest, fourteen or fifteen pints in a day, he said—though when one evening we consumed half that number together he came home giggling feebly. Still, he had gone at it with sufficient vigour to qualify eventually as an exhibition case at the Radcliffe Hospital at Oxford—'burnt away the lining of my stomach, man, it did.' They put him on the water-wagon, so he drank five bottles of concentrated 'egg-flip' in one evening at six shillings a time, and forthwith found himself back as an exhibition case again.

Sergeant Apex, when I met him, had been in the army sixteen months, which he reckoned was four months too long. He had charge of an 'awkward squad' of forty men, including an Irish boy who had incautiously tried to knife a twenty-stone bombardier, who, in turn, said Apex, had nearly killed him by kneeling on him. All boys together, in fact. To Apex this was tame stuff after the expedition to Narvik, and especially the return therefrom, which he made in the destroyer *Devonshire* in company with the Norwegian royal family and a few millions in gold. They were concerned in the action in which the *Glorious* was lost, but the tale was mainly remarkable for his description of what seasickness can do to a man. 'Dee-ah God, it was 'orrible,' he said.

It was their duty, it appears, to man the anti-aircraft guns on the front of the ship, but only two men were capable of reaching them. Eventually these lay unconscious beside the guns, one of them 'out' for two days, lying as though dead, with his mouth open. The occasion called for stern measures and Apex, on finding, by means not disclosed, a quart jar of the official rum ration, drank two-thirds of it neat. On regaining consciousness twenty-four hours later, he not unnaturally found that his 'thrort was on fiyer, man'.

He mentioned a point which I found intriguing, old as it may be to those who have experienced the Far North. In Narvik and Tromso, he said, it was light all day. On asking the time and being told, say three o'clock, it was customary to ask 'Day or night?' And when the expedition drew towards home, a great crowd lined the ship's rails simply to catch a glimpse of real old-fashioned darkness again.

To one who came straight from a number of years in civilized London it was a happy chance to share one's billet with a man so refreshingly raw as Apex. He had a stimulating disrespect for authority and for the more urbane conventions of life. When he felt like going on the early morning parade before breakfast, he did so; when he did not, he stayed in bed: an attitude which I held in respectful awe but dared not emulate. When you went out for a drink with him, there was always the engaging prospect, as the evening wore on, of a free fight, for some trifling cause of which the participants would have little recollection next morning. On one occasion at 'Uncle Tom's Cabin', a large red-brick hostelry well known to North Blackpool holiday-makers, a man was incautious enough to hit him on the head with a bottle. Apex smote the man on the ear, rendered him unconscious, and would, I gather, have trampled him to death if he had not been pulled off by two chuckers-out.

Disappointed at the apparent ignoring by the War Office of his application to become a parachutist, and piqued further by the loss of one of his stripes for an improper observation over the counter to one of the girls in the N.A.A.F.I., Bombardier Apex applied to be a gunner in the merchant navy, and great were the celebrations when it was learnt that he had been accepted. He returned on leave to South Wales, and the last I heard of him was that an escort had been dispatched to retrieve him. Trouble with the police, it was said.

Rigours of Active Service

It was during one of the most austere stages of the war that a friend showed me a letter.* It came from a man we both knew well, then stationed in Egypt. He had struck up a pleasing acquaintance, it seemed, with a young Syrian widow who owned what was virtually a palace, somewhere down the Nile. Three slaves took his hat when he called, he said, and 'it requires six more to relieve me of my Sam Browne'. His letter, the last sentence of which needs to be read rather slowly, concluded: 'her road transport problems are solved by a white Mercedes, an all-black Packard, and an open Cadillac. I generally remain after the guests have gone, to discuss the war situation.

'Standing there with this exquisite Syrian, with the moon on the Nile like molten silver, a radio playing Beethoven in the background, and two coal-black eyes gazing up at you, a scarlet rosebud mouth, and a husky voice with a fascinating accent saying: "You are 'appy?" brings home to you, my dear Lewis, the rigours of active service.'

* Alas, the writer of this letter was burnt to death in the Turf Club by a Cairo mob some years after the war.

Below Stairs

A rich ore of comedy was to be mined in the murky below-stairs depths of the Blackpool boarding house-cum-hotel, 'Eldorado', in the basement of which fourteen of us were billeted, to the great distress of the management and ourselves. The man Ledger, for instance. How they passed him for the army, even in those days, is just one of those things. Ledger was not 'a bit wanting' or 'not all there'; he was stark, staring crazy. And dangerous, at that.

(Incidentally in the same intake we had another man who was eventually carted off to a lunatic asylum; a man who had one leg an inch shorter than the other; two men with double ruptures; one who had kept himself alive for years on milk and fish; and a host of other crocks, the details of whose obvious disabilities now escape me—all passed as A1 by medical boards.)

Ledger was about twenty-five years old, and had been a miner all his life. His speech was pretty well unintelligible. 'Thar say?' he would say for 'Do you see?' and 'tray' for 'three'. When at last they discharged him, he stole my greatcoat to hand in, and tried to keep his own for Civvy Street—almost the only spark of sanity the poor fellow ever showed.

In charge of the miscellaneous gang in 'Eldorado' was Bombardier Chivers, another young Nottingham miner, this time with his head screwed on very much the right way. Now everyone has heard of lunatics who say they are Napoleon, or Jesus Christ, and so on, but it does not fall to the lot of many of us to hear one seriously do so. It happened at tea one day when, after a hard day's training, we sat down to half a tinned pilchard each, generously provided by the proprietor of 'Eldorado'.

'Ah'm Jasus Christ. That's who Ah am,' said Ledger.

The man beside him intimated that he did not accept this proposition, whereupon Ledger, with foam slobbering horribly from between his teeth, seized the largest knife he could see, caught the man round the neck, and held the knife to his throat.

'Ah'm Jasus Christ!' he said. 'Thar say?'

The situation, time-honoured manifestation of lunacy though it might be, was pregnant with potential tragedy. It was saved by Bombardier Chivers. Looking calmly up from his miserable pilchard, he said:

'In that case you can set about turning these few small fishes into food for fourteen men.'

There is no beating about the bush with men like Chivers. We were riding along the front in a crowded tram together one day, standing in the doorway. Sitting beside us on one of those occasional tip-up seats was a little old man of, perhaps, seventy odd. He talked to us for a bit, told us the history of a carved walking-stick he was leaning on, and then said:

'And how old do you think I am?'

Before we could offer our respective estimates, he added proudly: 'I'm eighty-three'. A fine achievement by the old boy, and I was taking breath to say so, but Chivers got in first.

'Won't be long now,' he said.

'Eh?' said the old man.

Again I wasn't quick enough.

'I said, it won't be long now!' bellowed Chivers. I could have murdered him.

There was, as I say, plenty of quiet fun to be observed below stairs at 'Eldorado', much of it in the kitchen, where a male chef was theoretically in charge. The real dictator, however, was an elderly body by the name of Maggie. If Maggie had not lived as long as the old man in the tram, she had at least passed the age when she had any further illusions as to the qualities of her fellow humans. It would have done the fat, self-satisfied residents, stuffing themselves in the dining-room upstairs, no harm to hear Maggie's crisp summaries of them as she sent up their food.

Her directness of speech and action led to frequent shindies in the kitchen. 'You —— off!' she said to the kitchenmaid, receiving in reply a well-aimed kick upon her aged posterior. The kitchenmaid ducked neatly as a bar of soap flashed across the kitchen.

On another occasion it was the kitchen boy who offended. 'Come 'ere, you undersized little pisspot!' yelled Maggie, seizing the boy's hair and shaking his head like a coconut. I even fell foul of her myself, on the subject of washing-up, which fell to each of us one day a week. I maintained (and still so maintain) that the object of plate-racks is to enable you to put plates away without drying them. Maggie held that they must first be dried with a dishcloth. Perhaps I should have known better, but I stuck to my point. Her final word was a swinging blow across the ear with a wet dishcloth.

The alleged disappearance from the boiler-house of a pair of socks belonging to the son of the proprietress, and a pithy comment thereon which reached her ears when it wasn't meant to, brought to an end my grisly stay at 'Eldorado' and with the acid reprimand of the billeting officer ringing in my ears, combined with jealous queries of: 'How did you work it?' from those condemned to stay, I shook the dust of this maudlin establishment from my feet, I trust for ever.

Passing the Buck

Our arrival to learn about Bofors guns was not encouraging. Saighton Camp, it struck us, was not ill-named. A nice fine drizzle was sweeping across a barren square of disturbing bleakness, and it was perishing cold. On the square itself sundry groups of men were being chivvied round guns with long spouts, or standing in little knots, stamping their feet and blowing on their palms, round box-like instruments on tripods, which we took to be predictors.

In the regimental office the time-honoured procedure was gone through by the clerk, namely lifting the head, noticing one's presence, then going on writing. We shifted humbly from foot to foot until the young gentleman in spectacles deigned to notice us. We announced our names and what we took to be the reason for our presence. 'Sorry,' said the clerk, 'No notification about you here,' and turned back to his writing. This, again, is part of the time-honoured formula. If you have had no instructions, nobody can 'get' you for doing nothing about it. 'Not me, sir. No, sir, I wasn't told, sir.' The back of the clerk's head, as he bent over his form-filling, showed unmistakably that he deemed his part in the episode to be over. We started shifting from foot to foot again, muttering feebly to each other as soldiers do before they have learnt the way of dealing with army clerks.

At this point the sergeant-major entered. If it had not been for his uniform and the brass emblem on his arm, one would have taken him for a head stable-lad—a sharp-faced little man of five feet nothing, with legs you could almost pass a football through when he stood to attention. He was under the impression, common to sergeant-majors, that one made oneself better heard in a small room by bellowing.

'Well, what is it?' he roared. 'Who are you? What are you doing in here?'

We said our humble piece.

'Never heard of you,' he said. 'No one's told me anything.' With that he passed into his inner sanctum, slamming the door. The clerk went on with his writing.

That, of course, was the moment at which in civilian life one stalks out of the shop and takes one's business to the rival on the other side of the road, vowing never to darken the doors of the offending premises again—but, alas, the army has no rival across the road. It was half an hour before we were ushered into the presence again. He had never heard of us, he repeated. It appeared that the fact of his now having done so afforded him little pleasure. Must have come to the wrong place, he said. No, he could not help. Nothing to do with him. Nobody had ever told him anything. Never heard of us.

The secret on these occasions, which I pass on with confidence for use in dealing with the horde of clerks and officials who intrude so much upon our post-war private lives, is: 'Never ask a question which permits the answer No.' Never ask, for instance, 'Can you suggest anything that I can do?' This is a sheer long-hop to leg and will be dispatched to the boundary, as it deserves, by any small bureaucrat. 'No,' he will say. 'I can't.' There is no come-back to this. It is not laid down as part of his job to make suggestions. He is, in fact, 'covered' if he does nothing. Your approach must be one that demands a positive answer and leaves no loophole. For instance, I turned the tide with the sergeant-major by saying, adroitly: 'What are your instructions, sir?' He wriggled uneasily on the end of the hook, but he was fairly caught. The buck had been passed, and a buck-passer of long standing he knew it. It is a sergeant-major's job to give instructions. Better still, we had slipped neatly into the desired position of being able to say in turn: 'Not me, sir. No, sir. The sergeant-major said we were to . . . etc.' As we made our way to a hut in which he had had to allot us a bunk, we rather felt we had won the first round.

'Quartermasters. Are they Human?'

I have, in fact, met two human quartermasters, which must be almost a record for a purely wartime soldier. The first I ever knew was human—a charming, philosophical Irishman, whom I liked because he used to have me drive him in my lorry to buy tomatoes for the sergeants' mess, and this made a nice change. Not only was he human himself, but he seemed to think that, until proved otherwise, the rest of mankind were probably human, too.

Quartermasters spend all their lives on the defensive. They are like bookmakers, for ever matching their wits against the daily assault of the sharpest brains among the enemy. They are the guardians of what the army nicely terms 'attractive stores'—anything from boots to binoculars—stores which, if quartermasters were not dead to all human feeling, would vanish like the summer snow. Their official duty is to 'issue' things. Their life work lies in thinking out reasons why they may decline to issue things.

However, let us not be too serious about these strange fellows, for they provide, if nothing else, an interesting study. Their inverted jargon is alone sufficient to justify their existence. To hear them using it as natural speech—without, so to speak, putting it in inverted commas—was to me a constant joy. I was always faintly surprised that they did not call themselves 'masters, quarter, mark I'.

I was in the regimental office one day when the 'Q' came in—an elderly 'regular' in whom the last spark of human sympathy had long since flickered and died.

'What's all this about a stove?' he said.

The clerks rose with alacrity. It was a moment they had been waiting many long weeks for. The side of the stove had worn thin with the years, and now a hole had appeared, showing the coals glowing within.

'It's burnt through the side, sir,' they said.

The 'Q' took up the ramshackle poker, thrust it in the hole, and wrenched it viciously to and fro. The hole, which had started at about two inches, became now so wide that the coals fell out and the stove was a total loss.

'Ha!' he said. 'Damage, wilful.'

There were cries of protest, and I could see he was slightly shaken. Being much too old a hand to be beaten as easily as this, he played for time by jabbing about in the ashes round the grate. Suddenly he seized upon the derelict metal stump of what had once been a knife. Perhaps a quarter of the rusty, worn-away blade was left, and just the iron stump of the handle.

'There you are!' he said triumphantly, 'A nine-inch cookhouse, large.'

Piteous protests from the clerks would not shift him. 'Not me, sir. No, sir,' they all said; 'it was the stove, sir. . . .'

'Never mind the stove. What about this nine-inch cookhouse, large? They've lost three nine-inch cookhouse, large, from the cookhouse only these last few weeks. . . .'

He was still holding his ground about nine-inch cookhouse, large, when I left. And when I departed from the camp weeks later, the clerks were still sitting in their greatcoats.

There came a day when the battery captain handed each of us a document, with the ominous observation: 'I expect you'll be pretty familiar with this by the time you've finished.' It is strange that I, who am at heart a most unmilitary man, should treasure so much a document 'issued' to me as a soldier. When I am weary of spirit, I have only to think of it to bring on a warm glow of nostalgic affection. Little did the battery captain think that for one, at least, of his twenty apprehensive pupils his document was to be a joy for a lifetime. The document was headed: 'ORDNANCE SURVEY OF ENGLAND AND WALES. SWINDON & CIRENCESTER. SHEET 104.'

It shows a fine tracery of roads like dark-red ribbons, and wiggly blue streams, and irregular light-green blobs for woods and spinneys. It covers that ancient, fertile and deeply romantic part of England called the Vale of the White Horse.

The Vale lies between the Berkshire Downs and the Cotswolds, and the White Horse was cut in the chalk, no one knows how many centuries ago, on the summit of the Downs above Uffington, scene of Tom Brown's boyhood in the holidays from Rugby. A friend of mine, who was a cadet at Shrivenham in the early days of the war, was among those whose first duty was to go daily to 'black out' the White Horse with turf, much to the indignation of the residents of Uffington.

I folded my Sheet One-O-Four, as we called it, to fit a portion of the respirator haversack designed for other things, and there it remained my stand-by and companion for five blissful months. I still know most of it by heart. Now it hangs, with various predecessors from 1790 onwards, framed on the wall of the room in which I am writing.

What immense fascination there is in a map! . . . Ever since writing that last word 'map' I have idled away half an hour without thinking, wandering in a sentimental journey away across the Vale on Sheet One-O-Four. I followed that wonderful road along the Ridge, and saw again in the mind's eye the little villages that cluster in the elm trees at its foot; Kingston Lisle, famous for the Blowing Stone, with which they will tell you, as you pay your sixpence to blow it, King Alfred summoned his warriors; Woolstone, Compton Beauchamp, Ashbury, Bishopstone, Idstone; Callis Hill, where, after seven straight miles, Ermine Street strides up over the Ridge to the Downs behind,

SL-F

looking from a distance like a white pillar—so steep that in the old days it took six horses to drag a load of hay to the summit, up to the 'Shepherds' Rest', which a hundred thousand sheep would pass in a single year on the way to the great wool markets; and Wanborough, where, in the same evening, we watched the tragi-comic contrast of the black smoke curling up from the meadows where they were burning a farmer's whole store of cattle because one of them had got foot-and-mouth disease, and a drunken man trying to ride a penny-farthing bicycle.

Gradually as we began to cover the neighbourhood in our travels, the picture on the map came to life, revealing a pattern whose background has not substantially changed since the day when the first Roman stood upon the Ridgeway and found the primitive English already living on the slopes below.

Often, standing up there, we used to imagine the emotions of the Romans as their long tramp brought them at last to the crest, and they saw stretched out below them in the evening sun the whole gorgeous panorama of the Vale. It must have made all the rigours of their journey seem worthwhile. 'Sanguineum mirabilis!' perhaps they said (ungrammatically) as they set off, with spirits renewed, down the last lap to what they called Corinium and we call Cirencester.

The Ridge held a strange fascination for me. It dominated one's whole outlook. Sometimes in the morning haze it seemed many miles away, a strange mystical world of its own. Then, when the light changed, it would draw close and might have been a few hundred yards. In fact, it was about three miles away. But, however far it might be in fact, the spirit could traverse the distance in a flash, and you could be standing once more on the crisp, springy turf up by the beacon beside the White Horse, with the wind in your hair and the wild thyme under your feet, looking down over the hollow they call the 'Manger' to the village of Woolstone. Readers of Tom Brown will recognize this hill. 'Most of you,' says the author, 'have probably travelled down the Great Western Railway as far as Swindon. Those of you who did so with their eyes open have been aware, soon after leaving Didcot station, of a fine range of chalk hills running parallel with the railway on the left-hand side as you go down, and distant some two or three miles, more or less, from the line. The highest point in the range is the White Horse Hill, which you come in front of just before you stop at the Shrivenham station. If you love English scenery, and have a few hours to spare, you can't do better, the next time you pass, than stop at the Farringdon Road or Shrivenham station, and make your way to that highest point.

'I pity people who weren't born in a vale. I don't mean a flat country, but a vale—that is, a flat country bounded by hills. The having your hill always in view, if you choose to turn towards him, that's the essence of a vale. There he is for ever in the distance, your friend and companion; you never lose him as you do in hilly districts.

'And then what a hill is the White Horse Hill! There it stands right up above the rest, nine hundred feet above the sea, and the boldest, bravest shape for a chalk hill that you ever saw.'

The Vale in Hughes's day was traversed by no great roads—nothing but country parish roads, and those very bad. One coach ran there, and that only from Wantage to London 'so that the western part of the Vale was without regular means of moving on, and certainly didn't seem to want them'. On the other hand, they had another means of locomotion—the canal. It supplied the countryside with coal, and 'up and down went the long barges, with the big black men lounging by the side of the horses along the towing-path, and the women in bright-coloured handkerchiefs in the stern steering'. Young Tom Brown liked the look of their cosy little cabins, but his nurse told him that the good-looking ladies of the barges were in the habit of enticing children into them and taking them up to London and selling them—which made him more than ever determined to get a ride if he could.

'Fiske Memorial'

A little incident at a Birmingham gun site will always stick in my memory. Twice a week two kindly ladies used to appear in a Y.M.C.A. van and hoot encouragingly at the foot of our tower—whereupon the monkeys would down tools and rush down for their bag of nuts. They sold us chocolate and cakes and razor blades and tea, and lent out books, and were a cheerful and highly acceptable link with the outside world, and I hereby pay my humble tribute to the labours of them and their kind. One day, as I sipped my tea at the counter, I noticed the crossed Union Jack and Stars and Stripes on the side of the van. Underneath were the words, 'Fiske Memorial'.

Billy Fiske! My mind raced back over the years to the time when we used to travel almost daily the twenty-one miles from Cambridge to Mildenhall in his monstrous supercharged green Bentley and reckon it a poor journey if we did not touch 110 miles an hour on the long straight leading to Newmarket; and to the days when his father had helped to send a team of us to play golf in the United States. Fiske had a wonderful eye for speed, and for seven years he defied all comers on the Cresta toboggan run at St. Moritz. When he was seventeen, he captained the American bobbing team in the Olympic Games—and won. Long before the United States came into the war, Billy Fiske gave his life for this country, the first American to do so, flying a Hurricane in the Battle of Britain. Now he lies buried in a little Sussex churchyard, and a plaque in St. Paul's Cathedral commemorates our gratitude.

I wondered what crisp comment this forthright little man would have come out with, if he could have seen me drinking a penn'orth of tea from the van that kept his memory alive.

Shot in the Dark

One night, dark deeds were afoot in the little Northumberland town of Haltwhistle. Up one of the narrow stone alley-ways behind the houses a shot rang out in the darkness. The alley-way was deserted, as such alleys are at that time of night, but citizens materialized apparently from nowhere and soon a goodly crowd was standing over the prostrate form of Sergeant Boffin. Gazing balefully up at the sympathetic company, he revealed that he had been shot in the ankle.

Sergeant Boffin, it has to be confessed, was not a very good type. He was fond of the ladies in a manner less wholesome and manly than the normal, licentious soldiery, and prolonged sojourn in the battery office, where he had charge of the paper work, had rendered him somewhat soft. (He was heard to observe when a sudden inrush of paper work looked like confining him late in the office one night: 'Bumph to the left of them; bumph to the right. Boffin will not ride tonight!') He was carted away to hospital, and it was not surprising that next morning, rumour having flown swiftly and lost nothing in its flight, all Haltwhistle was busy *cherchant la femme*. It became generally accepted that, in emerging from one of his not infrequent back-street amours, Boffin had been overtaken by a jealous husband.

There was much muttered whispering in the mess and the barrack-rooms, but no official acknowledgement of the affair, which was held to reflect no great credit on the battery and therefore best left unmentioned. A later discovery, however, added such fuel to the fire that the mystery could no longer be suppressed. It was found, I fancy by a police officer, that, whereas the unhappy Boffin had undoubtedly had his trousers on at the time of the shooting, and whereas the bullet had caught him fairly high up in the ankle, it had not, in fact, passed through his trousers. So what now, my dear Watson? You know my methods. Apply them!

I was not privileged to share in the investigations that ensued. Suffice to say that the finger of guilt veered inexorably to the victim's twenty-year-old brother, Gunner George Boffin. All manner of charges were laid against him, including being in illegal possession of an army revolver and ten rounds of ammunition, and feloniously shooting his brother in the ankle to save the latter the inconvenience of serving in His Majesty's army abroad. The sergeant was in due course charged, and limped away on crutches, with his foot in plaster of Paris, to serve eighteen months. Gunner George, languishing in irons awaiting his court martial, intimated that nothing would do but that Mr. Longhurst should conduct his defence.

As I had never spoken to the man and did not know him by sight, and furthermore had no legal background whatever, I felt this to be something of a compliment. On the principle of trying anything once, I accepted with alacrity. Such a request, in any case, no officer is entitled to refuse. If the truth be told, I shall always be grateful to Gunner Boffin for giving me the opportunity.

I went to interview the accused in his cell. A large, rather flabby, but by no means ill-looking youth, he had been whiling the hours away by drawing naked ladies with the stub of a pencil. Rather well done, they were. He seemed almost more interested in his art than in his predicament. After a certain amount of 'playing for position' he decided to come clean and told me the story of the fatal night. I think there is no doubt that he wished he had not done it, but equally that he was secretly rather intrigued to be the focus of so much attention and notoriety. His home background had been poor and his education perfunctory, and the influence of the films left him not wholly displeased with his role of local Al Capone. I asked him, for instance, how far he had been from his brother when the latter lifted his trouser leg and held out his foot to be shot at.

'About nine feet,' he replied.

'Surely it was a pretty good shot in the dark at that range?' I said.

His face lit up, and a light of honest keenness brightened his eye.

'Oh, I am a good shot, sir,' he said. 'I'd always get 'im at that range.'

The business meant a great deal of very hard work. The professional lawyer knows the procedure of the court and merely has to work up his brief. Though I had passed the ordinary military law exam (top, in fact!) as a cadet at Shrivenham, I had to learn the procedure, and very complicated it all is. However, I went to it with a will, because I felt that with the exercise of a little imagination one could get a real insight into the legal mind and the atmosphere of a lawyer's life—and, after all, almost anyone, given nine lives, would spend one of them as a barrister.

Though I cannot remember the legal niceties of it now, I recall that the great point was whether my 'client' should plead guilty or not guilty, and after much delay it was decided that it should be not guilty, for some technical reason, for, of course, it was not disputed that ' 'e done it'. He was incarcerated for a while in a dark dungeon at Fort

Fareham, while we were temporarily at Hamble, and the court martial took place at Newcastle.

There was evidence of mental instability in his record and he had once attended hospital at Northampton for trouble of a mental nature. Furthermore, a previous psychiatrist's report indicated that he might not be responsible for his actions. Much play must obviously be made of this. Unfortunately the psychiatrist was a lieutenant, and a later one, a major, had recorded that he could find nothing wrong with Boffin. Never mind, we must do our best. I had a word with the lieutenant just before the court martial. To my dismay he confessed that he 'thought he just remembered the fellow, but had been called away at the time, and had only seen him for about five minutes.' He was in a state of considerable apprehension. Without wishing to be unkind I can only say that he rather confirmed the current Army opinion of 'trick cyclists'.

The court martial taught me many things—one of them being an admiration for the disciplined patience of the lawyer. One after the other the witnesses came up, were sworn, and gave their evidence.

'Any questions?'

'No questions,' I would reply.

Then came the nervous psychiatrist. 'Did he seriously aver that in his opinion the accused was so mentally unbalanced as to be wholly un-aware of his actions at the time?' It was a straight question, and I am afraid that, after much humming and ha-ing and fidgeting with his tie, he could only give one answer. Our only hope was reduced to my speech in mitigation of sentence.

This went off reasonably enough, and I could see that I had scored a point by saying that, while I could not suggest that if one had tapped him on the shoulder as he poised the pistol for the fatal act and said: 'Do you think that what you are about to do is right or wrong?' he would have replied anything but 'wrong'—still, his mental history showed that he was not so acutely aware of the rightness of right and the wrongness of wrong as the rest of us. Indeed, I think this was fair.

At any rate, when the court broke up, the president was kind enough to ask whether I had any legal experience and, when I replied that I had none, to say: 'Well, I only wish that people with legal experience would stick to the point in the same way that you did.' My cup of gratification was full when, on walking up and down outside for a final word with my client, he said that he was quite satisfied that nothing more could possibly have been done for him. He got eighty-four days. Even so, I gathered, he would employ me again!

Shooting Gallery

Anti-aircraft experts always maintained that if ever they got targets that flew straight and level, at a constant speed, they would knock them down like ninepins. I am afraid I used to bait the enthusiasts in the mess on this subject. Well, here at last, with the flying bombs, was the acid test. Here was a great profusion of targets that really did fly at a constant height, course and speed. What about it?

The coast road beside the golf links at Littlestone, so familiar to holiday-makers though now deserted, had become, I suppose, the greatest shooting gallery the world has ever seen. On the way down we had driven through the incredible balloon belt near Sevenoaks, where every open space, even bits of railway embankment, had its balloon detachment encamped therein. Here it was the same story with guns. For miles along the foreshore there were guns of every calibre and kind. Heavies, with men and girls living under canvas; Bofors six in a row, wheel to wheel; batteries of rockets; Oerlikons; even tanks, track to track on the pebbles, each with a man in the turret manning twin machine-guns. It was a glorious free-for-all. Even the crackpot inventors who used to come to the War Office with 'the final answer to the anti-aircraft problem—here in this suitcase', were given a pitch and told to do their worst. An American battery also took part, and I was told that one of them was seen potting at a doodle bug with his revolver. It probably was not true, but such was the extraordinary atmosphere of the whole show that it quite well might have been. Magic rays, drain-pipes, revolvers, shotguns, catapults—it was all in. The old cautionary Rules for Opening Fire went to the winds. Anything that came from the other side of the Channel was fair game.

The final set-up was that the fighters had the first crack—from over the enemy coast to a line in mid-channel marked by coloured buoys. From then on to our own coast it was the guns. They in turn were not allowed to fire over land, where the next belt was reserved again for fighters. This stretched as far as the balloon barrage at Sevenoaks. After that, there was nothing for it but the sirens and the rescue squads.

The brigadier at Littlestone, a large Irishman with his foot in plaster of Paris, sent me along, after a few nostalgic memories of Killarney and County Kerry, to a 'heavy' site some miles down the road. Again it was the same story—every field, every space on the beach, occupied by some sort of weapon pointing out to sea. Our site was a bare patch in the open marsh, with a few huts and a wooden contraption which carried the predictor and served as an observation tower.

Neither officers nor men had averaged more than a couple of hours' sleep for three or four weeks and, so far as one could see, there was not much chance of their doing so in the measurable future. All through the night there were alarms and turn-outs, but nothing came our way. At last, at the first break of dawn, the whistles got everyone stumbling to his post again, and one could sense that this time it was the real thing.

The scene is one of strange beauty, the picture of which has stamped itself ineffaceably on my mind. There is that solemn stillness before the dawn when you can positively hear the silence. Away in the east the blood-red early light is shimmering on the calm ripples of the sea and above it the sky is turning mauve. On either side it is still too dark to see, but, down below, you can detect the outlines of the big guns and an occasional vague figure beside them.

It is impressive to reflect that for miles on either side men are standing to all manner of weapons in the darkness, all gazing in the same direction, all waiting for the thing that is now but a moving speck on the plotting boards to take shape on the horizon. There is a thrilling air of expectancy and you find you have been holding your breath. Any minute now!

At last, far, far away in the dawn, there appears a tiny pale light, for all the world like the first morning star. It is moving very slightly across the sky, even as another star, not bearing man's devices of death, may have moved over Bethlehem two thousand years before. But such thoughts follow afterwards. For the moment all we know is 'This is it!' and in a minute or so, in that purposeful sort of way that doodles have, the first target of the day comes hurrying along.

A second later a fantastic cannonade shatters the silence. From every open space within miles men are shooting at this thing. Deafening cracks, accompanied by sheets of flame, rock our wooden platform. Black puffs smudge the sky all round the doodle, some desperately near, some not so good, one or two, where a man has mis-set the fuse, a mile from the mark. It seems incredible that anything can live in this, but it does. On it flies, and now the Bofors are in range. For men who have not had a target for a year, and then only the quick ten-second flash of a Focke-Wulf, this is their dream come true. Their tracers climb into the sky in hundreds and I find myself in a burst of fellow feeling thinking of the respective No. 4's with their foot clamped down on the foot pedal, ramming the shells into the autoloader. It seems that even now the doodle will get away with it, but suddenly someone gets it. Throwing its head back for all the world like a pheasant, it glides to earth and goes off with a colossal orange flash somewhere back on the marshes.

Never mind that now. Look out, here comes another! The cannonade goes on. Almost the first salvo hits it and a mile out to sea it disintegrates in mid-air, inaudible against the noise of the guns. Another is on its tail. This makes a more dramatic exit. Someone knocks out its gyro control and sets it on fire. Fizzing like a comet and leaving a long trail of black smoke, it careers drunkenly upwards, loses impetus, and spirals into the sea.

One or two slip through. Behind us, inland, the fighters are droning up and down on their beat, waiting for what may come their way. One of them sees a doodle (pilots, of course, cannot hear them like people on the ground) and the pilot, heaving out coloured flares to attract the rest of the pack, sets off in pursuit. (Later the rule became 'One bomb, one fighter', on account of the unhappy occasion when a procession was observed to be flying at four hundred miles an hour in the direction of Sevenoaks. It consisted of a flying bomb, followed by four fighters, followed by a flying bomb—the old tale of 'the fox lying fifth' come to life, in fact!)

On the morning in question the guns shot down seven out of the ten I was lucky enough to see. I have shot pheasants, partridges, duck, snipe, geese, grouse, and many other flying things, and been thrilled enough in the process, but never in the world has there been a 'stand' to touch the coast of Kent! After a shave and breakfast at brigade headquarters I said farewell and went out of the front door with another officer. Up and down the coast the cannonade began again. It had clouded over and they were firing unseen. Suddenly there was a fiendish noise like the simultaneous tearing of a thousand mighty sheets of calico, and a salvo of rockets from the first fairway of the golf course passed over the roof. They vanished into the cloud, and seconds later we heard the 'woop-woop-woop-woop-woop' familiar to Londoners. We gazed out to sea. A second or two passed and out of the cloud plummeted a doodle, straight into the sea a few hundred yards off the shore. I could have thrown my hat into the air.

Eight out of eleven! And people were still saying: 'Why don't they *do* something about it?'

THE WORLD OF SPORT

Death in the Forest

'Tomorrow,' said Valentine Viscount Castlerosse one bright September day in Killarney, 'you will go deer-stalking.'

Next day the rifles were produced—two gleaming Mannlicher .303's—and, having driven as far as the car would take us, we set off in single file up the mountains which, with the lakes of Killarney, make one of the loveliest pictures in all the world.

An impressive retinue, as I remember thinking. His lordship, vast and perspiring, propelling himself with his thumb in the cleft of a tall hawthorn stick; myself; Matt Lyne, keeper of the forest, with rifle and telescope; John Lyne, also with rifle and telescope; and a fifth man carrying a small pail like a jam jar.

The significance of this pail was, to me, a mystery, and I hesitated to display my ignorance by asking. Later I discovered that it contained the ice for his lordship's whisky and soda.

For an hour we climbed up through the woods, till at last the trees gave place to the craggy, barren mountain tops that are the last stronghold of the wild deer. We sat down beside the path to refresh ourselves and scanned the distant slopes for a sign of our quarry. For myself, as I surveyed the wondrous loveliness of the scene, I should have been content not to spot a deer all day, and at first glance it seemed that this would be so, but the eyes of men who spend their lives in the hills see things that are invisible to us who grope for our daily bread in the cities of the plain.

Matt and John Lyne fell to discussion. Not whether any deer were to be seen, but which of the deer that both had already detected offered the best opportunity for attack. They could tell a young stag from an old with the naked eye. To me they were no more than microscopic, reddish-brown specks on the distant hill.

A plan of campaign was instituted whereby Matt and I should make a detour of about two miles over the boulders and bog to get downwind from a stag on the far hill-side, while Castlerosse, John, and the man with the pail ensconced themselves beside the path farther on.

I soon discovered that the country, apparently so barren of life, was in fact alive with Japanese deer—Japs, as they call them—speckled, large-eyed, graceful creatures, and the enemy of the deer-stalker only in the sense that they warn the main quarry of his approach.

The first excitement occurred when we surprised a buck of this species—they stand about the height of a Shetland pony, with two pointed horns—but, though we cast ourselves to the ground, he was away before I could do anything more aggressive than take a picture of his retreating rump.

We trudged on for perhaps three-quarters of an hour, making all manner of minor detours to prevent showing ourselves to the stag we were stalking, and then came the Moment. Prostrate on our bellies, we crept to the top of a small rise, and peered through the fringe of grass.

Not a beast in sight. The deer had vanished.

' 'Tis those damned Japs,' said Matt.

After one or two further short sallies we returned to our base, where a silvery tinkle of ice showed that his lordship was already finding the heat oppressive. Refreshment was taken and further plans laid.

These consisted in Matt and I getting on the march again, this time to the summit of the mountain that towered behind us. 'Certain to be deer up there somewhere,' it was said.

It was not long before we sighted another buck and set out to stalk him with another long detour that took us downwards to the fringe of the forest (in the purely arboreal sense: why the barren hills on which the deer live should be termed a deer 'forest' I have never gathered). As we crept on, I began to appreciate the unique fascination in the art of stalking. It has the real, primeval element of the chase—the battle of wits between the skill, patience, and persistence of the hunter and the naturally endowed wariness and fleetness of foot of the hunted. And the two, it seemed to me, were pretty evenly matched.

The pheasant, hand-fed with corn till the morning of execution, then levered off the ground by the beaters, has little chance against the marksmanship of a practised shot. The stag, on the other hand, has every chance. His hearing is acute, and with his eyes he can detect the movement of a man's cap in the grass half a mile away. In fact, if he so much as suspects the presence of the hunter, he wins.

Stalking demands infinite patience and a certain degree of low cunning—the mentality of the man who, in the Great War, would lie all day in no man's land, disguised with a covering of branches and old tin cans and sniping at the enemy, rather than that of the man who more willingly rushed over the top with his bayonet.

There are two canons of etiquette which all good stalkers observe. One is: Never fire at a moving beast; the other is: Never fire till you are well in range. In other words, once you have stalked your stag so successfully as to get him standing still, unaware of your presence, within, say, a maximum of two hundred yards, the rest should be a mechanical formality.

This, of course, presupposes that the stalker is a first-class shot with a rifle. If he isn't, he has no business to be stalking at all, for the prospect of leaving a wounded stag to a lingering death on the hill-side is not one that appeals. The vital target on a stag is a spot only nine or ten inches wide—and not clearly defined like an artificial target in black and white—just behind the foreleg. And when you've been creeping on all fours, crawling on your belly, leaping from one rock to the next, and all the time toiling up a mountain-side; and when the suspended excitement of perhaps two hours' endeavour comes at last to a head as you rest the rifle on a rock and draw a bead on your quarry, that vital spot becomes very small indeed.

Your heart thumps wildly and your hand is trembling. A little voice whispers: 'Suppose you miss it now!'

I hope I shall not be considered unduly vain if I declare that if there's one thing that I *can* do (or could do then!) it is shoot with a rifle. It is a comparatively simple art that a few people will never master, but for the vast majority it is just a question of practice. I started at the age of nine and have kept my hand in ever since. That's all there is to it.

And so, when at last Matt and I got within range of our buck, at perhaps a hundred and eighty yards, I began to wish that I had had time to have a sighter or two with this rifle before we had started. Should I advance the sights from 100 to 200 yards and aim a bit low—or leave them at 100 and take a full sight on the bull's eye—or leave them as they were and take a normal aim? A couple of preliminary shots would have told me, but there had been no time for preliminaries and now I had to guess.

I guessed wrong. I put up the sights, aimed low, and fired. The bullet ricocheted from a rock an inch or two above the animal's back, and it made off with great speed across the mountain. I, too, was extremely wild.

The shot, echoing across the valley, disturbed a herd of deer, which ran providentially within range of his lordship. To my intense mortification he shot one neatly through the heart. We returned to find him standing over his victim (a picture which later illustrated his 'Londoner's Log' in the *Sunday Express*), and while Matt got out his jack-knife and set about the gory operation of 'paunching' the stag, I had to confess my own unhappy tale.

By this time a man had turned up with a pony, the stag was duly heaved onto its back, and the party set off for home. Having climbed, as it seemed, up and down every mountain in Kerry, I was stiff and aching in every joint. On the following Sunday the 'Londoner's Log' concluded:

'Finally, Mr. Longhurst has been out stalking. He started the day most jauntily and finished nobly, and yet when 8.30 p.m. struck, namely, the dinner hour, I said: "Where is Mr. Longhurst?" and received the reply that "Mr. Longhurst is trying to get down the stairs".'

Next morning I procured a rough and ready target and fired a dozen sighters at it in the ancestral park. That day, having got the hang of the rifle, I shot three buck. But still no stag.

On the following morning we climbed to a neighbouring forest, and there encountered one of the most remarkable little men I ever did meet. His name was Dan Donohue and his age was seventy-nine. He lived in a primitive little cottage high up in the Kenmare forest, and had been keeper of the forest for more than half a century, and his father before him.

A wizened, round-faced little man with a high-pitched, sing-song voice that was difficult to understand, he was the best stalker in all Ireland, I was told. Having lived in the forest all his life, I believe he knew more of the ways of deer than the ways of men.

We spent a barren, tantalizing morning, but why should I worry? I had passed that morning in the presence of a genius in his craft. At seventy-nine Dan Donohue had the eyes of a hawk and the agility of a mountain goat. Furthermore, it proved impossible to tire him. When, as dusk fell, we tottered gratefully into the motor-car, he set off at the same lively pace on the three-mile trek up to his cottage. Half a century younger, it was all I could do to keep up with him. He leapt from rock to rock without pausing, using his stick in the most uncanny manner as a kind of third leg.

It was almost at the top of the highest mountain in the forest that the grand success was at last accomplished. We overtook our quarry, a big solitary stag, standing majestic and unaware in a glen below us. I squirmed my way down to the point where a ledge of rock jutted out over the glen, and knew that the moment had come.

I drew a bead on the stag. Then, instead of pressing the trigger, I laid down the rifle and gazed at this magnificent creature I was about to kill. Death seemed a monstrous penalty to exact for his negligence. We had won the game, according to the rules, and had crept successfully upon him without revealing our presence. Who was I to say that the beast should die?

Here was no mere verminous rabbit or sparrow or pigeon, no enemy of man, but a noble specimen of God's handiwork—the Monarch, indeed, of the Glen! My mind was a turmoil of opposing emotions. I could kill him, that was certain. He was nearly two hundred yards away, but I knew that I should not miss. A squeeze of the trigger and the deed would be done.

Had I been alone I should have taken a photograph of the beast to prove my victory and let him go. But faced with the prospect of explaining away such faint-hearted unorthodoxy to my host and, more especially, to old Dan, my courage deserted me. I raised the rifle again and a second later the stag was dead.

As it fell, there rose from the grass beside it a second stag. I shot that too. And I knew how the Ancient Mariner felt when he shot the albatross.

Dan Donohue was beside himself. '*Good*, gentleman, *good*,' he kept saying. We went down to examine the victims and found that the first was a 'royal', in other words it had twelve points to its antlers, and this was indeed a memorable début, for to shoot a royal ranks high among deer-stalkers—though, as I imprudently pointed out, you shoot first and count up the points afterwards.

My guilty conscience seemed to detect a puzzled, reproachful look in the glazed eyes of the two dead beasts. I reflected, with little satisfaction, that they had died not because I had been clever enough to shoot them but because I had not the moral courage not to.

No such thought, however, entered the mind of Dan Donohue and he launched himself with enthusiasm into the usual operation with the jack-knife. Moved perhaps by the same strange primitive instinct that inspires the Abyssinians, he attacked first the stags' genital organs, and with a wild frenzy flung them over his head.

The operation complete, we returned to the valley for congratulations.

I have shot my stag. I shall never shoot another.

Later one morning we stood in the bright September sunshine on the western demesne of the Kenmare estate, looking down across the green turf and the gorse to where Mahony's Point juts out into the lake.

'Do you think we could make a golf course here?' said Castlerosse.

'We could make the loveliest golf course in the whole world,' said I. And that was the beginning of the Killarney Golf and Fishing Club.

We wired for Sir Guy Campbell, the golf architect, and a fortnight later stood in the same spot, this time with Sir Guy. A curious profession his, and one that demands a much wider range of knowledge than you might suppose. The golf architect has to combine the eye of the creative artist with the hard-headedness of the business man; he must have the imagination to visualize a series of golf holes in a tangle of heather or gorse or forest, and, what is infinitely rarer, he must know how much the operation is going to cost. He must be familiar with all manner of grasses and know the soil on which they will flourish and what to do about it if they won't. And he must be a man of infinite tact, to deal with club committees who have one thing in common, that they reckon they know more about his job than he does himself.

Castlerosse and I swore that Sir Guy should have a free hand when he came. Hire the best man at the job you can find, and let him get on with it. That was our motto. I noticed, however, when the time arrived, that the architect hardly got a word in edgeways as he listened to our suggestions and advice.

When the moment came for him to survey the site for our course I was a little nervous. Perhaps I had been swayed by the loveliness of the scene into painting too rosy a picture. But the light of inspiration came into his eye as he gazed on the clumps of gorse and the pine-trees and the thickets and streams. A golf architect thinks and talks in terms of 'features'—and here before him were 'features' enough for half a dozen courses. Never mind the beauty of the background. You can't make a golf course on a background.

Two hundred acres of deer-cropped, rolling parkland, untouched in centuries by the hand of man. What a prospect for an architect! 'This is the most exciting thing I have ever done,' he said. So we set off to 'beat the bounds' as he called it, touring the boundaries and gradually working inwards. With us came Pat Lyne who was a kind of estate foreman. He was equipped with long bamboo stakes to mark the tee and greens, and showed a rare enthusiasm for the job. I am satisfied that he had not the remotest idea what we were up to.

We splashed through streams, scrambled through undergrowth and explored the sandy shore of the lake, and bit by bit a golf course was born. At the end of the day some wonderful holes had been devised, but alas, there were only fourteen of them, and we had to start all over again.

We thought we would build the club-house down on the end of Killeen Point, so as to be handy for the fishermen's boats, and to let the golfers sit on the lake shore in the evenings and contemplate the almost indescribable loveliness of the mountains in the sunset. No man would willingly leave a scene like that till it was too dark to see, and the profits from the bar must mount accordingly.

The narrow neck of land leading down to the Point had to accommodate not only the first and last holes, but also the road down to the club-house, and we questioned whether there was room for it without taking it too near to the reeds bordering the lake. Pat Lyne reassured us.

'It will be quite all right,' he said. 'There used to be a road here before, but it has not been used for some time.'

'How long?' someone asked.

'Oh, t'would be about four hundred years,' he replied.

In those few words you have the whole spirit of Killarney. Every rock and stone and path has its legend, and what is the passing of four hundred or five hundred or a thousand years? The man was perfectly serious. It was common knowledge that there had been a road down to Killeen Point four hundred years ago. It might have been yesterday.

The big coverts on the boundary, where the woodcock live in winter, were another problem—but not to Pat. 'We'll be having them all out by the roots. I would not be frightening me of that at all,' he said.

They have a picturesque way of putting things in that part of the world that would bring joy to the heart of the etymologist. We stuck in our bamboo stakes, for instance, and after a few inches came, to our great delight, to gravel. The stakes were rather insecure and the horses came and pushed them over.

'I will come tomorrow, please God, and *substantiate* every one of these,' said Pat.*

* Later when I spent my honeymoon in Castlerosse's house (my wife and I being shown by Dennis, the old butler, into separate rooms—the sort of thing you simply take as it comes in that part of the world) the estate agent kindly borrowed an ancient two-seater for our use. I asked whether it was insured. 'I think it must be,' was the reply. 'You see, there are four of them *implicated* in this car.'

Next day we began again, and this time fitted in all the eighteen holes, including one across to Mahony's Point, which I believe may become one of the accepted masterpieces of golf architecture. You drive across a sandy bay to a green set in a clump of pine-trees on the shore. On the right is the lake; on the left a bank of rhododendrons. A 'do or die' shot—but what a lovely place to die in!

Back in London we found a brawny Scot, in the person of Hamilton White, to take charge of the construction of the course. A few months later he wrote to me: 'I have made golf courses in England and Scotland and almost every country in Europe, but Killarney is queen of them all.'

Sic transit gloria . . .

It was ten o'clock on a lovely October morning and the scene was Westward Ho! The flat expanse between the golf club-house and the sea, which they call the 'Burrows', was shimmering in the sunshine, and red sails glided along above the level of the sandhills as the sailing barges and fishing boats made their way into the little harbour at Appledore. The world was at peace.

On the first tee down below the club-house a small group of people were waiting. Many were women, for the English women's championship was just beginning, but among them was a goodly sprinkling of men. Of the men, those that weren't caddies were golf journalists.

Golf journalists on the first tee at ten in the morning? Yes, indeed. Every one of them. And what had lured them forth at this unaccustomed hour? Why, the rumour had gone round the village that at ten o'clock that day a lady intended to play golf in trousers.*

One or two even went so far as to suggest that not only did she play in trousers but that she only used one club. This was ruled out as an unworthy attempt to paint the lily. Trousers, yes; or one club, yes. But trousers and one club—come, come, sir!

No one you meet has ever seen a ghost; on the other hand, there's no one who doesn't know someone who has. So it was with the mysterious lady. No one had seen her, but every one had it first-hand from someone who had.

Ten o'clock came, and no apparition. The name was called once. No reply. It was called again. No reply. The know-alls wagged their heads with a chorus of 'I told you so', and were retiring to the club-house for refreshment, when along the little lane that crosses the links a couple of hundred yards from the first tee there appeared a big yellow motor car.

The car stopped, and out into the headlines stepped Miss Gloria Minoprio.

* This was 1934—though I remember it as if it were yesterday. It is difficult at this distance of time to believe that an almost national sensation, far beyond the realms of golf, should have been caused by the appearance of a lady in trousers. Miss Minoprio later married but, alas, died in Nassau in the late 1950's. It has always been my regret that I never really got to know this clearly remarkable person. When I won a continental championship in 1936, I was gratified to receive a telegram of congratulation from her and replied accordingly. It was only fifteen years later that I learnt that it had been sent by General Critchley.

The deserters hastily retraced their steps from the bar, while among the ladies in waiting arose a clucking and fluttering as of an agitated flock of Leghorn pullets.

'My *dear*, do you see what I see? . . .' 'What a figure! . . .' 'What trousers!'

'Well, *really*!' cried the Ladies' Golf Union.

'Good God!' said the journalists.

Meanwhile, the object of their astonishment made her way composedly and with what dignity her costume would permit across to the waiting crowd.

She was clad from head to foot in dark blue, and, yes, she wore trousers. Close-fitting, exquisitely tailored trousers, very tightly cut, especially—er—behind. She wore them, as did our grandfathers, with straps beneath the insteps of her blue suède shoes. A neat blue jacket and a little blue turban completed the streamline.

A slim, graceful girl, with delicate, sensitive features and figure divine. She had bumps, to quote Mr. Damon Runyan's rudely graphic description, where a doll is entitled to have bumps. Only one thing marred the picture. On her cheeks should have glowed the rosy bloom of youth and health. Instead, they were heavily, almost grotesquely, powdered in white. She might have been wearing a white mask.

With her was a young caddie carrying, rather sheepishly, a scarlet spare jacket, a ball bag, and—not one club, but two. But rumour had spoken truth, and she only used one of these clubs. The other was a spare in case of accident.

She said 'How do you do?' almost inaudibly to her opponent. At the end of the match she said 'Thank you.' So far as I am aware that was all she did say.

Tapping the ground with her solitary cleek to show the caddie where she wished him to tee the ball, she prepared to play her opening stroke. It must have been something of an ordeal. If so, she certainly showed no sign of it.

She had, it turned out, a careful, precise style of play that might have been learned studiously from the text-book. Nothing very dashing about it, no undignified vigour, but quite efficient. She did not hit the ball very far—no woman does with an iron club—but she hit it for the most part nice and straight.

That morning the champions played in solitude, their supporters lured away by magnetic Minoprio. I forget the name of her opponent, but there was no doubt as to which was the more nervous of the two.

The prospect of losing to a lady in fancy dress using only one club is enough to shake the stoutest heart. Might take a lifetime to live down.

Recovering from their initial shock, those of the quickly gathering gallery who were interested in the technique of golf settled down to assess Miss Minoprio's capabilities with her solitary club. They proved to be considerable. Her long game was steady and, though the long shaft of her iron made her look rather clumsy, her putting was at least up to the average usually seen in a women's championship. Her approaches, low along the ground, were quite effective.

But the time came, inevitably, when she was faced with strokes beyond the capacity of Bobby Jones, Cotton, or the devil himself, to execute with a straight-faced iron. She could not loft the ball, except in a full shot; she could impart no 'stop' or back spin; she could get no distance from anything but a smooth, clipped lie. To lob the ball over an intervening hazard was beyond her.

There was much speculation as to what would occur when she got into a bunker. The truth is that it is quite simple to remove the ball from a bunker with any kind of club if the sand is soft and loose. Hit hard, three or four inches behind it, and the deed is done. So in the fine seaside sand of Westward Ho! Miss Minoprio performed with no little distinction, and some who had come to mock remained to marvel. But on firm or rain-sodden sand, or, indeed, on any hard surface, she was pathetically powerless.

That her average score would have been reduced by anything from half-a-dozen to ten shots in a round by the use of a normal set of clubs, no reasonable critic could doubt. She went through the motions well enough, but the instrument she used was too ill adapted for the purpose. She lost her match by, I think, five and four, and I was able to telephone to the *Evening Standard* what I believe to be almost the only Latin tag to find its way into the sporting pages of that journal—'Sic transit Gloria Monday.' (I repeated it shamelessly for five years with only one variation. One year she defeated a young girl who was so nervous that she could scarcely focus the ball. So when she was beaten next day the tag became 'Sic transit Gloria Tuesday.')

The yellow car had been driven across the 'burrows' and was waiting near by. She stepped in and was whisked away, not to appear in public again until the next women's championship, and the company settled down to debate her reason for imposing upon herself the ludicrous handicap of playing with one club.

One school of thought held that she was doing it for publicity.

Certainly her unusual attire lent weight to that opinion. If so she certainly succeeded, for her name and picture have featured in almost every newspaper every time she has appeared in a championship. But those who seek publicity like inevitably to bask in it when achieved. Miss Minoprio, so far as I know, has never entered a golf club-house during a championship; has never played in a tournament other than the two championships; has never made friends with other golfers.

And again, why the extraordinary outfit—admirable though it may be for golfing comfort? And why the mask-like countenance? Here a very strong school exists which holds that she plays golf while temporarily hypnotized, or entranced, either by auto-suggestion or by a friend. That is possible. And if she is not in a state of semi-hypnosis, that at least is as good a description as any of her appearance and demeanour.

She spent some months studying yoga in India (and incidentally she is a conjurer of the highest order, though the point is hardly relevant). After her début at Westward Ho! she wrote to tell me she had bought thirty copies of the *Tatler*, in which I had written about her, to distribute to her friends. We exchanged three or four letters. Later, while walking round in a championship, I introduced myself as her correspondent. She blinked with surprise at being spoken to. She had the vacant, far-away look of Lady Macbeth walking in her sleep. She seemed scarcely to understand what I was trying to say. 'Oh, yes . . . yes,' she said, looking vaguely into the distance over my shoulder. I faded away.

The Ladies' Golf Union, aghast at her first appearance, issued a proclamation that they 'deplored any departure from the traditional costume of the game', but the last laugh was against them. Nearly half the field in women's championships today turn out in trousers.

But none of them fit like Gloria Minoprio's.

Fox-hunt in Australia

Every Australian sheep station has its official rabbiter and that of John Baillieu, pre-war Oxford golfer, at Yarram Park, some 200 miles inland from Melbourne, one Charlie Coffey, is in addition the M.F.H. As he uses the same animals for both purposes, he may also be said to be M.R.H. On a recent visit to Australia I had the privilege of a day out with Charlie and, while it might not have done for the Quorn, it lingers as an experience not lightly forgotten.

The pack duly met in the back yard, nine of them all told—or should it be four and a half couple?—and a fine miscellaneous collection they were. They must reflect, between them, the lineage of every breed that has flourished in Australia since Captain Cook. Three are specialists: Michael, quarter pointer, quarter retriever, half completely anonymous, is, as it were, the chief detective and head burrower. Sandy, a tall, bushy-tailed, yellowish-white animal, is the long-range expert, and Nip, close-cropped and short in the leg, undertakes the role played in more aristocratic circles by the hunt terrier. The rest are strictly utility.

Barging like bus passengers in the rush hour, they scrambled into the back of the station wagon, grinning all over their faces at the day's prospect, and away we went, up a long red-dust avenue between two rows of magnificent gum trees, for all the world like the approach to a stately home of England, then away across one paddock after another —some green and flourishing, some still awaiting the hand of man— down towards the lake where a few days previously the M.F.H. had discerned a family of foxes.

The scene here is strangely like an English park, open, but liberally sprinkled with venerable trees, many of them ring-barked by the early settlers and now dead, but still gauntly dignified. Here and there you can see a cloud of white birds circling round a tree top, clearly visible at two or three miles' range in the virgin atmosphere, their raucous screeching floating back across the still air. These are the cockatoos so familiar at home a generation ago. With the recent lifting of the psittacosis ban they and other members of the parrot family—the lovely little roselles which flit about the garden and the incredibly speedy parakeets, one of which, when we were doing 30 m.p.h., shot past us with only an occasional flip of its wings—might be turned into one of Australia's more profitable exports. Every English family has a soft spot in its heart for the old poll-parrot.

The scene of operations turned out to be an enlarged rabbit burrow on the banks of the lake, complete with the usual tell-tale evidence at the entrance. There had been four cubs, said Charlie, but they were getting on and they might be gone by now. Michael took his official place at the head of the burrow, while the others stood aside in a comically deferential sort of way. 'He'll tell me if they're there,' Charlie said.

As plainly as if he had delivered the statement in writing Michael indicated that they were and a tremendous burrowing and scrabbling began, Charlie weighing in with the long-handled spade, pausing only when the burrow was divided and further indication was required from Michael. For some minutes the work went on, interrupted by sharp 'chi-ikes' as some enthusiast took a glancing blow on the nose from the spade, and soon the burrow was open for eight or ten yards. Four yards back from the opening Sandy, the long distance ace, for whom the penny dropped slowly at this sort of work, dug furiously on his own, receiving shower after shower of earth full in the face from the hind legs of the others. You cannot be an expert at everything.

Over the next few minutes I could willingly draw a veil. Peeping out from the bottom of the burrow there appeared a furtive, frightened, and poignantly appealing little face. My heart melted and my mind went back to the day, years before the war, when after much weariness of the flesh I had contrived to draw a bead on a gigantic stag, in the mountains above Killarney, and then only brought myself to shoot the beast because I had not the moral courage not to! No such faint-hearted unorthodoxy, however, entered Charlie's head and a moment later he had yanked out the first of the four cubs and flung it high in the air, to be instantly despatched in a howling scrimmage of dogs. As the third was pulled out, the fourth slipped away and made a bolt for it, but the wretched creature had not gone thirty yards before amid much yelling and hullabalooing it was brought down.

So much for the family, which Charlie, with positively surgical skill, set about demasking with his jack-knife. The Australian Government pays 7/6 per mask skin. (Why not brushes? 'God knows,' said Charlie.) He was delighted not only with the prospect of 30/- but also with the sport he had provided. He had taken out a friend from Tasmania who had never seen a fox, he said, and of course they never set eyes on one all day. 'So I got 'im one later and skun it.'

Now for the luckless parents. They were never with the cubs during the day, it appeared, but never more than a mile away. The master whistled up the pack, who were cooling themselves off in the lake with just their heads showing, like water buffalo, and away we went again, this time for something uncommonly like the real thing. With the pack fanned out on either side we ranged at twenty or thirty m.p.h. across what might have been Newmarket Heath, freely bestrewn with tussocks reminiscent of the Rushes at Westward Ho! and with a background of deep blue mountains. A vivid, unforgettable scene, and air like champagne.

I dare say we had gone a mile when someone detected a lithe, russet shape streaking through the tussocks some way ahead of the pack.

Charlie let forth the Australian version of Tally Ho! ('There he goes, the ——!') and at the same time Sandy, picking up the scent, gave tongue to summon the rest. From then on we had a perfect view from our mobile grandstand.

Outpaced before long, the fox doubled back, and the last sight I had of him was when he leapt four feet in the air among the tussocks, twisting and turning as he jumped. They brought him down in the open a hundred yards from the car, a huge dog fox, and Charlie got out his jack-knife. Alas, poor Father!

To my secret relief we failed to find Mother, who is doubtless raising another family by now, and, as we jogged home, I got Charlie talking about his singular pack. A pointer-type was limping pathetically along beside the car, looking up at us, and if ever a dog was 'thumbing a lift' this one was.

'He's putting it on,' said Charlie. 'Always does that when he sees a car. He'll sit for an hour beside the road when he knows the foreman is due to drive by.'

Another with quite a severe cut on a leg drew the comment. 'He won't hurt. Sew it up when we get back. What with? Bit o' wire. Put sixteen stitches in one of 'em the other day.'

His training methods, it seemed, were simple and direct. 'If they don't come, I give 'em a charge of No. 12 (i.e. 12-bore). Reckon I shot that pointer twenty times before he learnt.'

A dog's hunting days, he said, ran to five or six years. 'After which, I said, 'I suppose you, er, sort of pension them off in honourable retirement?'

'Nah!' said Charlie. 'Shewt 'em.'

One day we went across the valley from St. Moritz to the Olympic ski-jump, and a more staggering exhibition of cold-blooded nerve and skill I never did see. The jump consists of an artificial runway, perhaps forty yards long, which levels out at the bottom and then curves very slightly upward. Below is a bigger slope, tremendously steep, on which the jumper pitches. If he pitched on the flat, he would break every bone in his body.

Away up at the top is a tiny black figure, balancing with his skis horizontal to the slope. Down goes the red flag, and the figure leaps round and dashes pell-mell down the incline, heaving with his body to increase his momentum.

As he reaches the bottom, he hurls himself into space, hauling himself through the air with his arms. Down and down he goes until at last his skis hit the next precipitous slope with a thud and he either falls in a tangled, slithering jumble of skis and humanity, or swishes downward at seventy miles an hour to pull up in a shower of snow just short of the spectators. Phew!

The great art, I gather, is to time one's leap about ten yards before the actual take-off. Do it right, and you hit the snow with the heels of your skis. Do it wrong, either too far back or too far forward, and you hit the snow with your person, at not less than fifty miles an hour.

The record on the St. Moritz jump is about seventy-five yards—but figures are cold, unemotional things. Perhaps it will bring it home better if I remind you that this means jumping downwards through space for substantially farther than the average distance between two telegraph poles. No wonder they told me a ski-jumper is 'too old at twenty-six'.

One of the boys who jumped sixty-three yards on the day in question was only sixteen. Two who tied for the tournament were little older. To show there was no ill feeling they went back to the top and came down hand in hand. They pitched side by side fifty-eight yards lower down.

All available practice jumps are child's play beside the Olympic jump, and I remarked to a young Swiss in the town, whom I had seen performing, that the first jump from the big one must be an alarming experience. To a student of the psychology of sport his reply was enlightening. 'It is not the first jump that matters,' he said. 'But if you fall on your first jump, that makes the second jump very, very difficult.'

As for the Cresta and the Bob, anyone who imagines them as a kind of glorified tobogganing is due for a sharp disillusionment. They bear no relation, in sensation, to the Englishman's conception of tobogganing as practised from time to time in England. A much closer parallel is motor racing.

I had my baptism on the back seat of a two-man Bob, and glad I was to have had it before essaying the Cresta, which you ride alone on what's known as a 'skeleton'. The Bob is a contraption resembling a motor-car chassis, guided by a steering wheel and weighing about twenty-five stones—or rather more than Lord Castlerosse.

The track winds its way down through the forest in a series of banked bends, some of them complete hairpins, and the first surprise is that its surface is not snow, but ice. So the steel runners, instead of making the swishing sound of a toboggan on snow, make a rumbling, roaring noise like a brewer's dray on a cobbled street.

The thing rattled down at an unconscionable speed. Trees loomed up beside the track and in a split second flashed by, and no sooner had one recovered from the sensation of sitting in a horizontal position high up on an almost vertical banking than one had thundered on to the next bend and was doing the same thing in reverse order. We dived at last into the finishing straight at substantially more than a mile a minute and pulled up in a shower of ice as I applied the brakes at the back. One minute, eleven seconds. Terrible. On all sides they were complaining that the track had never been so slow.

Next morning—the Cresta. At the risk of boring the tiny minority who have ridden the track for themselves, let me describe the scene. It is early in the morning—early, that is, if you have not got to bed until four. You can only ride the Cresta from half-past eight till the sun comes over the mountains at about eleven and softens the ice.

You join the little knot of silent folk at the top of the run, write your name down on the list of starters, and set about equipping yourself for the fray. The equipment consists of special boots with metal 'rakes' sprouting from the toes, for retarding progress where necessary; metal knee-, elbow-, and knuckle-protectors; and a crash helmet (compulsory). You finish by resembling an ice hockey goal-minder.

Your toboggan has a little sliding seat and steel runners, which are smooth except for a few inches at the back where they are grooved.

The idea is that on the corners you slide the seat back, clasping the front of the toboggan with the top hand and the back of it with the lower hand. The weight is thus thrust back on to the grooves at the back of the runners, enabling you to get a grip on the ice and push the nose of the machine down with the top hand. Or not, as the case may be.

The run itself is about the width of a narrow-gauge railway and the straight stretches are enclosed by two-foot walls of solid frozen snow. The corners are, of course, banked almost to the vertical and each has its name—Bank, Stream, Battledore, Shuttlecock, and so on. The length in all is 1,320 yards, and the all-time record is held by an old friend of mine, Billy Fiske, who shot down in 56·7 seconds.

Before leaving for St. Moritz I had discovered two schools of thought regarding the Cresta. The one maintained that to go near it was equivalent to suicide, and that, in any case, I should never have the nerve. The other rather pooh-poohed the whole affair, holding that, after all, it was only tobogganing. As I stood stamping my feet on the snow on my first morning, I wished that some of the latter gentlemen could have been there in person, with their name next on the list.

The weird outfit, emphasizing the need for protection against violent injury or even death; the sight of successive riders flashing out of sight round Shuttlecock half a dozen inches from the rim of the banking, and the cries of 'He's over! . . . No, he's not!'; the experienced hands reminiscing of the time when old So-and-so went over the top at such-and-such a corner and broke five ribs; the kindly advice to take especial care first time down or you've only yourself to blame . . . ; these and the chill of the sunless early morning must fill the least imaginative novice with apprehension.

They were using a course of about a thousand yards, starting from a point known as Junction, the upper three hundred yards of the track being not yet completed, and the record to date was 47·9 seconds. My turn came at last. 'We don't mind if you take a minute and a quarter,' were the last words I heard, 'only, for God's sake, be careful!'

'The next rider,' said the voice of Colonel Hodgson at the microphone, 'is Mr. Longhurst.' The moment had come.

I cast myself on to my little steel craft and made off down the ice rut, wondering where the hell I should be in a minute's time. For the first few yards it was difficult to keep the thing from ricocheting from one wall to the other. Then we really got going, and the next few seconds remain a confused memory of wrestling with a toboggan that seemed to have come to life with only one ambition, to wriggle away from under me. We shot together up the first banking and round, right-handed, on to Battledore.

'Get off Battledore as quick as you can,' they had told me, but there was no time to think about that. I shot off it, down into the gully, and was tossed, like a cork on the ocean wave, on to the left-handed banking of Shuttlecock. Raking desperately with the left foot I managed to get round, and after one more bend found myself emerging into the long straight that leads down under the main road and the railway.

This time I was able to avoid bumping the walls and the speed increased, I suppose, to sixty or seventy miles an hour. A wild, exhilarating sensation. I should not have cared if it had reached a hundred. I wondered if I ought to be raking in readiness for the big banking I could see at the bottom, but decided to let it rip. I actually, I remember, started to sing, though neither I nor anyone else could hear.

I got round the bend, too high to be comfortable, and retain a confused impression of rounding a series of others before diving into the finishing straight where the experts touch eighty miles per hour. Yet of all the crowded sensations experienced on that first run, I remember most clearly the one that came immediately after the finish. The rider has no hope, of course, of pulling up for himself at that speed, so they construct a vast embankment to assist him, so steep that it would be quite impossible to remain on it stationary. As you hit this embankment it is as though some invisible giant had put his hand beneath your stomach and heaved you into the air. And even after eighty yards of it you have to rake hard to pull up.

I had come down with no serious hitch and waited anxiously for the voice to announce my time. 'Fifty-seven seconds.' Congratulations all round. Best time of the year for a novice. The thing was dead easy.

The next run was better, fifty-four seconds, and, inflated by this minor triumph, I was taken in hand by the president, Harry Hays Morgan. 'I'm going to find you a faster toboggan,' he said. 'Believe me, it will make all the difference.' He retired to the hut and unearthed a shiny green 'skeleton', sleek and streamlined.

Determined to do credit to my mentor and at the same time break all known records, I waited my turn and set off again. But, alas, the new craft took unkindly to its new master—if 'master' is the right word—and bucked and slithered and wriggled and ducked to get rid of me. We remained together round Battledore and were bumping and rattling our way round Shuttlecock, when of a sudden a strange unearthly silence held the air. Gracefully and with the greatest of ease, the Cresta, I, and Mr. Hays Morgan's beautiful toboggan parted company.

At the starter's box the bell tolled twice to signify disaster, and the voice announced: 'I am afraid Mr. Longhurst has gone over the top at Shuttlecock.' After flying through the air for what seemed eternity I pitched on my back, in a shower of snow, ice, small stones and what not, in the straw providentially provided at that point.

Remembering the secretary's instructions, I stood up in the straw, like Ruth amid the alien corn, and waved my arms to signify that I was unhurt. Retrieving the toboggan, I trudged ingloriously to the summit. Perhaps I was not so hot, after all.

Third Time Lucky

Breathes there a man with soul so dead who never to Providence hath said: 'Before I die, can I please catch just one salmon?'

It was in late April, just before the spring meeting at St. Andrews, that, through the courtesy of a fellow member of the Royal and Ancient Club, Mr. Gordon Ferguson, I was able to launch the first of a series of skirmishes with the salmon in the Tay. After much dashing of hopes and one complete heartbreak, our efforts recently reached a triumphant conclusion.

The scene in April was the Benchil and Catholes beats of the Tay some miles inland from Perth in the neighbourhood of Stanley, and here, as the river dashes along a gorge between wooded hills, the prospect was one to deflect the eye of the most earnest of salmon fishers. The world was in full flower. From time to time a silvery monster would leap from the water and fall back with a splash. The sun shone benignly down, and rarely, I reflected, had life been quite so good.

Many readers will be arch-experts upon the ways of salmon and how best to lure them to their doom. Some, though I doubt it, may be able to explain why, if salmon never eat anything when they come up the river to spawn (nothing ever, apparently, being found in their insides) they should be expected to snap at a fly or a long-deceased prawn.

For myself, I had, it is true, on a memorable occasion, seen two salmon hauled from the Lune, in Lancashire, by a member of the Royal Liverpool Golf Club on an apparatus floated largely by gin corks, and had often stood on the viaduct near the little village of Arkholme gazing down at the fish queueing up in the pool below—but as to catching them, I knew nothing. I was prepared to do what I was told.

There are, it seems, three alternative courses of action (apart from netting, cyanide, Mills bombs and the Hoylake method outlined above). These are trolling or harling, i.e. sitting in the boat and trailing the lines therefrom; casting with a bait; and casting with a fly. Harling in winter can be a perishing business on account of the inaction—except for the boatmen, who toil like galley slaves in the vigorous current and do not seem to notice it—but in spring it is the idler's dream come true, and I remember feeling almost guilty that Fate and my kind host should have called upon me to be sitting dreamily amid such incomparable beauty while others laboured in the boat or on the Stock Exchange.

Most of the time was spent, however, in prawn-casting, and this, after a few misfires, proved to be a most satisfying occupation. Without conscious effort the apparatus could be made to whizz gracefully some thirty yards from the boat, after which one let it run round with the current and then, provided it did not get caught up in rock or weed, wound it in again.

I could not help comparing the action with golf, in which game it has long been an axiom of mine that 'the harder you hit, the less far it goes'. This, it turned out, was also true of prawn-flinging. If the contraption went thirty yards without much effort, how far would it not go with a really good hit at the top of the swing? The answer was 'about fifteen yards, and crooked'.

Sometimes, in a supreme effort to span the Tay in one cast, one forgot first to adjust the patent reel, whereupon the prawn would whirl round and round on six feet of line like a minor comet, cracking like a whip and nearly decapitating one's host at the other end of the boat.

After generations of experience salmon have developed one remarkable knack. The prawn is fixed on with nine hooks and a long needle, the whole lot is bound round with copper wire, and it must rotate in the current at something like four hundred revolutions a minute. Yet twice a salmon had extracted my prawn in a twinkling of an eye, spitting out clean and bare the remainder of the cocktail—the nine hooks, the needle, and copper wire—as a dog rejects the pill cunningly concealed in a wrapping of roast beef.

Eventually I was standing contemplating the infinite and thinking of nothing in particular when a screeching of the reel and a mighty tugging indicated that this, at last, was it. Panic, alas, set in for a moment among our little crew, some ducking, others offering unintelligible advice in a strange dialect. However, after a few alternate rushings and windings, we settled down to see the thing through. My right arm was trembling like a leaf, but I remember I had reached the stage, oh fatal thought! of deciding to have one half smoked and the other with mayonnaise and cucumber, when a searing sensation in the forefinger indicated that the line, rushing out again, was cutting through it like chalk through cheese. An agonized yell—and all was over. Prawn and all.

A little later we suspended the proceedings to listen on the portable wireless to the Guineas, in which my host's brother, who once won the

Derby with Airborne, had a horse called Palpitate running. I had placed a bet on it via the local post office and, the security of Her Majesty's telegraphic system being what it is, the whole village was on it, policeman and all. The big field got off to a good start, all except one, which happened to be facing the wrong way at the time. Palpitate.

Three days were spent with never another touch. No doubt about it, they said, autumn was the real time. Late September, perhaps, to coincide with the meeting at St. Andrews? Yes, that would be admirable. Pretty well a certainty, in fact.

So there we were, based again on Birnam, where at the foot of the hotel garden they will show you a vast oak guaranteed to be a survivor of the wood which 'came to Dunsinane' in *Macbeth*. The forests and the bracken were just beginning their full autumn glory and there was a tang of wood smoke in the air. This was just the time last year, it was recalled, that Mr. So-and-so pulled out the 30-pounder, just where we were about to fish, below Dunkeld; and so, I declare, should we have done—had there been any water in the river. For the first time in recorded history, the majestic Tay had shrunk almost to a trickle. Islands had appeared where islands had never been seen before and there were places where one could almost wade from bank to bank.

No, when you really came down to it, winter, they said, was the only real certainty. You remember when Mr. Whatsisname had one with his first cast and got six on the first morning? That was in February, before the netting began. In February they almost fought for the privilege of hooking themselves on your line.

So February, this time, it was. Euston 7.20 and the old familiar thrill, which I hope may never dim, of the sleeper to Scotland. Waking at 4 a.m., I looked out on the Border country, with the snow-clad hills bathed in the full moonlight and the conical haystacks casting dark shadows.

The single line up to Dunkeld, in daytime so much like a toy railway threading its way through toy fir trees, took on an air of mystery as the driver, silhouetted against the light of his furnace in the darkness, handed out his hoop to the signalman in the box. In imagination I had foreseen snow, ice, frozen fingers, and the Tay as a raging torrent. Instead, we stepped out after breakfast to a world of vivid sunshine, unbroken blue sky, and a beauty beyond my poor powers to describe. In Scotland at this time of year the sun never climbs very high in the sky, so that even in mid-morning the scene is spotlighted, as it were, from the side rather than from above. Winter colours, pale in England, stand out here as though in the early days of coloured postcards. The hills on the horizon seem little more than an hour's walk and you can count the gulls flocking behind a tractor as it turns up the gleaming chocolate-coloured earth a mile away.

We were on the Lower Scone beat this time, where the river widens out towards Perth. Here we were met by the senior boatman, Cowie, and his assistant Menzies, and Cowie at once struck a note unique in my limited experience of fishermen, for whom the water was right yesterday and may well be right tomorrow but has never in recorded history been right today. The water, he said, was 'just right'. There was enough of it but not too much. Its texture was right, its temperature was right, and, no, the sun did not matter. We stepped into the boat with a lively surmise, scarcely able to believe our ears.

Although on these open stretches there is naturally not the same amount of wild life, there was still enough to keep one's interest, as the bait—on this occasion a large yellow sprat—revolved invisibly under the water. Mallard, as many as a hundred at a time, would let us come within the length of a cricket pitch before moving higher up the bank. Not far away a big whitish goosander and his bronzy-brown mate dived all the morning, while a dipper made frenzied dashes up-river and splashed into the water, where, said Cowie, it was able to 'run along the bottom by altering its centre of gravity'.

Half the morning passed without incident and then the fun began. First blood to mine host was a 10 lb. salmon—not large, maybe, but one of the most perfect fish that even Cowie had set eyes on—a poem in streamlined silver and just right for the glass case in the office, in which the captor had always sworn to preserve his first salmon.

Thereafter we suffered much from kelts. The kelt, for the uninitiated, is a female salmon which has been up the river and spawned and is now returning, exhausted, to the sea. The poor thing is elongated like a conger, its scales are liable to be a rather odious shade of mauve, and its gills are certain to be covered with maggots. Nevertheless, you are not to know this when it turns and snaps at your prawn and, to the beginner, the first mighty rush is the same authentic thrill. Furthermore, until you can haul it within distance of the boat, no man knows whether it is a noble and magnificent fish straight from the sea, a matter of boasting for years to come, or some miserable mother-to-be who is on the way to retirement.

My own first one, after much heart-thumping, turned out to be a kelt. It was hauled ignominiously ashore and after having a mouthful of hooks extracted with a pocket knife—which it did not seem to mind—was relaunched and swam away. I should have liked to linger over it a little; to photograph it perhaps, or even weigh it—but it obviously was not the thing to be seen in the company of a kelt.

Next morning everything went my way. First a truly gigantic kelt—and what a pity we did not meet when it was on its way up the river! Then another tremendous run, a good deal of distant surface-splashing —always a good sign it was said . . . certain to be a 'fish', as against a mere kelt . . . this is it! . . . and then, released as though on a catapult, the sprat shot out of the water like a tracer bullet and lodged in my host's coat.

However, we had not long to wait. Another screeching of the reel and off we went again. After a few animated rushes the fish retired to the deepest point of the river, and, as I believe the expression is, sulked. Clearly another —— kelt.

After much heaving and contradictory advice the sack of coals was induced to come to life and the fray continued. How many minutes later I do not know (and never again will I believe anyone who states exactly how long he was playing a salmon) a monstrous form was to be seen from the boat. Forty pounds if it was an ounce. A whale-like tail flapped out of the water and was gone. A flash of silver down below— ominously mauvish it seemed to me—but in a moment there were cries of: 'It's a fush! It's a fush!' I hauled the creature gingerly towards the boat, trying to keep from my mind the fatal 'half smoked and half with mayonnaise'. A second later the meat-hook had flashed in Cowie's hand, Menzies had knocked the victim on the head with a cosh, and there, inert in the bottom of the boat, was beyond doubt the finest salmon ever extracted from the Tay.

What matter if they said it was in 'rather poor condition' and had 'probably been up before?' It had sea lice on it, proving it to be on its way up now. What matter if it was a little elongated and had half a fin missing?

'It's a fush,' they had said. To me it was and will ever remain, '*The* fush'. Seventeen and a half pounds.

In Praise of Bull Terriers

Several millions of Englishmen, and for that matter Scotsmen, Irishmen and Welshmen, are unable to contemplate life without the company of a dog. Of these a small, discriminating minority are unable to contemplate it without the company of a Bull Terrier.

I joined their ranks when, on my return from some expedition to the Far East many years ago, my wife met me at the door with an anxious expression and had got as far as: 'Honestly, I don't know *what* you'll say, but really I just couldn't. . . .' when the legs were cut smartly from under her by a bustling white whirlwind, and into my life there entered Sunshine Something-or-other Something of Ormandy, better to be known as Sally.

Never having worried much about dogs' pedigrees (any more, I hope, than they have worried about mine) I was not greatly impressed with the 'Sunshine Something-or-other', but the Ormandy seemed to strike a chord and I was gratified later to learn that the Sally who had joined our Chelsea alley was a product of the strain made famous by my old friend and golfing companion, Raymond Oppenheimer. Indeed, her grandfather was none other than that patriarch of the Ormandy family, Boris Something-or-other, now somewhat in his dotage, whom I had so often seen waddling about the Oppenheimer drawing-room at White Waltham, Berkshire. Raymond is so advanced an expert on Bull Terriers as to be invited to America to judge them, and to so practised an eye our Sally is doubtless no great credit to her grandfather.

However, it was of Bull Terriers in general that I meant to write, and the strange fascination that they exercise over people—strange, at any rate, since they are not themselves specialists; neither hunting dogs, nor lap dogs, nor one-man dogs, nor show-the-owner-off-to-other-people dogs, like Borzois.

Perhaps it is that they talk so plainly—mostly with their ears, partly with their eyes and tail. Of course, like other doting owners, I like to think I know everything that my dog is thinking (and I am pretty sure that the dog knows everything that I am thinking), but the Bull Terrier owner can claim no peculiarity in this matter. Everyone else can see what a Bull Terrier is thinking.

Perhaps it is their absurd combination of toughness and sloppiness.

At one moment the tough bruiser that you can thump on the chest with closed fist, the terror of every cat in the neighbourhood, the dog that will charge full tilt, nose-on, into a closed door and never bat an eyelid, the creature that will sit on your foot rather than on a pile carpet and lay its head on a brick rather than a cushion. At the next moment a creature of unbelievable sloppiness, lying in abandoned attitudes, being pulled about all over the place by the children, and coming all over coy at being told what a beautiful dog it is.

Cats and Bull Terriers, of course, go together—the one generally about six feet in front of the other and both flat out. 'We are fortunate,' I remember remarking once to Raymond Oppenheimer, 'Ours doesn't seem to pay any attention to them.'

'Ha!' he replied. 'You wait. Just you wait!'

I must not offend cat lovers by suggesting that there is any merit in chasing their beloved pets, and indeed nothing would induce me to encourage the decease of one, though if you have lived in a Chelsea square and found the night hideous and the house reeking with them, your patience will have been sorely tried. Be that as it may, the fact is that Bull Terriers do chase cats—though the female of the species is much less deadly than the male in this respect—and ours proved to be no exception. Indeed, I think they are the abiding passion of her life. If, when she has been apparently asleep for the past hour, there is the faintest suspicious sound outside, she will open half of one eye in the manner immortalized by Cecil Aldin's drawing and peer up with a question that needs no words. I have only to whisper 'I believe it was,' and the room is turned into a raging commotion as she scrambles for the front door.

The ground speed of cats never ceases to amaze me. The distance from our front door to the ruined church at the end of the square, a cat sanctuary protected by a six-foot wooden fence, is perhaps eighty yards, and I swear that many a cat has done it in six seconds. Yet, while the dog appears to be racing at the speed of an express train, the cat lollops along in front with long slow bounds, tail curved upwards and sideways and slightly kinked at the end—and the cat inevitably wins. And if the start is too short and the cat turns to see it through, the mighty cat-hunter, the terror of the square, comes back two sizes smaller, licking the blood from criss-crossed scratches across the nose and trying to pass it off with an expression of 'I could have got it if I had wanted, but you called me off.'

I read somewhere with much interest that Bull Terriers, if caught young, can be trained into admirable retrievers, and I often wonder if this is true. Personally I have not come across a case, but my experience is limited. Judging by our Sally, I should have thought it inconceivable, since she has less nose than any variety of dog I have known. The other day when she put up a cock pheasant in the woods, the bird sat calmly a few feet up in a hazel bush, comically craning its neck to watch her every movement as she bustled about unawares below. Then she pushed a rabbit out of some thin brushwood a foot from her nose and never realized it had gone. And within a minute or two a very large deer passed across within a few feet and she neither saw nor scented that.

All the same, a Bull Terrier as retriever is an intriguing thought, and I should love dearly to see the faces of one's fellow guests as one turned up at a shoot with one. Perhaps someone can enlighten me.

Judging again by limited experience, Bull Terriers are poor wives and poorer mothers. Sally went up the aisle only once—with a handsome brindled bridegroom by the name of Sammy. And when the offspring arrived some of them had to have stitches in the scruff of their necks from being flung about by mother.

Nevertheless, if their domestic qualities leave something to be desired, Bull Terriers have many virtues. One is that they are, on the whole, silent dogs, and do not unnecessarily yap or bark. Another is that their wave-length seems so delicately attunable to that of man, and this makes them not only the perfect silent companion but also the perfect watchdog. Our own is friendlily disposed to the entire world and I often declare that, if the time came, she would lick the burglar's hand. Yet when on the one occasion on which my wife, left alone, had cause to suspect the motives of a caller at the door, without a word being spoken the dog's hackle rose to a black ridge on her white back and it would have been a brave malefactor who had tried any tricks.

One final virtue, if virtue it be; I will back a Bull Terrier to dispatch a piled dish of raw horsemeat in less time than any other dog, large or small. Our domestic record, timed, is twelve seconds. After that she looks you full in the eye, emits that rumbling sound which is always said in China to signify appreciation of one's host's fare, and wags her tail.

'A dog,' said Sherlock Holmes, 'reflects the family life. Whoever saw a frisky dog in a gloomy family, or a sad dog in a happy one? Snarling people have snarling dogs, dangerous people have dangerous ones.'

If Holmes was right, then I am one of the nicest fellows in the whole world.

Much Grousing on the Moor

The Glorious Twelfth appears to have ushered in a somewhat inglorious season. There is much beating about the heather and waving of flags and tramping up barren hillsides, and lovely ladies with shooting-sticks, tweeds, and red fingernails adorn the butts as elegantly as ever—but, alas, on many a moor there are no birds. Plenty of grousing, but no grouse.

One tale of woe reports how an Anglo-American party paraded with no fewer than a hundred beaters, 'flankers', and flagwaggers, and a firing squad of eight, each with two guns and a loader. Total bag, eight and a half brace—or half a bird per barrel.

Indeed, so varied are the perils which apparently beset the grouse that it is remarkable not that there are so few but that there are any. The first hatch are automatically written off either by the early snow or because it lingered so long. The young heather, always in short supply, is infected by a parasite which eats away the internals of the survivors. Stoats, jays, magpies, crows, egg collectors, hikers, and disgruntled ex-employees destroy the eggs, and foxes claim a bird apiece per day.

Why, then, should adult, over-taxed citizens spend their remaining capital in pursuit of these elusive and much persecuted birds? A recent, and on the whole unproductive, day on a moor in Yorkshire has, to me at least, revealed the answer. It is that for sheer elevation of spirit, for casting off the cares and frustrations of current life, and generally recharging the human battery, nothing in the world touches a fine August day up on the moors.

The memory lingers on. I see myself again in the end butt, with the other nine out of sight over the brow of the hill. Alone in silence and sunshine. I have twenty minutes to let the scene sink in, before the sheep on the crest a mile away give warning by uneasy movement that the beaters are on their way.

Down below, the River Wharfe winds its way through a rich valley dotted with sycamores. On the far side is Ilkley Moor, music-hall legend to the mere Southerner, where, they assure me, half the population of the West Riding walk at week-ends and still the grouse survive. Behind us the Blubberhouses Moor conjures up visions of the irate Lord Walsingham in '88, blazing furiously away with three guns and two loaders to 'larn' the Prince of Wales.

His Royal Highness, it appears, had declined his invitation and gone instead to Bolton Abbey, where he could be 'sure of there being some birds'. Whereupon Lord W. strode up in dudgeon to his moor and in a one-man fusillade despatched 1,070 grouse, thus proving his point and placing his name imperishably in the record books.

Not that the lure of grouse shooting lies only in swooning at the scenery. The practical side of the business, especially to the untutored, is a fascinating challenge, much akin to that of golf, in that you have to do it all yourself and have no one to blame, not even a caddie, for your own failures. The two pursuits have much in common—except that, whereas the Lockes and Cottons of this world say 'Head down', my old friend Bob Robertson, who has been teaching shooting for so long that he can see almost where each of the pellets goes, digs one in the back and cries 'Head up!'

'Eye on the ball,' however, and 'Follow through' are injunctions common to both. Simple enough with clay pigeons or practice swings at the daisies, they border upon the impossible when driving off the first tee at St. Andrews before a critical multitude, or when the air is suddenly black with flying, swerving objects which a moment ago were but specks on the horizon.

On the other hand, the golfer may envy the shooting man one thing. He does at least have a second barrel.

Shooting Memories

Having been shooting for upwards of thirty years with weapons ranging from the catapult to the Bofors, I have at last been presented with what every good shooting man, I now learn, has possessed since childhood—a game book.

This is a handsome, leather-bound volume with gilt letters on the cover and innumerable columns under which I am to list the creatures I shoot and the fish I catch. These include ptarmigan, over which I do not anticipate unduly troubling the scorer, and Various, under which is numbered the humble pigeon, a bird too proletarian to rate a column to itself.

Turning the pages of my new possession with a loving anticipation, I find myself in a dilemma. Am I to try to recapture and insert the highlights of the past, or am I, as though starting a diary in August, to begin from now?

If the latter, the opening entry must be discouraging—something like: 'Trudged a mile and a half with 100 cartridges through a foot of snow to a wood near Huntercombe, where yesterday the air was darkened by about 20,000 pigeons. Stood for 1½ hours. Saw nothing, heard nothing, and in the end felt nothing. Total—Various: nil.'

A poor beginning indeed, and altogether unworthy. Clearly we must go back—back, for a start, to 4.42 p.m. on a December afternoon just after the war, and a moment of which I had been dreaming for six years. I am hidden in a gorse bush on the lake-side fringe of some flooded water meadows at Killarney. Half an hour's hard rowing has brought us to this lonely, silent spot and the boat lies concealed behind us in nature's perfect boathouse, a cavern worn away by the water in the rocks. Away over the lake the sun has gone down in splendour over Carrantouil and the McGillicuddy's Reeks, and the afterglow reflects magically on the water. Farther across my two companions wait in similar ambush.

A few duck flight in on whistling wings; a distant clock strikes the quarter hours; the rest is silence. As we lie in wait, all are thinking the same thoughts. Will they come tonight?

And then, far away yet unmistakable, we hear it, the sound that sends a shiver up the spine, sets every nerve on edge, and remains completely indescribable—the cry of the wild geese.

Soon I can see them, twenty or thirty in V formation at perhaps 300 feet. As they reach the lake, they break up, tumbling and gambolling through the sky like the rooks at bedtime. Re-forming lower down, they make their way out over the water, and crouching in my bush, I turn to follow them by their cries. Soon the raucous yelping with which they arrived turns to the squeaky quee-quee-quee-quee that means they are coming in to land.

'They're giggling. They're coming in!' whispers Pat Lyne behind me.

We have turned a full circle before we see them again, lower now and surely within shot. They pass over the bushes in which one of my companions should be hidden. Good heavens, don't say he has moved! I feel like shouting. Suddenly two vivid flashes stab up into the violet half-light. A goose falls vertically, almost 'pouring' down from the sky, like the barrage balloons hit in the war. It pitches with a resounding thump, and another falls farther away in the water and we hear the dog splashing his way in search of it.

Ten minutes later it happens again—the distant cries, the wide cautious circling, the suspense, and then suddenly the air is black with them. Six years I have dreamed of this moment. Lord, what if I miss them now! But all is well and I reflect, as we row back in darkness, that no smugness in the world equals that of a man who returns home clutching the neck of a wild goose.

Killarney, and Kerry in general, will figure high in my game book. Duck rising from the little bays around Ross Castle, or plummeting over the fir trees between the inland pond and the main lake. Snipe zigzagging over the rushy fields and peat hags, pursued in company with the versatile and indomitable Dr. Billy O'Sullivan, hotel proprietor, gun-dog trainer, greyhound breeder, rugby footballer, and captain of the Irish golf team.

And woodcock—they have a column to themselves, I am glad to see. No shooting man has lived till he has attended a 'cock' shoot in Kerry, preferably up in the wilds of Glencar, away from human kind, where the salmon river dashes through the valley and the woodcock shelter in the holly bushes on the hillsides.

We arrive to find assembled upwards of twenty beaters, who will forgive my describing them as the rural Irishmen of the caricatures. One in particular remains in the memory. He has a battered hat, incredibly long arms, and a six-inch grin which reveals a solitary tooth sprouting from his lower jaw. We know him as the Original Man.

We marshal ourselves in U formation and thus proceed through the holly; guns and beaters happily intermingled, each with little idea of the whereabouts of the other. 'Rattle dem bushes, bhoys! Rattle dem bushes!' exhorts the head man, and the 'music' begins. This, startling as it is to the novice, is nothing to what follows when the first luckless 'cock' flits brownly from the bushes. Everyone stops. 'Ma-a-ark!' they all yell, irrespective of whether they have seen it or not, and soon you find yourself yelling too. I once found myself trying to shoot a wood-cock with two dozen people yelling 'Ma-a-ark!' and a donkey braying its head off ten yards away.

No less disconcerting was an expedition to shoot snipe in Egypt, the scene of the operation being the village of Ekiad, some two and a half hours from Cairo down the road beside the Ismailia Canal. Few people any longer measure the fun by the size of the bag, and here along the Canal, in the vivid, smokeless light of early morning, were many of those glimpses of colour, contrast, and beauty that are the by-products of a good day's shooting.

Nor could there be a more ideal companion with whom to enjoy them than Nicholas Strekalovsky, a Russian artist long resident in Egypt, whose pictures of bird life, and of the fantastically coloured rocky coast of Sinai and the Red Sea, once induced King Farouk to buy the contents of one of his exhibitions en bloc.

Guided by one Mohammed, spit image of Viscount Montgomery in a darker shade and head bailiff on the British Embassy's duck shoot, we turned across the desert and pulled up eventually in a mud village beside a smaller, palm-fringed canal. Here the car, an imposing affair sent along by Prince Abbas Halim in one of those spontaneous gestures of hospitality so characteristic of the Arab world, was instantly sur-rounded by small boys who materialized from nowhere, like accident spectators in a deserted street.

Neither the long walk through the palm groves, following the little irrigation channels, nor the threats of 'Monty' and his adult henchmen served to throw off these juvenile assistants, and a dozen were with us to the end. Two nearly got shot, but the merriment of the others at this episode, together with the way they dashed through the mud as retrievers or jostled each other for position in order to catch the spent cartridges as they were ejected, added much to the general enjoyment.

Snipe grounds look much the same the world over. Take away the palm trees and the sunshine, and for Mohammed read O'Sullivan, and we might have been back in the rushy fields of Killarney. Indeed, it is migratorily possible that some of the snipe we disturbed may themselves have lodged in the peat bogs of Kerry.

The first few yards as one splashes through the still, lifeless rushes, waiting for the 'zzt! zzt!' of a startled snipe and the tiny zigzagging target, bring moments of suspense which one does not have to be a shooting man to appreciate. The opening stroke is made no easier when the bird's sudden appearance is greeted by a chorus of yells and shrieks from directly behind. One child clutched my arm, another prodded me in the back, the more experienced crouched, like miniature wicket-keepers, to catch the empties, while all jumped frenziedly up and down, yelling 'Abou! Abou!'

It took me some time to gather the significance of this. It sounded almost like 'A vous! A vous!' The answer is that it was—but they cannot pronounce a 'v'.

Discharging two barrels without effect, I made some irate comment, and this was greeted with howls of glee and giggling and poking in the ribs. The snipe shot skywards and started circling, whereupon the chorus squatted down in the rushes making osculatory noises calculated, erroneously, to lure it down again.

We saw immense numbers of little jack snipe, each a couple of good mouthfuls, but dear at the price with cartridges at 235 piastres a hundred; and some of the more handsome 'painted' variety; but no great number of 'full' snipe. They are capricious creatures; here today, or rather yesterday, and gone tomorrow. They are like fishermen. If it isn't the temperature, it is the wind; and if it isn't the wind, it is the water. Things are never right for them all at once.

After shooting about thirty and seeing a remarkable variety of bird life, including the elegant hoopoe, long ago exterminated in England, we sat beside the Embassy's lake and watched, not without temptation, large parties of duck circling overhead, undeterred by the fact that 2,000 of their kind had perished there on the previous Sunday morning.

The day ended with a glutinous feast of figs, dates and sweet tea laid on in his home by 'Monty', while the rest of the village, mingling among the assorted livestock, gazed in with awe from without. I was remarking on the age-old, idealistic tranquillity of the scene when a deafening blast of hot American jazz roared out from the next room.

'Monty', with great pride, had turned on his new radio.

Not all my game book memories, of course, will come from so far afield. Perhaps the strangest will relate to a day's shooting in a deserted village. It was a sleepy little hamlet on the remote fringe of the coast of Suffolk, and this was just after the war's end. Six years before, the Army had descended on the village and, together with 2,000 acres of wild gorse, heather, and bracken, swallowed it whole. The hall became headquarters; barbed wire and sentries encircled the condemned area; and the inhabitants, sadly nailing boards over their windows and locking their back doors for the last time, moved away to neighbouring towns.

My companions were a member of the Army staff and P. B. Lucas, later to become Member of Parliament for Brentford and Chiswick and our 1949 Walker Cup golf captain, who was then commanding the R.A.F. station at Bentwaters.

All day, in pursuit of such pheasants as had not been scared away by flame-throwers, mine-destroying tanks, and surreptitious rifle practice, we wandered at will and met not a living soul. Down past the silent churchyard, where the rude forefathers of the hamlet slept in their unkempt graves; past the church farm; through the dilapidated 200-year-old cottages, and along past the 'Chequers'.

We had an excellent day. I will not enlarge upon what Sherlock Holmes might have called 'The Singular Episode of the Captain, the No. 4 Cartridge and the Tame Goose'—but we got a dozen pheasants, some duck on the evening flight in the marshes, a hare or two, and as many rabbits as, standing up in the car on the way home, we cared to shoot in the glare of the headlights.

Grouse in Lancashire—only rarely, alas; guinea-fowl and a gigantic, illicit bustard in the Sudan; pigeons in Cambridgeshire with the redoubtable 'Squire' Hicks, at seventy-nine, firing nine shots in a failing light and coming in with eight birds; the time when six guns moved a solitary pheasant from copse to copse, missing it, till someone said to the keeper, 'Do you think we shall tire this pheasant out?'; and the two great stags at Muckross—a column now closed, for I will never shoot another.

How the memories crowd in and what a labour of love it will be to recapture them! But how many will be lost? If only someone had given me a game book when I was a boy!

'Getting up' in Nassau

A highly exhilarating sport in the Bahamas is water ski-ing, which is by no means so difficult as it may seem, for even your humble servant was able to do it after a fashion. As a change from catching cold on the sands or fishing from the pier, it could be more widely practised from our own shores. For skill, thrill and grace there is nothing to touch it—especially against a background of dazzling sand, palm trees, and the clear, buoyant waters of Paradise Beach.

The paraphernalia consists of two skis, wider than the snow variety, with rubber pouches for the feet; thirty yards of rope with a wooden bar at the end; and a speedboat. Beginners, and those susceptible to cramp, also require a beach, on account of the underwater contortions involved in putting on the skis while out of one's depth. The performer lies on his back like some water-logged beetle, his skis protruding from the water. The rope is flung to him, the motor 'revved up'.

To the novice who has just seen others hauled violently out of the water, only to be flung instantly back in a shower of legs, skis, rope and, in one case, the bathing pants themselves, this is a moment at least as awesome as the start of one's first ride down the Cresta. In riding the Cresta you may not know whether you will finish, but at least you know you will begin. In water ski-ing the beginner's concern is to make a start at all—to 'get up', as they call it.

The impression of my first attempt is still vivid. A tremendous tugging on the shoulders as the speedboat roared away; showers of foam; much bumping, heaving and struggling for balance, and suddenly—a moment beside which holes-in-one, centuries, and tries-between-the-post are but poor barren affairs—I was 'up'.

An astonishing sensation! Riding the great trough of water thrown up by the boat, one feels the surface as solid as beaten snow. The skis duck-and-drake across it with a hard, bumping sound. It seems uncanny, faintly irreligious, to be standing on the water in this way.

Mr. Billy Butlin, my companion on the other rope, was a more experienced performer; a ten-handicap man, as you might say. But suddenly the dragging of his rope on the water indicated, though I did not dare look round, that Mr. Butlin was no longer attached thereto. The inquest revealed that he had been 'seeing if he could do it on one leg'.

It is unnerving for the novice thus to witness the downfall of the more expert. It causes him to be cast forcibly on the face of the Atlantic at thirty miles per hour, the mouth wide open like the scoop let down by railway engines when picking up water at speed. He emerges to a silent, liquid loneliness, a mere head bobbing in the bay, uttering feeble oaths, alone in the ocean with a pair of upturned skis and no idea how it happened.

A high-class exponent in the Bahamas was the colonial secretary, Mr. F. A. Evans, whom I had not seen since the days when he was a classical scholar and rather better half-back at Charterhouse. He performed splendid evolutions in a pair of flowered knickers, and local opinion had it that never had a government official been seen to move so fast.

More expert still were the professionals, who start off with only one ski, or jump over each other's ropes, or lift young ladies at full speed on to their shoulders in attitudes which, though skilful, might not have done for our grandmothers. At the moment, however, they were gnashing their teeth, for the newsreels had just shown a young boy ski-ing first with miniature eighteen-inch boards scarcely bigger than rulers, and then with his *bare feet*. The only trouble about it, he said, was the acute tickling sensation.

I Gotta Horse

The revelation in the *Sunday Times* that I am the owner of part of a racehorse has brought ribald comments from my friends, to which I reply loftily, 'Not merely an owner. A Winning Owner.' Being a Winning Owner means that, if you back your horse when it wins and not too heavily when it loses, you may with luck come out just about all square. What it is like to be a Losing Owner hardly bears contemplation.

My first, and last, incursion upon the Turf has taught me the truth of what I had already suspected, namely, that although 'certainties' often win, there is in fact no such thing as a certainty. All that you can be certain of is whether your own horse is trying. Ours, I may say, is always trying, if only for the fact that we cannot afford for him not to be. Unfortunately other equally impoverished owners are liable to be trying, too.

Our horse is a smallish chestnut called Infatuated, possessed of an exceptionally nice disposition, though not destined, I am afraid, to earn us anything for stud purposes. My senior owner, so to speak, is Brigadier Peter Wreford-Brown, with whom I arrived at the same house on the same day at Charterhouse, where later, if I remember, he used to make a book among the Lower School. Our horse is trained by Toby Balding, son of the great polo player, at Weyhill.

Before coming to the hazards, thrills and disappointments of being a racehorse owner, I may perhaps intrude a personal note. I am not the first Winning Owner in the family. My mother's uncle, William Gilbert, having won the 2,000 Guineas with Sailor Prince, invested the last of his dwindling fortune on this horse in the Royal Hunt Cup in 1886. He also had another horse running called Despair, ridden by a boy.

He won the Royal Hunt Cup all right, but, alas, it ruined him, for the winner was not Sailor Prince but Despair. I like to think of the wretched boy, as he is led in by my great uncle to the plaudits of the crowd, saying, ' 'e was away with me, sir. 'Onest, sir. I couldn't 'old 'im, sir.' To complete the story Sailor Prince ought to have been second, but in fact he was nowhere.

In view of this we felt it only appropriate that my mother, who is eighty-five, should be registered at Weatherby's as owner of the family half of Infatuated and so, after a good deal of 'Don't be so ridiculous; me, at my time of life!' it became. I cherish the memory of her, cheque book open and pen poised, saying solemnly, 'But what would the Rector say?' To which I am afraid I replied: 'I know exactly what the Rector would say. He would say "Is it going to win at Plumpton on Easter Monday?"'

Our first venture was at Newbury, where I at once began to sense the vanity of being an Owner. You turn importantly into the car-park marked 'Owners, trainers and jockeys'; watch your horse being saddled up; walk importantly into the ring and talk to the jockey, in our case Bill Palmer ('Haven't had a winner in my family for seventy-six years,' I said. 'I'll do my best, sir!' he replied); and furthermore you get a free lunch or, if too excited to eat it, the equivalent of 7/6 in sandwiches, which comes to one round of smoked salmon and one of ham.

We hoped that at the best we might get a place. They were half way round the second time before we were so much as mentioned by the commentator, lying about twelfth among an apparently impenetrable mass of horses. Then it was eighth: then fifth: then fourth. Surely he could catch just one more!

Then suddenly, as they came over the last hurdle ('flight' to us racing men), it was 'Infatuated and So-and-So.' I have a wonderful picture of him taken at this very moment, which Palmer will be able to show with pride to his grandchildren as a masterpiece of poise and motion. A few seconds later I was lifting my hat to the pair of them as they passed the post, winners by twelve lengths—and 16 to 1 on the Tote.

We repaired to the winner's enclosure and I fancy that I was still there, in case anyone had not seen me, when they brought the next winner in. The racing Press got hold of the story of my mother's uncle and she found herself featured in nearly all the papers next day, one account being headed in inch-high letters 'Mother's Joy'.

Infatuated then won a race at Warwick, beating a horse that cost ten times the £600 we had paid for him, and was an odds-on favourite at Wye, his value apparently increasing by about £1,000 a month—but there, alas, ended our saga of success. He got within an hour of Wye racecourse when they abandoned the meeting, thus robbing us of a certain £300. Then he got to Plumpton and they abandoned the meeting at 1 P.M., robbing us, as we like to think, of another £300.

Never mind. All would come right at Fontwell—but a lovely sunny day turned out only to be what we still remember as Black Monday.

It was my first experience of being a Losing Owner and I found it painful, especially to the pocket. All that I had gained went down the drain.

'Never mind,' said my mother, 'so long as the little horse is all right. . . .' She was right. If ever he fell and had to be destroyed, I know I should never set foot on a racecourse again.

Since then he has won a race at Chepstow, paying on the Tote, of course, almost double the 5-2 starting price at which we backed him. Maddening, but I suppose one must not complain. Having won three races, we are still a little in hand and Infatuated is worth double what we paid for him. The trouble is that we have become so fond of him that we could not bear to sell him.

Those who fancy themselves in the role of Winning Owner may care to see last month's training bill:

Training fees at 10 gns. per week *re* Infatuated to 23rd	£34	10	0
Keep at 6 gns. for remainder of month . .	6	6	0
Veterinary supplies		10	6
Shoeing	5	14	6
Infatuated to Wye (Abortive trip, allowance being paid by Totalisator Betting Board) .	10	10	0
Infatuated to Plumpton (ditto) . . .	8	10	0
Infatuated to Nottingham	29	0	0
Infatuated to Warwick	17	10	0
Infatuated to Chepstow	22	10	0
TOTAL .	£135	1	0

Every time Infatuated runs for £300, I nearly have a heart attack. What it must be like to have one running in Wednesday's Derby for £30,000, I hardly like to think. Still, it is always something to be able to say, in a modest little way, 'I got a horse. . . .'

ADVENTURES IN OIL

The Unsung Hero

The brothers Thomas and Edwin Morgan, after four days of fruitless search for a non-existent lode of silver, were trudging wearily back along the thirty-mile trail to Rockhampton in Queensland, Australia. They settled for the night in a desolate stony valley, relieved only by a few stunted palms and a stream trickling down into the River Dee. The time was midsummer 1882.

As Thomas prepared the camp, Edwin wandered off down the valley, swinging his pick, as prospectors will, at any odd rock that took his fancy. One such was a black boulder which had obviously rolled down from the hillside—and the chip which flew off it glinted. Edwin put it silently in his pocket and, saying nothing to the guide, returned with his brother to Rockhampton. Soon the two of them were back, their eyes standing out of their heads. 'There seemed,' they said afterwards, 'to be more gold than stone.' One sample sent for assay for them by the manager of the Queensland National Bank showed gold at the rate of 3,700 ounces to the ton.

It was, in fact, one of the greatest individual gold strikes in history.

The bank manager consulted Mr. William Knox D'Arcy, the son of the local solicitor, who, together with the Morgan brothers, formed the Mount Morgan Gold Mining Co. with a nominal capital of a million pounds. By 1886 the £1 shares were worth £17 and towards the end of the century D'Arcy returned home to England with a fortune.

Edwin Morgan by the chance blow of his pick had released directly to the world a flow of gold which was to yield tens of millions of pounds and which continues to this day. What he released indirectly made all the gold seem a mere drop in the ocean.

Within a year or two D'Arcy invested the major part of his fortune in financing an expedition to search for oil in Persia.

As his commander in the field D'Arcy chose a man of remarkable tenacity and character. His name was G. B. Reynolds. Then rising fifty, he had had a certain amount of experience of oil-drilling in Sumatra and had been in the Public Works Department in India. He was destined to overcome hardship, frustration and disappointment calculated to break the spirit of a dozen younger men and at the end of it all to pass quietly from the scene as one of the great unsung heroes in the history of oil.

As all the machinery and equipment had to be sent from England via Basra and Baghdad, Reynolds, travelling out through Russia and Tehran, decided to make his headquarters in Baghdad. The prospect that confronted him as he rode out to survey the scene of operations may well have caused his heart to sink. A barren, inhospitable land; no roads worthy of the name; little or no water, either to drink or for the boilers when they arrived; tribesmen of uncertain temper; and all the time the sun blistering down at more than 100° in the shade. In England there were long delays in assembling all the drilling gear, stores and equipment, and when it did arrive the Turks would not let the heavily loaded wagons pass over the bridge at Khanaqin, though it was manifestly strong enough; nor, they said, must they cross over into Persia by any route except the one via Khanaqin, which happened to be impassable at the time. Meanwhile Reynolds spent much of his time haggling with the local chiefs, who made it abundantly plain that, whatever else the Shah might think he was including in his Concession, he was not conceding the use of their land without some sort of payment to them.

Sixteen months after his engagement Reynolds was at last able to report that drilling had begun at Chiah Surkh and by the end of 1902 the first well had reached 300 feet. A pipeline route to the Gulf was being surveyed and in a matter of months, perhaps even of weeks, the rigours of their present life would be rewarded. In the meantime it was rigorous indeed, and at the range of a mere half-century we may look back at this little band of pioneers and in spirit lift our hats to them. They were a motley and miscellaneous crew. There were the two Canadian drillers, McNaughton and Buchanan; a number of Polish drillers; an American engineer named Rosenplaenter, who was appointed to take charge when Reynolds went on leave; an Indian doctor who might have been the original 'Failed B.A., Calcutta'; a labour force consisting mainly of tribesmen who had never handled machinery in their lives; and the inevitable assortment of cooks, bottle-washers and camp-followers in general. They had two tin sheds as office and dining-room, but for the rest everyone lived and worked in tents.

McNaughton, who stuck it through to the bitter end, received many an honourable mention in dispatches, but the rest, strangely, seem to have possessed little of the adaptability to be expected of men who volunteer for such a job. The Poles downed tools so often on the grounds that it was a 'Saint's day' that Rosenplaenter had to send home for a Roman Catholic calendar. They had no authority with the Persian labourers. 'Our two Canadian drillers,' Rosenplaenter was pleased to report, 'are handling them with tact and discretion and have at once been recognized and accepted as masters.' Later they were joined by other Canadian drillers, of whom Reynolds, exacerbated by complaints relayed from home, wrote sourly: 'A more helpless crew I seldom saw.' One of them complained that he could not eat gooseberry jam and that they had run out of Provost Oats for breakfast—'being too casual to readily make a substitute out of wheat or rice, any amount of both being available.' Another complained that he incessantly had only cold boiled eggs and dry bread, and when Reynolds asked him where were all the tinned rations he had been given, found that he was sitting on the box containing them. 'He ought to have brought his mother out,' Reynolds said. Nor was Rosenplaenter any more complimentary about his own countrymen. 'The average American driller is quite unfit to be sent to a country like this,' he said, 'as he will not suit himself to new circumstances and conditions.'

We shall see some of these characters in a more favourable light later on, but in the meantime if tempers were short it was understandable. Even in this age of air-conditioning and the refrigerator those who work in Persia count their service not in years but in summers. In the summer of 1903 indications at No. 1 well, though a layer of hard-grained rocks had been reached which 'cut their bits all to pieces', may have been encouraging, but life in general was very much the opposite. Rosenplaenter, for a start, had a Baghdad boil on his ankle, which, he said, 'interfered considerably with his locomotion'. It will also, as anyone can testify who knows that part of the world and can in imagination carry his mind back to what it must have been like sixty years ago, have interfered considerably with his temper. At seven in the morning the temperature was 110° in the shade—'what the thermometer would read during the noon hours we cannot even guess'—and already five of the small band of Europeans, together with a Baghdad mechanic, had been touched by the sun and one of them was dying. For the last six days grasshoppers had swarmed across the country like locusts and devoured every trace of green pasture. The river was full of them and the water stank. Their bodies lay all over the camp and everywhere the men went they trod their way through a squelching mass of dead insects. Every half-hour they skimmed them from the water tanks. Smallpox had broken out at Sekhuan, where they got their food and water. Their dwindling stock of firewood for the boiler was constantly being raided and then the boiler itself collapsed, its tubes corroded by the sulphurous water. Letters from home, always the dearest consolation of the exile, had failed to arrive because the carrier and his camel had died en route—and, to cap it all, some idiot had just dropped a fourteen-pound sledge hammer down the well. For Rosenplaenter life was far from rosy.

They struggled on in the blinding heat, encouraged in August by striking salt water and some gas with the 'true oil gas smell' at 1,665 feet in No. 1 well and by an explosion of gas at only seventeen feet in No. 2 well, which was promising and fortunately did not harm. Early in November their drinking water was down to two or three days' supply when at last the rains came. They worked on with spirits revived and at last in January 1904 a great moment came. Oil! Oil surging up through No. 2 well at the rate of 120 barrels per twenty-four hours. As they drilled deeper, it spurted up over the top of the derrick.

At home D'Arcy was metaphorically throwing his cap in the air. 'Glorious news from Persia,' he announced. 'It is the greatest help to me.' He had already sunk £150,000 of his own money into the Concession, quite apart from what he had spent in obtaining it. 'Every purse has its limit,' he had said, 'and I can see the limit of my own.' He had approached the Rothschilds in Paris, Sir Ernest Cassel and Joseph Lyons & Co. in England, but financiers, he found, 'would have nothing to do with the matter till oil is found.' It was all he could do to keep the bank quiet, he said—at the same time lodging with them another 10,000 shares in the Mount Morgan Mine. He had even interviewed a group of Americans who had come over to bid for the Concession. Still, things were different now. The 'glorious news' had changed everything and now the stony-hearted financiers would assuredly come in.

Alas, poor D'Arcy! In May the well at Chiah Surkh ran suddenly and completely dry.

In the meantime Reynolds after four long years of unavailing toil in the wilderness, still accompanied by the faithful McNaughton, was preparing the second assault. He was due to attack with the most primitive weapons what must have seemed at times one of the most impregnable fortresses of nature. He assembled his forces at Ahwaz and in December 1905 set off for Shardin. His caravan consisted of seven 'jims'—primitive carts with four iron wheels and a long iron frame for carrying pipe or casing—six four-wheeled American carts and two two-wheeled carts, mostly drawn by mules. There was, of course, no proper road and when they came to irrigation channels the only way they could cross them was to unload the tall smokestacks of the boilers, lay them in the channels with the water passing through them, and so use them as improvised bridges.

The two alternative sites in the new area, Shardin and Maidan-i-Naftun, were about eighty miles apart, and it was Reynolds's opinion that the latter was the better prospect of the two. His instructions were to begin at Shardin but he soon asked for permission to open up a camp at Maidan-i-Naftun as well. 'You must understand,' he wrote, 'that if you do drill there my work will be more than doubled on account of the travelling required between the two places, but I came out here to see this business through and unless you let me drill there I shall not think I've done so.' He was certainly a glutton for punishment.

Month by sweltering month the drilling went on at Shardin, with apparatus that would be regarded as mere museum pieces by the drillers of today. In the intervals of supervising the work, Reynolds was prospecting for a road to Maidan-i-Naftun. After unbelievable difficulties he managed to get it open in August 1907.

In the same year Reynolds was joined by two notable companions; one destined to give a lifetime of service not only to his employers but to Persia, the other a skilled and reliable observer who has left behind him an eyewitness account by which we can recapture the scene and spirit of the pioneering days.

The first was Doctor M. Y. Young. The second was Lt. Wilson of the 18th Bengal Lancers, later Sir Arnold Wilson, at one time Member of Parliament for Hitchin, and author of *S.W. Persia—A Political Officer's Diary, 1907-1914*. He was on service in India when towards the end of 1907 he was detailed to proceed to South-West Persia with twenty men, 'ostensibly to reinforce the guard of the Ahwaz consulate but in fact to protect the drillers until the attempt to find oil was successful or abandoned.'

The more one sees of Reynolds through the eyes of these two men who laboured beside him and shared the hopes and disappointments of his rigorous life, the more does his stature rise. Dr. Young found him living in austere simplicity in the poorer quarter of Ahwaz. His living-room was furnished with a camp-bed and table, a couple of chairs and a bookcase, all made by the local carpenter, while in the adjoining office he had a large table, a typewriter, two or three chairs and two zinc trunks for his files and official papers.

Reynolds at this time was in his middle fifties. The youthful Wilson, who found that he had been at school at Clifton with Reynolds's son, described him as 'a great man, with remarkable gifts for organization and management, who inspires real respect in Englishmen and Canadians and real affection in Persians and Arabs'.

Reynolds had at this time been drilling in Persia for five solid years, three of them at Chiah Surkh and now two at Shardin. By September 1907 the two wells had reached 2,000 feet without a vestige of reward and for months everyone had known in their hearts that this venture too was hopeless. Once more they downed tools and abandoned the quest. Having completed the road that very month, they moved to Maidan-i-Naftun for what was clearly their final attempt. They picked on a barren ledge overlooking a shallow sort of stream that might have trout in it but, in fact, according to Wilson, tasted of Epsom salts and acted accordingly on strangers. The water was handy for the boilers and at the foot of the ledge they were encouraged to note—you can see it there today—a dark stain in the water denoting a seepage of oil. It was only one of thousands in Persia, but it was something. The verdict of a geologist sent from home was less encouraging. He thought they would find enough oil to use as fuel but did not recommend that the well be carried to any great depths. A mile or two from this inhospitable spot were the ruined walls and stone staircases of what was known locally as the Masjid-i-Sulaiman, or 'Mosque of Solomon', relic of a civilization dead these 2,000 years. Later they adopted this as the name of the place, and as M.I.S. it has been known ever since.

Here they began again the all too familiar routine, setting up the tents, the office, the humble canteen and the rig, and by the end of January 1908 they were able to begin drilling. A few weeks later they enjoyed the momentary reward of all who labour in the hills of Persia, the precious few weeks when suddenly the barren landscape blossoms in a riot of jonquil, sweet-scented nightstock, tulip and anemone. Then the sun is too much for them and in a moment they are gone.

Wilson, who had not yet experienced a Persian summer, waxed lyrical over this sudden unexpected bounty of nature. 'The hills and plains,' he wrote, 'are carpeted with flowers; in the valleys here and there are great beds of wild narcissus. My men, like Persians, bend low to their stirrups to smell them as they ride slowly through, sometimes putting up a wild pig or two. I can remember no time when my mind and eyes and ears enjoyed during all my waking hours such a feast of beautiful and interesting things.'

A year later he knew better. 'I had hoped,' he wrote, 'to be out of this blasted country by the end of the spring. . . .'

Meanwhile, day and night, the drilling went on. Towards the middle of May, when No. 1, as the first well was called, was down to 1,100 feet, there came, according to Wilson's *Diary*, what must to Reynolds have been the most heartbreaking moment of his life. For six years he had toiled in the wilderness. He had endured unceasing hardship, frustration and often physical danger. He had survived the two massive disappointments of Chiah Surkh and Shardin. Now, to quote Wilson again, he was handed a cable from the directors of the Syndicate, saying that 'funds were exhausted and the decision reached finally and irrevocably was that he was to cease work, dismiss the staff, dismantle anything worth the cost of transporting to the coast for reshipment, and come home.'

So, three thousand miles apart, bitter and disillusioned, two groups of men sat cursing their luck. Instead of enjoying his retirement as a country gentleman in the lush climate of Edwardian England, D'Arcy's only reward had been several years' hard labour and the loss of a quarter of a million pounds. Burmah Oil had sacrificed the services of some of their best men and a hundred thousand pounds or two into the bargain. The Admiralty were back where they started, still converting ships to burn non-existent oil. Meanwhile in the barren hills of Masjid-i-Sulaiman they cursed more freely, as is the custom and privilege of the man in the field when confronted with unintelligible and apparently insane decisions by the general staff at home.

Having duly given vent to his feelings Reynolds had to decide what to do. His solution was in the circumstances masterly. It would not be safe, he said, on account of possible errors of coding, to rely on the telegram. Instructions of such importance could not be acted upon without written confirmation. This with luck would take about a month. In the meantime drilling went feverishly on.

A fortnight later Wilson, sleeping in the open outside his tent, was woken at half-past four in the morning by unaccustomed noise and shouting at the No. 1 well nearby. He got up, ran across, and found oil spurting fifty feet above the top of the derrick. It smothered the drillers and their Persian crew as they danced wildly round the rig, yelling and choking—partly with excitement, partly from the escaping gas. The day was the 26th of May, 1908, and, though we may be sure that not a single schoolboy will find it in his history books, it was in fact one of the most significant dates in world history.

'I have the honour to report,' Reynolds drily wrote, 'that this morning at about 4 a.m. oil was struck in the No. 1 hole at a depth of 1,180 feet. . . . Particulars re gravity and quantity of oil flowing will follow but unless I get this away at once I shall miss the post.' (The oil incidentally proved to contain a good deal of sulphur and stank abominably, though to Reynolds it may well have smelt like nectar.) By the same messenger he sent cables to be dispatched from Basra, a week's journey away. Wilson, unaware of this but giving him by courtesy a start of forty-eight hours, cabled the news to Major Cox at Bushire. He had no code, so he wired: 'See Psalm 104 verse 15 third sentence, and Psalm 114 verse 8 second sentence.' Cox, being fortunately possessed of an Old Testament, decoded: 'That he may bring out of the earth oil to make him a cheerful countenance,' and 'The flint stone into a springing well'. He cabled the Legation in Tehran, whence the news was flashed to the Foreign Office—some days before Reynolds's messenger had so much as reached Basra.

D'Arcy, recalling his 'Glorious news from Persia' when oil had begun to flow at Chiah Surkh four years before and dried up a few days later, received the intelligence with understandable caution. 'If this is true,' he said, 'our troubles are over—but I am telling no one till I get the news confirmed.' This time, however, it was the real thing. Reynolds and his men had penetrated what proved to be the biggest oilfield then known to man.

Rig 20

May Day 1951 marked, for the Anglo-Iranian Oil Company, an episode which illuminated, in more senses than one, their darker days in Persia.

At five o'clock in the morning the driller and his crew on Rig 20 at Naft Safid were having a particularly trying time. The notices 'Danger. Well Drilling In' were up and they had been drilling through the hard impervious rock in which the oil was trapped thousands of feet below, which is a hazardous job at the best of times, when the detachment of some small part of the gear at the bottom of the well involved them in a 'fishing' job, with a matter of possibly only a few feet of rock left to drill. They were pulling the fishing tool, with a length of drilling pipe attached, out of the well, when mud and gas came roaring and surging up and blew violently out. This is a moment when you ask no questions and make no comment. The driller and crew leapt for their lives. They were hardly clear when the gas, rushing up through the eight-inch hole at a pressure of 2,500 lb. per square inch, suddenly ignited into a flame more than 1,000 feet high. In fifty years of drilling in Persia it was the Company's first oil-well fire while a well was being drilled. It was also, till that time, the biggest and most spectacular in the history of oil.

The news reached Britannic House in London in the afternoon and by 4 p.m. the New York office was being alerted by telephone to seek out the best man in the world to deal with the situation, namely Myron Kinley. By 2.30 p.m. on the same day of the fire, allowing for the difference between Californian and Persian time, he was found at his home and by 3.30 was on his way to New York. After a few hours for consultation in the New York office he took off on the afternoon of May 2, and spent that and the following night in the aeroplane to Basra, where he was met by one of the Company's planes and flown to Naft Safid. He arrived there eighty hours after the fire had started, having travelled some 9,000 miles.

Myron Kinley is, or was at that time, a plumpish, baldish, genial-looking man of fifty-five, completely belying by his appearance the extraordinary activity in which he was the world's most renowned specialist. As evidence of past exploits he bore a partially crippled leg, a damaged arm, and the disadvantage that no insurance company would insure him.

Rig 20 is set in a natural amphitheatre perhaps a couple of hundred yards wide. I remember that my first impression on seeing it was that if you searched the oil wells of the world you could find no more spectacular setting for a fire. The hills rise up like grandstands on every side, broken only by a small gap through which the road curves itself into the arena. By the time that Kinley got there the whole place was an inferno, unapproachable by this road or any other means. The outside temperature was now 250° Fahrenheit, the well was giving off 4,000 million thermal units of heat—in other words enough to heat two-thirds of the homes of the whole of England—and while the main flame was roaring vertically upwards others were shooting out side-ways and directly up the road. Before he could so much as advise, Kinley must look closely at the well, and before he could do this they must have unlimited water and a new road.

After a general mobilization from Abadan and Fields a road was hacked out in four days, and twenty-two miles of six-inch piping were laid to bring water from the Karun River. Not far from the blaze they were able to sandbag a natural depression and turn it into a reservoir. Meanwhile the rig itself and the machinery had long since collapsed into a tortured tangle of metal—it remains there as such today—and from time to time great jets of flame would shoot suddenly from un-suspected quarters, as though snapping at would-be extinguishers of the fire.

While the preliminary work was being done on the water supply and the road, Kinley was directing work on a lengthy mobile canopy made mainly of asbestos sheeting, behind which he proposed to advance and inspect the well-head. He knew from long experience exactly what he wanted and despite the misgivings of many present he knew that it would work. The result was similar to the 'testudo', or 'tortoise', behind which Roman soldiers used to advance upon a defended fortress a couple of thousand years before, except that in this instance it was to be pushed forward by a tractor.

Before Kinley and his volunteers could advance, the canopy and the surrounding ground had been doused continuously by the fire hoses. Then they themselves were submitted to the same treatment. The noise of the fire—it was a high-pitched screaming sound rather than a roar—made it impossible to hear yourself speak within 200 yards, much less within the canopy, so they filled their ears with wax and rehearsed their orders by means of signs. As the time came to move the canopy gradually forward, firemen behind portable asbestos shields soaked the contrivance and the men in it continuously with water, while other firemen in turn gave 'covering fire' by soaking the ones in front. It was like advancing behind a creeping barrage of water. Kinley's object was to get close enough to the tangle of wreckage to see where to place an explosive charge by which he hoped, for a start, to clear the well-head and turn the flames into a single vertical jet. He was within twenty yards when he found all progress blocked by a red-hot conglomeration of pipes and casing stacked beside the well.

Next day, volunteers somehow managed to cast a chain over these and drag them clear by a crane, and the way was now open for the introduction of Kinley's next device, which was a long metal rod, protruding, like a fishing-rod, from a bulldozer. To the other end of it was welded a tank containing a forty-gallon drum, with the space between the two filled with water. Volunteers, swathed from head to foot and hosed continuously, staggered up with fifty-pound loads of high explosive to fill the drum. Under the canopy, in a temperature still above 200°, the Field Superintendent, Eric Martin, placed the explosives in the drum, Kinley gave the signal to move the whole contraption forward to the heart of the flames and steadily the drum was lowered to the desired position. The arena was cleared; everyone withdrew to a safe distance; Kinley signalled by lowering his arm, and the charge was fired. The explosion thudded in men's ears—they could hardly hear it against the din—and in a fraction, they saw the side jets vanish, leaving, as Kinley had hoped, one vast vertical flame.

Then they saw a demonstration of the forces of nature about which people talk with awe to this day. It is the highlight of a spectacular film made on the spot, and is inevitably received by audiences with a momentary silence, followed by a gasp of wonder. As the explosion caused the broken well-head to disintegrate, it left the way open for the full force of the gas to escape upwards. Down in the hole was half a mile of four and a half-inch drill pipe. A second or two after the explosion came the fantastic sight of the whole half-mile of pipe shooting up from the hole like a long slender rocket. It shot away high into the sky, far above the thousand feet of flame, and here, twisting and turning and writhing like a serpent, it broke as though into mere pieces of string and fell slowly to earth.

Rig 20 had at this time been blazing for a fortnight but it was another week before Kinley reckoned it safe to launch the second phase of his attack. In this he hoped with another explosion to snuff out the flame. He moved all the firefighting equipment round to the old road, made further canopies and shields and a second reservoir, and caused water to be poured into the well cellar and all over the surrounding ground and red-hot wreckage continuously day and night for a week. Meanwhile special equipment of vast strength was going to be necessary in order to cap the gas, should he succeed in blowing out the flame, and this was being flown from Britain and the United States. Men who took advantage of the respite to retire to a rest-house far from the scene found that the screaming of the well vibrated in their ears as though they were still within hearing.

Kinley in the meantime was preparing his second bomb, 500 lb. of gelignite this time, and hanging, as before, on the end of a 'fishing-rod'. With hoses playing on it from every side it was advanced foot by foot to the very base of the 1,000-foot column of fire. Once again Kinley lowered his arm, the plunger was pressed, and suddenly the mighty flame, which for three weeks had made it possible to read a newspaper at midnight a mile away, was out. It was instantly replaced by an equally vicious column of screaming petroleum gas, visible like steam. The second stage had been accomplished and the supremely dangerous work could now begin.

This involved cutting away some of the casing which was still protruding from the well and fitting a base on which could be clamped the huge four and a half-ton hydraulically operated valve by which they hoped eventually to bottle up the gas. So long as the gas shot vertically upward it was comparatively safe, and now that the temperature had reverted to the mere 110° normal in Persia at that time of year men could approach close to the foot of the column. When it came to lowering any kind of machinery over it, however, jets of gas must clearly rush out sideways and here would come the moments of extreme peril. One spark from one man's shoe on a flint would light such a holocaust as would instantly destroy Kinley and all those working near the rig and possibly the firemen too. For several days he was content to pump water continuously on the site and particularly into the well cellar, which they were going to have to enlarge in order to cut away the casing.

Eventually, Kinley and volunteers from the Company's Fields staff cut the casing, working within a few feet of the outlet of the gas, and after much difficulty managed to get the base fitted round the jet and cemented in. They were thus ready for what every man knew would be the most deadly peril of all, namely hoisting the great valve into position and clamping it down on the base. It was lifted by a crane and controlled by four gangs of men pulling on hawsers in different directions. Gradually they manœuvred it into position, and, with feelings it is not difficult to imagine, brought it into contact with the gas jet.

The effect was like putting one's finger over the nozzle of the garden hose. Gas sprayed out in all directions and with such tremendous force as to hurl showers of rocks and small stones as though they were leaves blown by a gale. Kinley and his men could not hear the clatter but they knew well enough that at this moment one spark from one stone would cause them to be ungulfed in fire and reduce in an instant to charred and unrecognizable remnants. For a while the four-and-a-half-ton valve was buffeted about like a ping-pong ball in a shooting booth. Then suddenly the single jet shot up again through the opening in the valve and all was well. The valve was lowered into place and clamped down. It was gradually closed; the jet subsided, and at last, for the first time in forty-three days, total silence reigned around Rig 20.

Flying Round the Rockies

I have twice flown across Canada and on the second occasion familiarity had in no way dimmed the impact of the recurrent theme of amazement that our ancestors should actually have 'walked there'. Flying at 300 miles an hour or more in one of the Viscounts that sing like boiling kettles over the length and breadth of Canada, one gazes down for hour after incredible hour at a land of unending spruce forests and lakes through which, even from the air, it seems impossible to pick a route by which man could have threaded his way. This monotonous land gives place at last to equally unending prairie, with road and railway stretching dead straight as far as the eye can see, the landscape broken only by isolated farmsteads and the tall elevators storing their several hundred million surplus bushels of grain. This country stretches roughly to the middle of Alberta, there to be halted first by the foothills and then by the mighty Rockies—a land formation uncommonly similar to the foothills and mountains of South Persia.

At first sight from the air, to anyone who has not yet sampled it on the ground, some of the foothill country might be mistaken for the highlands of Scotland—a land of fir trees, lakes, and what might well be heather. In the valley where the river curves round beyond that distant hill, for instance, it would surely be no surprise to come upon Balmoral Castle. The British have always looked upon such countryside as a scene of beauty, and this would certainly be no exception. Only the glint of the sun reflecting continuously from the ground between the trees gives a hint, from the air, of its true character. It is in fact 'muskeg'.

The muskeg of Canada must be one of the dreariest and most desperate territories in the world. It presents an obstacle more formidable to man almost than the Rockies themselves and would at least as easily stop an army. It is a land of forest, deadfall and bog—the deadfall being the intricate carpet of dead treetrunks, some sunk long since in the bog, some half-submerged, others higher up and waiting their turn. To hack one's way through such stuff on dry ground would be backbreaking enough. To do so in conditions where a false step may at any moment see a man up to his neck in slime and swamp is an impossibility, and only when the muskeg freezes is it passable at all. From Alberta it stretches unbroken for a thousand miles to the Arctic.

It is doubtful whether the motto 'Look before you leap' applies with greater conviction anywhere in the world than in the hitherto unproven parts of Alberta, where in searching for oil a million dollars can be tossed away as easily as leaving your small change on the dressing-room table. Those who are responsible for the 'looking', therefore, carry an unusually heavy burden of responsibility, almost as heavy, so it seemed to me, as those who finally on their advice sanction the 'leap'. The two men who carried this initial responsibility in the Triad Oil Company were seconded from British Petroleum—the chief geologist, A. N. Thomas, and the chief geophysicist, Dr. T. C. Richards, both of them backed by long experience in the Middle East. Mr. Thomas, being a good Welshman, was known, in accordance with the national practice of identifying people by the nature of their work— Evans the hearse, Jones the post, Morgan the milk and so on—as 'Thomas the Stone'. His geophysical opposite number, though boasting so far as I know no Welsh ancestry, became known inevitably by the complementary counterpart, 'Richards the Tremor'.

In Canada the geologist stops at about the time of year at which the geophysicist is ready to begin. The ice and snow which drive the one from his rock faces and outcrops mean that the other can at last move around in the frozen muskeg. What is more, the rivers now make the most admirable highways along which he can travel at surprising speed on tyre, track or sledge. When the thaw comes in the spring, both are confined to barracks for two months while the rivers melt and the surface of the earth turns gradually into the consistency of glue.

Much of Triad's geological research was being done high up in the Rockies and to watch it in progress made me wonder once again whether it was too late to take up geology as a hobby. The camp which I visited, with Thomas acting as guide, instructor and chauffeur, was about 5,500 feet up in the Rockies, beside the Red Deer River. Forty miles out from Calgary we turned north and drove for another fifty miles through the foothills, leaving our signatures in a little box attached to a vast wooden gate marking the entrance to the Provincial Government's forest reserve. The forest rangers, I gathered, liked to have a record of all who enter the reserve, partly to know who is in there and why, and partly to know where to look for them if they are lost. As though to emphasize that this was the beginning of the 'real thing', a moose dashed through a field of standing corn beside the road, hurled itself at the wire fence on the other side, fell over, and at the second charge burst down the fence and disappeared in the forest.

A bridge near the Red Deer was the rendezvous with two of the young fellows from the camp who had brought down a Land Rover for the last fifteen miles of the journey and in this we bumped, slithered and splashed for the best part of an hour, climbing steadily through the silent, and to me altogether abominable forest, and skidding merrily towards the edges of the bank overlooking the river in a manner calculated to set a middle-aged author wondering what he was doing there at all.

However, all was worth while. We emerged eventually into a scene that was pure Switzerland—a broad valley with green meadows, the river dashing its way down along one side and the Rockies towering in the background. The camp itself brought back many a wartime scene: the brown tents and the various dark green vehicles camouflaged almost invisibly in a clump of pine trees below the track. On the other side of the track, perched on a convenient knoll, was the helicopter—a mere bubble of glass, a couple of blades, an exposed engine and an orange-coloured framework apparently of Meccano.

In the main tent I was soon being introduced at close quarters to a variety of heavily bearded young men, some with strong Canadian accents, others with the unmistakable intonation of England and the Old School Tie. Seven or eight of them were geologists, either qualified or in training; one was the official palaeontologist (which means, for those not well up in their geology, a man who deals with fossils); one was the helicopter pilot and another his resident engineer. With one exception none was yet thirty and few were twenty-five.

The exception was Stan, the man who could make or mar their three months' unbroken stay in the wilds. Stan, a lean, leathery figure in blue jeans, to which in bygone days one could see a gun attached at either hip, was general camp-minder and cook. While paying compliments to his cooking, they were quick to impress upon me that his real claim to fame was that he was the champion wild-cow milker of the world. At the Calgary Stampede, it appeared, he had set up an all-time record of twenty-eight seconds. Pressed for details, Stan said laconically: 'The flag goes down and you dash at 'er.'

Stan's exploits as lightning milker were, I need hardly say, but light relief to a background of serious and immensely painstaking work, on the strength of which someone, some time, was going to have to take a deep breath and decide where to hazard some millions of dollars. Their object, broadly, was to suggest, from their observations high up in the Rockies, the likely location of rock structures which might hold oil deep down under the ground some thirty or forty miles away in the foothills or the plain. Their work lay, literally, in measuring the Rockies with a tape measure. They would find exposed surfaces with recognizable strata and measure them to within an inch, setting down the results in their notebooks and passing on the information each evening to one of the party whose job was to convey it to the yard-long coloured charts, so familiar to those who spend their lives trying to detect, or drilling for, oil. In Alberta alone there must by now be several hundred thousand of these charts. How many years, one wonders, will it be before they reveal their final secrets?

In addition to their measurements they brought back with them a more concrete result of their labours in the shape of small jagged lumps of rock containing fossils. Nothing sounds more prosaic than a fossil—and indeed their fate was prosaic enough, for they were wrapped up in toilet paper by the palaeontologist, inserted in little canvas bags, numbered, dumped together in a sack and sent down to Calgary—but to me they were fascinating beyond measure. There were shells of all shapes and sizes, tiny limpets, molluscs and every kind of marine life, some of them so flawless and lifelike that it seemed that, if one could prise them off the parent rock, one could almost hand them over to Stan to cook for supper. Yet all of them lived and died a hundred million years ago when the Rockies were under the sea. To hold them in one's hand and marvel at their perfection made one suddenly feel uncommonly small.

All this work was made possible, of course, by that aerial maid-of-all-work, the helicopter. Each of the three teams consisted of two men, a qualified geologist and a university trainee—the best practical training in the whole world, Thomas declared—and every morning, Sundays and week-days for the four months' season, the teams would be taken to work in turn and brought home in the evening as regularly as the commuters on a suburban train in Toronto. The difference lay in the fact that the 'station' at which they arrived was probably a small ledge several thousand feet up in the Rockies, often barely big enough to accommodate the rotating blades.

The pilot, a handsome, gay young fellow with a fine red beard, was moved by an infectious and thoroughly serious-minded enthusiasm for his craft, to which I fell a ready victim. It is indeed a curious sensation, this sitting in a plastic bubble, able to survey at the same time the sky above, the mountains beside, and the valley beneath your feet—apart from the narrow metal bar on which the latter are resting and from which you hope most sincerely they will not suddenly slip. For the first time man can now not only fly like the birds but hover like the hawk—and even, I believe, unlike any known respectable bird, fly backwards. Furthermore one does so without that faint but inevitable sense of apprehension felt by all air passengers at take-off and landing, for all their pretence of continuing to read their newspapers. In a helicopter you cannot detect even the moment at which the metal skids leave the ground and you are airborne. There were, on the other hand, moments when I could have wished that the straps with which the chief geologist and myself were jointly bound to our seats—neither being in our athletic prime—had met by more than one inch, and that the pilot had refrained from cautioning me, being the outside passenger, not to lean against the plastic door as 'they sometimes open'. Such faint-hearted thoughts were put in their place, however, when he added that in the summer they liked to take the doors off altogether, so that they could lean out and take photographs. Their greatest delight, I gathered, was to perch the helicopter on the edge of a vertical precipice and then drive off directly over the edge. What a thing it is to be young!

Island in the Sun

Like most people, I dare say, who have not been there before, I approached Trinidad with a lively sense of anticipation but little more knowledge than that the West Indians sing Calypsos and play the brightest cricket in the world.

I found it an enchanting island—though whether it presented the same hospitable aspect to Columbus when he discovered it in 1498 is a matter of doubt. There is much to be said, when approaching the beauty spots of this world, for arriving in the dark and waiting for the full revelation in the morning. When I woke in the morning, the picture framed in the window revealed a tiny vivid blue bay with a two-masted yacht riding at anchor in the bright tropical sun. Wooded hills encircled the bay and not a ripple disturbed the water, so that one could count the multi-coloured fish round the jetty. What a haven, one could not help reflecting, for a buccaneer in the old days! However, lest all this should sound irrelevant, let me add that in this idyllic spot—pure Somerset Maugham in its way, especially when sudden rain clattered on the roof and left the whole scene steaming—is the rest-house in which the senior staff of the Trinidad Petroleum Development Company take it in turns to refresh themselves from their labours.

When we had taken a motor launch round the Islands and inspected the neighbouring coast of Venezuela and taken in the full beauty of the scene, not excluding the lepers' colony and the prison, each on their separate islands—and even they looked romantic from afar—one began to wonder how anyone who came here for a rest ever dragged themselves back to work.

The island is shaped somewhat in the form of a square, seventy-odd miles deep and fifty miles wide, with two elongated points at the left-hand corners. The hills and islands of the top left-hand tip reach within six miles of a similar promontory jutting out from Venezuela and any-one can see that the two lands must once have been one. The southern promontory is usually known as Devon and Cornwall, on account of its extraordinary geographical likeness to that part of England, and the celebrated asphalt lake is beside the sea in a position corresponding with Bristol. The neighbouring town happens, however, by some slip on the part of the early settlers to have been named Brighton.

Though all Trinidad has at some time been prospected for oil and anywhere in the island you may come across derelict equipment rusting in undergrowth or jungle, the oilfields of today are confined, if one may continue the English parallel, to Devon and Dorset, Hampshire and Wiltshire, and a small area round Dover—in other words all in the south. For ninety years, since the very earliest days of the world oil industry, Trinidad had been a continuous temptation and the ruin of individuals and companies good and bad. As any oilman will tell you, the best thing, if you are going to fail, is to do it completely and conclusively, write off the loss, and try elsewhere. With seepages everywhere, mud volcanoes bubbling with gas, and a whole 130-acre lake of pure asphalt, it is only human to fall for the policy of 'one more try'. It is the one more try that so often leads to the bankruptcy court.

The T.P.D. interests are centred around Palo Seco, in the south. The so-called 'camp' consists of fifty-five houses, all separated from each other and overlooking in varying degrees the blue waters of the South Atlantic. In the centre they have a most delightful thatched-roofed version of the inevitable club, complete with several hard tennis courts, one of which is floodlit; a school for the children; and a kind of bandstand in which dusky nannies sit in a solemn, dreamy circle, gossiping while half-naked children of all colours play games on the grass. The temperature was a balmy 90°—it was the hot season, they said—shorts and a bush shirt were the normal wear, and the sun was high in the heavens when work began at seven in the morning. Oil has a habit of being found, or searched for, in the vilest places, but even my host George Walling, the General Manager, who remembered Palo Seco when there were only five houses, had to agree that this was not one of them.

In South Persia oil dominates both the scene and the minds of those who work there. It is bound to do, since, if it were not for the oil, none of them would be there. In Trinidad the oil exists side by side with other and older forms of life and remains for the most part discreetly camouflaged. Many of the wells are in coffee or cocoa plantations overshadowed by tall immortelle trees which were planted to provide shade fifty years or more ago. These exquisite trees have umbrella-like tops—not unlike some of the 'gum' variety in Australia—and to climb to some vantage point and look down on a whole sea of them topped with blossom of bright orange is one of the sights of this world. There are in fact some thousands of wells in Trinidad and on the average they are only 500 feet apart. The result is a kind of filigree of pipelines running alongside the roads, with smaller lines branching off unobtrusively into the bush or jungle, each marked by a kind of tombstone bearing the number of the well whose contribution they are bringing down.

Farther east from Palo Seco, T.P.D. have spent some years, and rather more than a million pounds, in opening up an area called Moruga—the point, incidentally, at which Columbus made his first landing. This is the real authentic jungle and it cost £100,000 to build eight miles of preliminary road. Now, there are the beginnings of a fine camp with half a dozen first-class bungalows and all the normal amenities of civilization. In residence we found a breezy cheerful character, Lt.-Cdr. Mounteney, who had been in the Indian Navy during the war. The jungle is highly sinister to those who are not used to it and is treated with the utmost respect by those who are. People talk simply of 'going in', as though they were entering a building, and indeed to 'go in' does give the sensation, within a few yards, of a door closing behind you—a door furthermore which, once it has closed, leaves no visible trace of its whereabouts in case you should wish to go out again. Stepping out of the bright sunshine you enter a cool, dark, silent world, populated mainly by monkeys, deer, some small creatures resembling hares and equally good to eat, and a variety of snakes. Mounteney, on hearing yells of alarm, had that morning gone hastily across to a native house and shot a seven-footer, but for the most part they retreat with the coming of man. We 'went in' together, Mounteney swinging his cutlass with a splendidly nautical air, though its main function was not to defend the party against wild beasts but, more prosaically, to hack chips out of tree trunks in order to mark the path.

The object of our incursion into the jungle was to inspect the mud volcanoes, or 'bouffes'. While most of them were in an open clearing, which they had made by destroying all the plant life around them, some were in the fringe of the jungle, for all the world like a big badger's earth in an English wood. These curious phenomena are exact models of a volcano in miniature. Some are seven or eight feet high, others only a matter of inches. They are made by the methane gas escaping to the surface and, when they erupt, they go 'bouffe' with a most human after-dinner sound. They are, of course, one of the reasons why men have for so long and at such cost been searching for oil in Trinidad. Where there is gas, there is almost certainly oil—but no one has found it yet.

Going Down Now, Sir!

A community so vast and varied as the refinery at Abadan is bound to throw up picturesque characters. One is J. V. Jones, a large, imperturbable Liverpudlian known to everyone as Diver Jones. By profession a deep-sea diver, he started in 1922 as the result of an argument with a diver in Liverpool on whose work he ventured a disparaging comment.

'If you think you can do it any better, you —— well come and do it yourself,' said the diver. Thus was Jones launched—or perhaps one should say submerged—upon his career.

He and his colleague, J. W. Q. Costain, have some remarkable exploits to their credit. On one occasion a vessel at Abadan got 400 feet of two-inch wire mooring cable round her propellers. They went down and cut the whole thing off with hand hacksaws—a fantastic achievement for two men considering the conditions. In five days they each worked for seventy-two hours and it took a fortnight for their hands to heal up. They were in diving suits from nine in the morning to seven in the evening.

Perhaps their greatest triumph was the *Safiyeh*, a 250-ton river tanker which was sunk in the Iraq rebellion in May 1941, just below the junction of the Tigris and Euphrates, in what is supposed to have been the Garden of Eden. They decided they would let their beards grow till they got it afloat. It took them a month and three days. They lived in a little motor-boat and kept themselves alive largely by an ice-making machine they took with them. Costain's diving log shows that he was actually under water for a total of ninety-two hours. The river temperature was 102°, or rather more than normal blood heat and he lost sixteen pounds in fourteen days. Jones lost a stone. They took a draughtsman and a shore boatswain from Abadan to work their life line—*neither of whom had ever done it before*. They had to train them in the art when they got there.

Social life in the Garden of Eden consisted of two games of cribbage each day after breakfast, and for the whole time, Costain said, they were beset by every creeping and crawling creature in Genesis. The labouring work was done by fifty marsh Arabs, who receipted their pay with thumb prints. At one point their crane driver sat on his crane for twenty-eight hours without taking his foot off the brake.

Towards the end, Costain, having crawled down through a hatchway into the engine-room—without, of course, being able to see anything—inflated himself to come up and found that he had become too large to re-emerge through the opening. He stuck there for three hours.

Such are the unsung heroes of war, though they may not thank me for saying so.

I was much intrigued by these two characters—it is not every day that you meet people who in the normal course of duty go diving in the Garden of Eden—and on the old principle of 'Try anything once' I managed to induce them to take me with them one day.

The scene of the operation was Braim Creek, an offshoot from the Shatt-el-Arab. Here, as indeed in the river itself, the water is so muddy that you cannot see your hand in front of your face and it was in this opaque font that I received my underwater baptism. They say that in clear seas, where you can see for forty or fifty yards with all the marine life around you, diving is a memorable experience, and I have no doubt it is. The beginner, however, is unlikely to forget it whether he can see or not.

We climbed aboard a kind of flat barge, manned by a number of Persians, complete with donkey engine, ropes, lengths of what looked like hosepipe, and three diving suits. The first move was to take off most of our clothes and put on great woollen trousers, leggings and sweaters. Sometimes, Jones and Costain said, they put on seven pairs of those leggings and still could not feel their feet when they came up. The woollen outfit is followed by a thick gabardine suit into which you have to be shaken, like something that will not quite go into a sack. Then you soap your hands and slide them through tough rubber wristlets. The suit, needless to say, has no openings at the bottom of the trouser legs; your feet fit into the ends, rather after the style of the 'frogmen'. So with the wristlets in position, you are now sealed up except for the neck.

The next step is to put your head through an iron ring like a horse collar, which is then bolted, with wing nuts and a special spanner, to iron plates inside the suit. Somebody forces your feet, which look like flippers in the stiff gabardine, into a grotesque pair of boots done up with straps and ropes, and someone else pulls a strap tight round your middle. You make as though to take a step across the deck, only to find the boots so heavy as to be apparently nailed thereto. In fact, you now weigh some 200 pounds in addition to your own weight, and I confess to a certain amount of apprehension at this point, for the deck was slippery and sloped downwards to the water, there was no rail, and I reckoned that, if I did slip, I should sink like a stone and no power on earth could save me. I was mighty relieved when they slipped a rope under my arms. One pull, they said, meant 'O.K.' and four 'Pull me up'.

At this point I paused to watch Costain descend the ladder and vanish slowly from human sight, till his existence and whereabouts were marked only by rings of bubbles. I lumbered across to the ladder and stood half-way down for them to lower the helmet over my head and bolt it to the horse collar. It was making a wheezing sound and emitting a faintly rubbery air reminiscent of the moment before the gas comes through at the dentist's. Finally they screwed the round, thick glass facepiece into place and there was nothing for it but 'Going down now, sir!'

Whatever else it may be, diving is no job for anyone who suffers from claustrophobia, especially in muddy water where you can see nothing at all and only changes of light tell you how deep you are. By pressing our helmets together, Costain and I could just see each other well enough to give the victory sign, but, though for a while we went hand in hand, I never caught another glimpse of him. You live in a little world of your own, smaller and more constricted perhaps, than anything your mind has ever dwelt upon: a little room, as it were, hardly bigger than an outsize football. It has a window in front and a window at either side and, when you turn your head, you feel that the windows ought to turn with it. But although they are only three or four inches from your eyes, they do not move with your eyes, as spectacles do. And the feeling that, although you can raise your hand to your head, you cannot touch it enhances the sense of constriction. If you have something in your eye or want to scratch your nose, you can get within an inch of either but by no power on earth can you touch them. So of course you want to. Desperately.

In this opaque water there is no means, other than an instinct which of course I did not possess, of telling where you are. The boots are so heavy and solid that you cannot tell whether you are standing on a firm surface or not, though the bottom of Braim Creek was too slimy to tell anyway. What is worse, you cannot tell which way you are facing, nor even which way up you are. Theoretically, all this is controlled by a valve in the helmet which regulates the outflow of air. Close it and you inflate yourself and rise to the surface, flat on your back and distended like a long-deceased fish. Open it out and you sink firmly to the bottom. The knack is to open it just enough to take the weight off your shoulders.

Costain and I floundered across to the slimy piles of the jetty, which we could feel but could not see, and I came to realize something of the measure of these men's achievement in staying under water for hours, hacking away at a steel hawser with hand saws or crawling into the interior of sunken vessels, all as though completely blind.

After a while I began to pant, as one does at high altitudes without oxygen. It got worse to the point of being alarming. I was going to pass out. I had no idea whether I was deep or shallow; facing north, east, west, or south, or lying face downwards. The muddy waters swirled across the window of my tiny world, closer, as it seemed, and closer, and there was no one to tell. Nothing for it but four pulls on the rope, and pretty unmistakable ones they were. The rope tightened and I inflated myself to help Diver Jones, who was holding it, to haul me like some inert porpoise to the surface. And never was a man more happy to see the light of day.

As I sat casting off the cumbersome equipment, I deplored my lack of staying power.

'You don't want to worry about that,' they said, 'we did not like to say so, but everyone passes out first time!'

And here is a curious thing. If I had been asked to give evidence on oath as to how long I had been underwater, I should have said 'Two or three minutes.' I should have been certain beyond the point of reasonable human doubt that three was the maximum. The answer was twelve and a half. Very strange.

Later they sent me a fine illuminated scroll to certify that I had 'qualified for admission as an Hon. Member of the Society of Underwater Workers, having been underwater for a period of twelve and a half minutes at Braim Creek, Abadan, Persia. . . .' It hangs framed on my wall. I am very proud of my Union.

Few, Forgotten and Lonely

The railway from the Persian Gulf to Teheran started from a place called Andimeshk, which, in the hot weather, was reckoned one of the worst in the world. 'Salts in the morning and take it easy,' was the recipe by which alone one of the senior inhabitants reckoned life could be made endurable. The wartime running of the railway was a crazy-sounding sort of international set-up, which had one essential merit. It worked. Up and down the flat sand which passed for a platform, British 'redcaps', trousers immaculately creased, boots gleaming, hats squarely on the centre of the head; American 'snowballs' with polished pistols; Persian gendarmes in light blue; and the Russian police with their flat caps and soft shiny boots; all strolled up and down in pairs. Meanwhile the local black market squatted on its haunches offering packets of Camels and Lucky Strike stamped: 'For sale only to U.S. Forces in Alaska. . . .'

Soon the train itself gave the impressive toot with which Hollywood films have made us familiar, and drew in to the station. The engine-driver—pardon me, the locomotive engineer—was American. He was wearing one of those long-peaked caps we associate with ski-ing, and rimless spectacles. From the side of his mouth, as he leaned nonchalantly out of his cab, there sprouted a large cigar.

The guard was Persian and the ticket collectors British and Iraqi—but, as I say, it worked.

And what a staggering bit of engineering this railway is, when all is said and done! My friend, Dick Costain, and other British firms had something to do with it. So did the Germans. So did the Americans. Anyway, as the line climbs its way upwards through the foothills, and as you look ahead and see barrier after barrier rising against you, the last massive defences indistinguishable from the average picture of the Himalayas, you would deem it impossible for any railway to thread and burrow its way through to the other side.

On and on it goes, snaking through the valleys, darting into more than a hundred tunnels, sometimes popping out of one straight on to a bridge over a gorge and into the rock again on the other side. The engine, panting along in front at a steady twenty miles an hour, becomes a familiar companion as the frequent curves bring it into the passenger's view. As the climb continues, the air becomes sparkling and cool and the scenery on occasions quite fabulous. From time to time the single track doubles itself at some wayside halt and another train is passed, this being *the* event in the lives of the local inhabitants. Small urchins, often of engaging countenance though dressed mostly in a single ragged garment like an inverted pillow-case with holes for the arms and neck, seek tips from the passengers with cries of ''Ullo, sergeant'. At one point we overtook a train of cattle trucks, each containing fourteen Russian ex-prisoners-of-war being repatriated, under armed guard, to their happy homeland.

All the bridges and tunnels had to be guarded and the soldiers who did it must have clicked for one of the loneliest jobs in all the war. Many were Indians. They lived in little encampments of half a dozen or so, one of them, I noticed, in a vast cleft in the mountains where a train emerged from one tunnel and fifty yards later popped into another. The sun can hardly have reached them for more than an hour a day, and their only contact with the rest of the world was through the tunnel.

I was reminded of Kipling:

> Few, forgotten and lonely,
>   Where the empty metals shine;
> No, not combatants, only
>   Details guarding the line.

They had said at Andimeshk that we were due in at eight o'clock next morning. As we came to a halt at Teheran, the station clock was striking eight. Good for the locomotive engineer!

Petroleum gas, formidable as it still is today—from 5,000 feet it can come up the well with a velocity capable of cutting through solid steel plate in a matter of seconds—must have been a terrifying hazard in the early days. Not only might it blow everyone to pieces if it caught fire, but, being heavy, it tended to flow, deadly and invisible, from higher ground down into the valleys. Foxes, jackals, porcupines, owls, and in one case a cow, dropped dead in the neighbourhood of the rig, and frequently the drillers were only dragged away in the nick of time, insensible. Later they wore gas masks and devised an escape apparatus consisting of a basket-and-slide into which they jumped at the first sign of danger. 'One inspiration,' Dr. Young reported, 'seems sufficient to cause insensibility and unless the victim be immediately removed into fresh air, the chances of recovery are small. Everyone who catches a whiff of it testifies that to be gassed by petroleum gas seems the most peaceful death that one can imagine. One moment you are alive. The next, you fade gracefully and painlessly into oblivion.' This, incidentally, confirms a curious feature of this gas, namely that, while its nauseously rotten-egg smell is unmistakable, in strong enough concentrations it is quite undetectable because it destroys the sense of smell. The animal world, however, by natural instinct transmitted now through many generations, has learnt the lesson, and despite the warmth of the innumerable gas flares no animals sleep beside them today.

In Persia one of the first tasks was to plan a route for the pipeline across 130 miles of uncharted hills and sweltering plain to the Gulf, and somewhere on its barren shores to find a site for a refinery. The problems were both practical and administrative, and Wilson summed them up in a sentence: 'The position of a Company which is working under a Concession from one Government (Persian) but depends on the goodwill of a provincial administration (Arab and Bakhtiari) and the military and moral support of a third (British and Indian) with a head office in Glasgow, dealing with the Foreign Office (in London) and a Foreign Department (Simla) through local officers (in Persia) is not easy.'

To survey the route for the pipeline the Company sent out Charles Ritchie. Like so many of the pioneers who have for centuries thrust out from Britain to the far corners of the earth, Ritchie was a Scot. He was employed by the great Glasgow firm of G. & J. Weir and had helped to lay some of the pipelines in Burma. His survey was so competent that he was sent back in 1909 to take charge of the laying of the pipeline but, though he lived to see it completed, it was to cost him his life. Wilson described him as one of the most remarkable men he had ever come across—'a tall, red-faced man, heavy-handed, impetuous and energetic, often quarrelsome and of uncertain temper', ready enough to vent his anger on Arabs, Persians or Indians who offended him, 'but equally truculent to his superiors; above all filled with a fiery determination to see the pipeline through ahead of schedule.'

It seems strange at this distance of time that, while Reynolds, who was very much the 'gentleman'—when at home in England he dyed his eyebrows, wore a monocle and always proceeded in full regalia to Ascot—had set a tradition of Spartan austerity; Ritchie, the teetotaller, non-smoker, sergeant-major type who could not abide seeing anyone around with nothing to do and whose only word of Persian was 'Yella' ('Get on!'), spared no expense to make himself comfortable. He hired the best house in Ahwaz and furnished it in fine style. He brought out a 14 h.p. Darracq, which caused a vast sensation among the inhabitants of South-West Persia and was indeed the first motor-car that Wilson had ever seen, and a fine Thames launch in which he used to go on shooting trips up the river. Later—he must really have been rather a splendid character and one's heart warms to him for it—he sent for an aeroplane. His imagination had been fired by Bleriot's flight across the Channel that summer, and the aeroplane was of the same make. Ritchie's knowledge of flying was nil but he made a diligent study of the book of instructions that accompanied the machine and saw no reason why he should not fly it. Taxiing across the sandy levels near Ahwaz he found himself suddenly in the air—whether on purpose or not is uncertain—and a few moments later was upside down in a gulley, with the machine wrecked and oil pouring out all over him. 'Quick, someone,' he shouted. 'Get a camera and take my picture.' He dismantled the machine and stored it for a while in his cellar; later it was returned to London, where its honoured remains hung for many years in the entrance hall of the Company's headquarters at Britannic House.

Though the pipeline was one day to deliver fifty million tons of oil in a single year and the deserted mudflats of Abadan to become a city the size of Sheffield, Ritchie himself was destined to live for only a year or two more. In 1914, in the prime of life, he caught smallpox. Some survived this hideous disease, though marked for life. Ritchie, calling for a mirror, looked at his reflection, turned his face to the wall, and died.

The Eternal Fires

Satisfaction is always to be gained from the thought that one is following in distinguished footsteps, but I must confess that it had not occurred to me that I might one day find myself following in those of none other than Shadrach, Meshach and Abednego, that indomitable and imperishable trio whose names remain imprinted in every schoolboy's mind to the end of of his days.

The eternal fires through which they walked, which are near Kirkuk, are today something of a disappointment. Hissing slightly, since they consist of self-ignited seepages of natural gas, they form a circle a few yards wide, into which it is possible to step with not too much discomfort, if with a certain amount of apprehension.

The flames are only two or three feet high, but the fact that in the memory of people still alive they were the height of a man indicates that in the time of Nebuchadnezzar they may well have resembled the roaring fiery furnace of the Old Testament—in which case the glory so long credited to Abednego and his two colleagues remains undimmed.

Though somewhat tamed over the years the eternal fires are still an awesome phenomenon, and the thought that in this very spot they almost certainly were burning in Nebuchadnezzar's day and were the object of personal comment by that idolatrous and contrite monarch and have been gazed upon with continuous wonder for five thousand years gives them a strange quality of 'eternalness', at the same time emphasizing in the mind of the beholder the shortness of his own expected span. Nor is this reflection in any way diminished by the certainty that they stank as abominably in the days of Abednego as they do today.

EAST OF SUEZ

Where Every Prospect Pleases

Late in the evening Maurice Murdock, brother of Richard 'Stinker' Murdock of radio fame, and myself reached the rest house at Sigiriya, far away in the country, and, turning through a white gate as though to an English farmhouse, found ourselves at a pleasant bungalow with veranda and flower garden. Some people, I gathered, complained that the rest houses in Ceylon had sadly deteriorated. To the traveller from home this was strange talk. We each had a decent room with its own bathroom and at this late hour they produced a dinner of soup, local fish, and roast wild boar, rounded off with that national speciality, the rum omelet, for which the lights are ceremoniously turned off while the manager in person immerses it in flaming liquid. What with this, and coffee and drinks on the veranda, I was hard put to it to detect where the deterioration had set in.

The object of this first leg of our journey was to see, and possibly climb—though I had mental reservations on this point—the Sigiri Rock, and for this purpose we were called at six. It was a delicious morning, the birds were singing and all was right with the world, except that only the base of the rock, a mile or two away, was visible and the rest was in low cloud. With an air of righteousness I resigned myself to sitting down on the veranda and doing my weekly piece for the *Sunday Times*, a contribution which had at least the merit of being the earliest I had ever penned for that organ. Bacon and eggs came up at eight and within the hour the view had cleared, to reveal the Rock in all its fantastic magnificence.

Mushrooming slightly at the top, Sigiri rises a clear 600 feet, for no apparent reason, in the middle of hundreds of miles of flat jungle. Though no geologist, I could not help supposing it to be, like the Bass Rock, Ailsa Craig, and the Giant's Causeway at home, the hard core left over from some vast volcanic upheaval many millions of years ago. It is its archaeological, rather than geological, interest, however, that makes it unique. The top of the mushroom, excluding the precipitous rim, extends to three acres, and for eighteen years, from A.D. 478 to 496, it was the home and fortress of King Kassapa I. The background to this extraordinary episode is, in parts, familiar enough today, though our measures to cope with it are not perhaps so direct. The rival sons of the old king; the sister married to the nephew and complaining to father that he had whipped her on the thigh—doubtless rightly; father having mother-in-law stripped and burnt alive; the son, Kassapa, doing away with father, by walling him up alive, and seizing the throne; and the other son, after fetching help from India, waiting eighteen years before he could lure his brother down from his citadel to do battle. This battle, incidentally, Kassapa would have won, had he not turned his elephant to avoid a swamp, thereby giving his followers the impression that he was on the run.

Today, Kassapa's fortress, apart from the roofs and buildings themselves, is virtually unchanged, and elephants could move back into the stables tomorrow. Round the base colossal rocks lie where they had already fallen 2,000 years ago. One is cut clean in two, the work perhaps of 500,000 man-hours. One half is carved with steps leading up to a flattened audience hall, complete with throne and stone-backed seats, the other has a tank or cistern cut in the top. Various steps lead up through the ramparts and after walking up through a series of beautifully squared-off terraces one begins to climb the main gallery cut in the solid stone, with overhanging roof and outside wall, round, as it were, the stalk of the mushroom. The inner edge of the outside wall was covered with a pinkish plaster 1,500 years ago and is still so highly polished that you can almost see your face in it. From here a spiral iron staircase put up in 1938—before that it was a rope ladder— leads up to some frescoes of almost the same age which, judging by the coloured prints, are not only quite exquisite but reveal that Kassapa's version of the female form divine varied in no respect from our own.

We reached at last the flat half-acre known as the Lion Plateau. Standing back to survey the summit, one is confronted with two perfectly carved lion's paws, of such dimensions that the single claws are four feet wide. When they were unearthed some fifty years ago they were thought at first to be rather ill-done elephants' trunks. Now they stand out in their full splendour and one can only gaze and wonder at the man who conceived things on such a scale. There is also on the plateau a small prosaic black shed with close-meshed zinc sides. This, it appeared from the notice, was the place you made for if attacked by bees on the way down from the summit.

For the moment, however, I had no time for lion's claws or bees. This was the moment of decision. The way to the summit, from which the view must be stupendous—and in any case, having got thus far, one wanted to see the old king's private citadel—led via a vertical iron ladder and thence across the sheer face of the rock by a series of hollowed-out footholds and a small iron rail, through which it was clearly possible at any moment to slip to eternity. Blondin doubtless could have done it blindfold and on stilts. For myself, I was reasonably confident of getting up. The prospect might then arise of passing the remainder of one's natural life there and having one's meals sent up through sheer inability to get down. Four Buddhist priests, vivid in their orange-yellow robes against the dark rock-face and looking about the size of ants, were clearly making heavy weather of it. On the other hand a couple of elderly Indian women in saris were managing it, and if they could, so, surely, could I. The die was cast and, with a small voice whispering 'Tis a far, far stupider thing you do now than you have ever done', I mounted the ladder. When it came to the little footholds, some of which involved actually crossing the feet, I confess to wondering whether I was not certifiably insane. I tried to comfort myself with the old anti-aircraft slogan, 'What goes up must come down', but the small voice added, 'Yes, but how?'

However, the summit once reached proved worth it, whatever the next hour might bring. Here at least the hackneyed tag 'Out of this world' was true. Up here was a little three-acre world on its own, connected with the rest only by these few tiny footholds. It must in Kassapa's day have been the most impregnable fortress on the surface of the earth. On every side you can see as far as the curved rim of the horizon, an endless carpet of green broken only by a few hills and what we should call lakes and are locally called tanks. Ramparts, walls, terraces, paths, and gardens remain as though they might have been abandoned only a century ago. The big water tank is in as good preservation today as it was then. Above it the king's throne is carved in the granite and one could imagine him sitting there alone in his eyrie, meditating like Napoleon at St. Helena on the world he had defied.

There is also a smaller tank, perhaps ten feet by five, carved on the very edge of the precipice. This was the Queen's bath—the King's bath being farther up and rather larger. Had she 'dropped off' in the bath and, on waking, stepped out the wrong side, she would have dropped a clear 500 feet.

Fortified and refreshed at the rest house and with both feet once more attached to mother earth we moved on to the biggest of the tanks, Minneriya, which really, since it occupies some 4,500 acres, might be given the courtesy title of lake. Another heavenly place, more like a lonely Scottish loch, Minneriya was dug out in the early part of the fourth century by a great Sinhalese king called Mahasena.

He dammed it up where necessary, erected 'modern' sluice gates and irrigation channels and by this means created a vast fertile region in that part of Ceylon. Later Ceylon, like England, went through its dark ages and the whole system fell into disuse. Now, 1,600 years later, the Government has been resurrecting Mahasena's public works and is trying to re-colonize the area.

Minneriya was on the way to the ruined cities—a form of architecture not normally in my line but in this case fascinating beyond description. The capital city in this bygone age was Anuradhapura. Like most of these polysyllabic Sinhalese names it looks formidable on paper and one does not consciously pronounce it on reading it, but it rolls off the tongue in the most pleasing way. Anuradhapura lasted as the seat of the Sinhalese kings for several centuries but was destroyed by the Cholas from South India in the eleventh—which is perhaps one reason why Ceylon, now that it is an independent Dominion, controls immigration from India with such a fine-meshed net—and the Cholas made the neighbouring city of Polonnaruva their capital. Eventually they were driven out a few years before William the Conqueror landed at Pevensey, and Polonnaruva settled down as the capital of the island. Its founder as a great city was King Parakramabahu I—another one to roll off the tongue—who reigned for thirty-odd years from 1153. In the thirteenth century back came the raiders from the mainland and that, for 500 years, was the end of Polonnaruva.

A hundred-odd years ago a few pioneers began penetrating to Anuradhapura and Polonnaruva, each of them several days' journey by bullock cart through jungle tracks, and as a result of their tales the Archaeological Survey of the Ceylon Government, then of course administered by the British, started their project of clearing and excavating the sites.

Nowadays, as you motor through the jungle towards Polonnaruva, the first signs of anything unusual after mile upon mile of thick vegetation broken only by an occasional tiny village are odd stone pillars here and there in the undergrowth beside the road, not unlike the pillars of Stonehenge. Gradually the forest gives way to clearings with occasional ruined buildings and then suddenly you find yourself in a park with green lawns and stately trees, for all the world like Chatsworth or Woburn, complete with lake like a half-scale version of Windermere.

In many ways the scene is curiously English. It might be Tintern or Glastonbury with, instead of a single ruined abbey, an entire ruined city. Parakramabahu left no small monument to his reign. Here, restored to what every sense told one must be true to the original of eight hundred years ago, are lawns, terraces, gardens, and roads. In the middle of the park, on an eminence covering about twenty-five acres, the old king built his personal citadel, surrounded by a wall with a fine gateway. The walls of his palace still stand to quite a height, together with theatres, picture galleries, a magnificent pillared pavilion, and the royal bath—a lovely recessed bathing pool built in three tiers, down which one stepped in turn to the deepest part in the middle. Most of the stone is a darkish red, like the roof tiles of an old English barn, and the general beauty of the scene and the delicate lines of the buildings, pillars, and carvings spoke of a refinement that few cities could boast today.

The citadel is, of course, only the heart of the ancient city. For miles around one can wander or drive among temples, pavilions, and courts, including a wonderful dagaba (as I believe the word to be)—that peculiarly graceful type of shrine which I can only liken prosaically to a Prussian helmet with a spike on the top. On one rock face they carved colossal images of Buddha, reclining, sitting, and standing. The recumbent one is forty feet long and all are perfect in detail.

We had taken with us a venerable gentleman who claimed to be the 'senior guide' and was much worried lest his position as such be usurped by some Colombo official when Princess Elizabeth came to be shown around. He showed us another great carving, this time of Parakramabahu himself—a figure of benevolent aspect, stout proportions, and long, drooping moustaches.

'In his time no poverty, no crime, no prison, everyone happy and fed,' he said. He chanted his information in a high-pitched, sing-song voice and had it word perfect. So much so that if one interrupted with a question he would go back several lines and start again.

'This building round the base of which runs a frieze of elephants in bas-relief carved wonderfully true to nature and of which the pillars are adorned with chaste designs is said by Mr. Longhurst to have been originally constructed by King Parakramabahu the first bit is known to have been. . . .'

'I beg your pardon? Mr. Longhurst?'

'Round the base of which runs a frieze of elephants in bas-relief carved wonderfully true to nature and of which the pillars are adorned with chaste designs is said by Mr. Longhurst. . . .'

'Mr. Longhurst?'

'Mr. Longhurst was the archaeological commissioner to the Government of Ceylon and was mainly responsible for the uncovering of the ruined cities. . . .'

And so it turned out. No relation, though.

Darkest Africa

An invitation recently came my way which I cannot see many people refusing. It was to visit the province of Darfur, on the western side of the Sudan next to French Equatorial Africa, where my host, Lieutenant-Colonel Peter Wreford-Brown, of the celebrated soccer family, commands that part of the Sudan Defence Corps known as the Western Arab Corps. It resulted in what I still look back upon as the happiest week of my life.

Darfur is a closed province—not because anyone has anything to hide from the world, but because in the outer parts of this vast flat stretch of scrub and sand, as big as the British Isles, there is no made-up road, no hotel, no shop, no signpost, no telephone, no anything, and the few authorities who govern and patrol it have other things to do than send out search parties. It also has other distinctions. Plumb in the middle of the African triangle, it is probably the farthest point, taken all round, from the sea; and its westerly boundary forms such a perfect profile of the late Lord Oxford and Asquith that one cannot help feeling someone did it on purpose.

During my stay my host and the Governor, Mr. K. D. D. Henderson, were due to visit two tribal gatherings in the south of the province. Several thousand men and women converge for these gatherings on one small village, bringing with them their horses, which the Government either buy, subsidise for being in good condition, or reject. Tremendous parades of homage and welcome are held, and a splendid time is had by all.

It did not take me long to appreciate the size of the country. On landing at the capital, El Fasher, five hours' flying from Khartoum, our next step was to bump and jog along a sandy track for eight hours in a truck, with Captain J. Sharpe, of the Western Arab Corps, till we reached Nyala. Here we had supper at the house of the District Commissioner, Ranhold Laurie, who, with another D.C. from the Sudan, John Wilson, put up one of the great sporting achievements of modern times.

Both had been great rowing men in their day. A few years previously Wilson, on emerging from his court, had been somewhat taken aback, in both senses of the word, to find the head of a spear emerging outwards through his stomach. It had been thrust through him from behind by a dissatisfied litigant, and by some miracle had not destroyed a vital part. He was flown out and duly recovered.

When they went home for their leave in 1948, neither he nor Laurie had rowed for eight years. Together they proceeded to win the Coxswainless Pairs in the Olympic Games.

Another three hours brought us in darkness through the apparently unending flat scrub to the thatched village of Abu Sela, headquarters of the Habbaniya tribe. Here I was in time to see a parade of horses, with Ian Gillespie, the senior veterinary inspector, who came to the province from the Western Isles fifteen years ago, acting as judge, and the Governor handing out the piles of silver stacked on the table.

The outstanding feature of the trip, however, was the tribal gathering of the Rizeigat at the village of Sidbu, a day's journey from Abu Sela. Here, as we drove in, an hour or so in advance of the Governor, we were greeted by a sight no longer surely to be seen elsewhere in the world—two thousand horsemen with nine-foot spears, lining the road for half a mile. We were really no more than the hors d'œuvres, but they gave us a royal cheer. The women kept up their high pitched lu-lu-lu-lu; children gazed in awe; the red-robed drummers on the ceremonial camels banged their red-draped drums with ivory drumsticks; and I am not at all sure that the police band from Fasher did not also strike up on their bagpipes.

All this, however, was merely a gesture of welcome. The main event was reserved for the morrow. Once again the avenue was formed. Together the Governor and the Nazir Ibrahim Musa headed a procession between the lines, the latter a tremendous old fellow with jutting beard, red robes, gold trappings, a five-foot whip hanging from his wrist, eleven sons, and daughters uncounted. Behind them rode an escort of sixty men in, of all things, chain mail. (How sixty suits of armour come to be in remotest Africa no one knows for certain, but many competent judges declare them to be relics of the Crusades.) Behind these, preceded by the mauve standard with the Cross of Lorraine, Wreford-Brown led a detachment of the Western Arab Corps. As the Governor passed, every man dipped his spear in token of homage, and it was a noble sight to see the spears going down on either side, like corn bowing before a ripple of wind.

When this was over, the Governor dismounted and the old Nazir, lowering his sword as he passed, led the whole parade past. What a sight it was! Riding nine abreast, with loose foals following behind their mothers, they took more than half an hour to pass, at intervals of no more than twenty yards or so, again dipping their spears as they passed.

As may be imagined, this was a considerable manœuvre, and I could not help wondering how much paper-work, operation orders, tele-phoning, rehearsals, and the rest of it would have been thought neces-sary at home for such a parade. Yet, so far as I could see, no orders were given at any time by anybody. There seemed to be no officers, no particular leaders. The thing just happened. The only exception was when at one point the ranks became a bit ragged (many of the riders not only had only rope reins and a halter, with no bit, but also were leading a spare horse, to say nothing of carrying their spear). The Nazir, by this time dismounted and standing with the Governor, beckoned to a red-robed elder beside him, another striking character, jet black with narrow slanting eyes and vivid white teeth, and spoke a word or two to him. Thereupon the old man walked fifty yards up the line and, brandishing his whip, restored instant order in each rank as it passed—without, so far as one could hear, uttering a word.

When all had passed, including the camels, the two lines reformed and the chain mail warriors treated the multitude to a *duffa*, in which they gallop, flat out, in pairs, and pull up short in a cloud of dust at the end. After this there was a formal tea party with the Nazir, followed by several hours of drum-banging and dancing and feasting, much to the satisfaction of the village vultures, who, after sitting so long like lumps of sacking in the trees, hopped gauntly down and tidied up the place to the last morsel.

Another striking event was the great lion hunt, which I had been promised before leaving England. Lions are vermin in Darfur, so that one had the prospect not only of a new experience and something to dine out upon for the next few weeks but also of doing one's good deed for the day. The inhabitants think highly of anyone who kills a lion, irrespective of how he does it. Thus, as much face is to be gained from potting a beast, unconscious, at a hundred yards as from the local procedure of cornering it, armed only with spears, and doing it to death by hand—or even, as did the brother of one of the men out with us, rushing in and stabbing it with a bayonet as it was leaping upon another man.

Early one morning we drove a dozen miles out from Abu Sela, where a very large, very black fellow stopped the party and conducted us through the scrub to a water-hole. Here we found the beaters, thirty of them, and a more splendidly bold and bloodthirsty crew you never did see.

All were mounted and all carried long spears with heads as sharp as razor blades. Some had stirrups, some had not. Of those who had, the majority preferred to insert only the big toe—for, of course, none boasted footwear of any kind. Their ancestors, many of whom fought with such fearless frenzy against the machine-guns of Omdurman, made no bones about it: their stirrups were often no more than a small metal ring for the big toe.

At the water-hole more horses were waiting—my own a fine white stallion with sheepskin saddle—and we rode for another twenty minutes, mostly through camel-thorn, to a wadi fringed with rushes and tall trees. A casual glance noted that many of these trees would, at a push, be climbable—especially when aided by that sudden charge of adrenalin which, the medical experts tell us, enables a man in an emergency to jump a ten-foot wall, and later not know how he did it.

The firing party, consisting of the Nazir Ali el Ghali, Captain K. Timbrell, Laurie and myself, disposed themselves strategically to cover the approach of the lion, which was to come 'padding up the wadi'. The Nazir and Timbrell squatted in the tall grass, while the not so intrepid white hunter, comforted by the thought that any animal which survived this barrage deserved anything it could get, concealed himself in the fork of a tree. With a good deal of glinting of knives members of the Sudan Defence Force squatted enthusiastically in the bushes around.

The beaters vanished and an air of utter peace descended on the scene—an atmosphere which all who shoot will understand, when the beaters have gone but not begun their task, when anything may happen in the end, but nothing assuredly will happen for half an hour, and the world around, provided you keep still, settles quietly down to its daily life again as though you did not exist.

Last-minute instructions were given to the novice: how, if there were two of them, he was to shoot the lioness—'the one without the mane'— as the lion would in that event push off, while the lioness in similar circumstances would stay and become awkward (a singular reflection, one could not help thinking, upon the King of Beasts), and how, if it came to the last cartridge, he was to hold his fire till the lion was at a point about fifteen feet away—as likely, one thought, as the novice counting ten before opening his pararachute.

Peace reigned and one was left alone in the sunshine, with one up the spout and five in the magazine and a highly charged sense of anticipation. I do not know how many times I drew a bead on the imaginary tawny shape slipping silently round the end of the wadi. But, alas, it never appeared. A cry in the distance, then another, and another, meant that the beaters were converging on us, and soon they were riding in on all sides from the scrub. The head beater, a terrific fellow who made one glad that, for this generation at any rate, peace prevailed in the Sudan, explained the situation with many gestures and in a language that I did not understand, and off they all galloped again to drive the other end of the wadi. Here too, however, the result was a blank.

So the horses were whistled up from their refuge half a mile in the rear, and we all repaired to the water-hole, there to lunch off ice-cold beer, hot soup, roast duck, and coffee, and so home to Abu Sela—only to be met by an urgent deputation as to what was to be done about the lion. It had just killed a bull, right on the outskirts of the village!

Having mentioned the menu, I must now lift my hat to Sudanese cooks in general. When you think what the average English cook cannot do with half a dozen gas rings, pressure cookers, fresh vegetables, electric light, and the rest of it, you marvel all the more at what the Sudanese cook does do, squatting over a small grid with a fire of sticks, a few pots, and the light of a hurricane lamp.

Each evening on trek the party assembled round the camp fire, composed of three or four small tree trunks, point to point, which blazed the moment you kicked them—each man with his table, chair, and such drinks as he either required or possessed. (Incidentally one's chair, in a land wholly devoid of furniture, is a precious and essential possession. As to drink, my experience was that at the end of the day one required, desperately, a small whisky with an immense quantity of soda, perhaps another—and then no more. A remarkable contrast to, say, Cairo or Singapore.)

The talk flows on, as camp fire talk always does, while Venus, bright enough to cast a shadow on her own, sinks down in the west and Orion climbs up in the east, and then, it may be anything from eight to half-past nine, people start calling for their dinner. A cheerful cry answers from the darkness and within five minutes there appears the soup, with little squares of fried bread. It is followed, perhaps, by a couple of teal, done to a turn, with gravy, potatoes and tinned peas. After this a soufflé and coffee.

How is it done? I do not profess to know. I can only say that if you value domestic bliss, do not come back and ask why it cannot be done at home!

In this kind of life sport becomes, not a special occasion, but part of one's daily life; though I am afraid it does not take long to accustom oneself, on seeing a party of guinea-fowl beside the track, to the deplorable practice of lining up as many as possible for one cartridge and then letting fly at them, sitting, from the window of the car. This gives great delight both to the driver and to the Sudanese perched precariously on the vehicles behind. To them it is not only sport, which they love anyway, but *lahum*—or meat—which they rarely get. Grinning widely (this is a country of smiling faces) they dash into the bush, knives flashing, to slit the throats of the victims, thus relieving their spirits on their journey to Allah.

Sometimes the guinea-fowl were too far from the track for this mean procedure, and in this case a miniature drive would be organized. They are unpredictable creatures, but when you do get them to fly over the guns they make a capital shot, like a not-too-fast pheasant.

We had not gone far before my companion suddenly stopped the car, dashed out into an open patch in the scrub with the .22, and opened fire on a, to me, invisible target. It turned out to be a great bustard. I take this to be the biggest bird that still flies. This specimen, however, stuck to the ground and was last seen with his long, dark, ostrich-like neck passing rapidly through the tall distant grass like a periscope. Later I shot one of the lesser variety, which we chased with the car. It stood nearly four feet high and was equal to a twenty-pound turkey, and just as good to eat.

Any sort of water-hole in this arid land was good for a quick inspection, with almost the certainty of a miniature stalk and a shot or two. The first that I remember was typical—a pool of perhaps an acre with taller trees standing out from the scrub, maybe half a mile from the track. As we approached we could see life on the water, so my host went round to the right, the driver to the left, and I to the middle. As I got near, a little too soon, up went three geese, perhaps a dozen teal, a number of ibis, birds with long black bills like outsize curlews, a heron, two cranes and the inevitable party of waders, which I took to be stilts, flying with their long red legs trailing out behind. The geese looked wonderful as they wheeled away in the sunlit sky and any moment I thought to see one of them drop, but they were just too quick. The teal came over me and I dropped one in the water. The driver's puttees were off in a flash and a moment later it was duly knifed. Not long afterwards we came on another pond, with another three geese, perhaps the same birds, and despatched two, one somewhat doubtfully with the .22—but a dinner is a dinner and you cannot eat it in the air.

On other occasions we had more organized duck shoots, and these were a joy indeed, partly because, if you are so minded, the very prospect of wild fowl quickens the senses, and partly because of the tremendous variety of birdlife that crowds round patches of water in a dry country. I have vivid recollections of standing at the water's edge beneath some big trees in the early morning sun. Across the narrow stretch of water the reeds and willows might have fringed a little bay at Killarney. The place was alive with geese and duck and the first shot sent them off, but they were driven to and fro by two guns at the other water a mile away. They presented a fine variety of shots (and incidentally, my first right and left at geese) and some of the teal flew like jet-propelled plummets—but it was not only that. The birds one did not shoot at were an equal delight. A couple of golden-crested cranes, for instance, kept coming back to within a few yards—such exquisite dainty creatures till (as so often happens!) they open their mouths, when their slow honk! honk! sounds like an aged London taxi-driver with a bulb horn. Innumerable doves flitted to and fro, cooing 'two-by-two, two-by-two' and sipping at the water's edge, and an old maribou stork with his huge bill trod fastidiously through the reeds and took off with a great flapping and creaking as though his joints needed oiling. On the other side of the lake the lowing of beasts indicated a village. And when, as we left, a couple of the women arrived carrying on their heads pitchers of fresh milk for us, merely as a gesture of welcome, the morning seemed complete.

After an all too short spell of what seemed at this time of year and by contrast with an English winter an almost idyllic existence, we returned to Fasher, where I was much fascinated by the residence of the Governor. It was once the palace of the Black Sultan, Ali Dinar, who declared against the Allies in 1916 and was overpowered and killed somewhere down past Abu Sela. His red velvet-and-gold chair of state adorns the Governor's office and a picture of his body hangs on the wall. The present dining-room was his main living-room and some of his furniture is there intact, including the most lovely little inlaid ivory table. This same inlaid ivory adorns all the doors and window-doors (the walls being three feet thick), and Mr. Henderson has had it cleaned up to gleam in its original glory.

Over the gateway is the wooden cage in which Ali Dinar was wont to confine, roasting in the midday sun, the more fortunate of those who incurred his displeasure. The others, more simply, went down the well. An elderly man now working as a messenger for one of the officers in Fasher worked for three years for Ali Dinar as a boy. When asked what he was like, he replied: 'How can I say? I never saw him. We were never allowed to look above our knees'!

Across the courtyard are the women's quarters, a superb barn-like hall with painted beams, wooden grill gates, sun balcony, white walls and black thatch. Half of it is now the library and in the other half, when I was there, tall-backed chairs were set out for Christmas Communion. More than anything it seemed emblematic of that peace and security which in the short space of fifty years a handful of British, with no hope of gain, had brought to one of the fiercest lands in the world.

Prisoners at Play

A familiar sight in Lagos is the working parties from the local gaol. A great many of the prisoners, I was often assured, are far from reluctant to undergo a spell 'inside'. For people whose philosophy is that you work in order to eat and, when you have enough to eat, you no longer work (and what an admirable philosophy too!), the steady security of prison life, the regular meals, the beds, made a strong appeal, and there was the story of one man who got left outside one night and spent two hours persuading the guards that he was entitled to come in.

These working parties intrigued me greatly. Mostly their job is cutting the grass, and beside the road you see perhaps a couple of dozen of the biggest and blackest men you ever imagined, each wearing a little pair of cotton shorts with his number stamped on the backside and brandishing a murderous implement akin to a billhook. They are standing in a row—all except two. These two stand behind and provide the music. The music consists of a pair of triangles, upon which two enormous men tap out a little refrain which has been jingling in my brain ever since.

Ting ting *ting*
Ting-a-ting *ting*
Ting ting *ting* ting
Ting-a-ting *ting*.

On and on they go, half asleep as they play, while the row who are doing the work take a pace forward in unison, slash their billhooks, and rise up to repeat the process . . . forward, slash, up . . . forward, slash, up. . . . 'Hi-ya, *hi*-ya . . . Hi-ya, *hi*-ya.' They keep that perfect time which is the deep characteristic of the negro races—but without the ting-a-ting ting, I was told, they might easily cut each other's feet off. With their billhooks flashing in the sun these vast black men looked a pretty bloodthirsty crew and one glanced instinctively for the guard. Ah, there he was! A little fellow propped up against a tree, nonchalantly swinging a small stick.

I mentioned this to a friend at home who had spent much of his life administering large tracks of West African territory and he confirmed the tale. He went farther. In his day, he said, the guard sometimes carried a rifle. On one occasion he was to be seen marching his prisoners back for the night, when he suddenly remembered that he had left his rifle leaning against a tree.

So he sent one of the prisoners back to fetch it!

Over the Sahara

In a reasonably wide experience of passenger flying I have only rarely found any acute awareness of being 'separated from the earth'. The feeling is perhaps accentuated by dusk or darkness, but I have often flown through the night without its coming into my head. This particular night I spent reading a remarkable book, *Wind in the Sahara*, by R. V. C. Bodley, an old Etonian who alternated a period of distinguished service as a British officer with years of seclusion 'away from it all' with a tribe of Bedouin Arabs in the Sahara. There is good descriptive stuff in the book, all the better for the sort of sincerity which makes a man give up the way of life to which he was born, in exchange for the austere rigours of life in the desert. I found my mind lured away to the Sahara. The pitiless sun, the blinding dazzle, the hopelessness of the lost and thirsting traveller, the bleached bones on the desert's dusty face . . . a familiar conception, though one so far removed from hum-drum daily existence as to be unreal. The fabulous, far-distant Sahara that every man knew about but none had seen.

And then I sat up with a jerk.

Far distant, my foot! It was, at this very moment, less than two miles away, and nothing in the world could alter the fact. Looking round, it was hard to believe. There they were, the mother, the baby, the air hostess, and now even the General, all peacefully asleep with not a care in the world. And two miles below, the very middle of the Sahara! What's more I could see it; a vague glow in the light of the moon, and of a startling whiteness when the lightning stabbed down from a thunderstorm on our own level a few miles away. One cough of the motors—and we might never be discovered, much less rescued. Reading the book, I had thought the mind to be translating itself over thousands of miles to join the writer and his Bedouins in the desert, yet all the time the body had been within a couple of miles, perhaps, of the very spot about which he was writing. I reflected that of all those who have read *Wind in the Sahara* I was probably the one who did it nearest the Sahara!

The Ship that Flies

I lived the first twenty years of my life within a few miles of Carding-
ton, in Bedfordshire, and one of my most vivid memories is of the
R101 droning smoothly over our garden one lovely summer evening a
few hours before it was burnt to destruction at Beauvais, and with it
the hopes of airship designers perhaps for ever. For all that, I have
never had the chance of flying in an airship. They will tell you it is
comfortable beyond comparison with other modes of air travel, and
certainly an inspection of the Graf Zeppelin in its hangar near Frankfurt
a year or two before the war seemed to confirm this opinion.

The air traveller of the present has no chance to test this theory. He
hands the palm to the flying-boat. For all your 'sleeper' planes and
suchlike I cannot believe there is anything to touch the fat, friendly
solidity of the flying-boat. She is not an aeroplane that happens to land
on water: she is a ship that happens to fly. Her captain is steeped as
much in the lore of the water as of the sky. She does not, as yet, go very
fast, but she ploughs steadily along at about 160 m.p.h. and you can
get anywhere in the world at that speed within a few days. What is
more, the wide ocean is at a pinch her landing field, and there is much
comfort in that. And how much more romantic it is to be ferried to
your flying-boat in a launch than to be driven up in a common bus;
and from your arm-chair inside to sit looking at the water as closely
as though you were in a punt, instead of gazing down from a height
on a stretch of dusty tarmac! And who is blasé enough not to feel a
schoolboyish thrill at the mighty splashing and churning of the foam as
the boat begins its take-off? The water roars and batters against the hull,
but, as the speed gathers, so the roaring subsides, until at a precise
moment, not to be experienced in land-planes, a sudden smooth stillness signifies that the great boat has left one element to fly in another.

At Bangkok the flying-boats come in to the broad Menam, which
is filled with a variety of interest by comparison with a sea base, not
merely because it is all confined in a small space but also because of all
the different river life which adds to the fun. Here, apart from the
appurtenances of the flying-boat base, the scene must be almost pre-
cisely as Siamese White saw it in the 1600's when a couple of tides
carried him up the twenty miles from the river mouth, or 'Bar of
Siam', as it was called, to the capital of Ayudhya. The wide coils of

the river, the low scrubby vegetation on the banks with the stilted homes of the water population lining every muddy creek, the astonishing variety of craft from canoes to houseboats criss-crossing the stream—none of them can have changed in these three hundred years.

Nor have the river dwellers found any good reason why their habits should change either, and to get the fairway clear from end to end for a big flying-boat to take off demands a nice mixture of threats, cajolery, and the ability to be in twenty-five places at once. The scene, in fact, is very much like that of a golf fairway in a big championship when, no matter how many stewards you have, there are always half a dozen idiots who think they have time to be 'the last across the road'. So, while one of the two launches was looking after the flying-boat, the other would be dashing up and down a mile of water harrying those who were on the fairway to get off it and dissuading others from trying to get across; but of course, directly their backs were turned, out would come some ancient family craft with the washing flying amidships, propelled by a solitary oar at the back and with no hope of making a crossing in less than ten minutes.

The station officer kindly invited me to take part in the ceremony one morning, and very entertaining it was. We dashed up and down, yelling unintelligibly through megaphones until at last the fairway was clear. Then came a most pleasing experience. We lined up side by side with the flying-boat, gave it the green light, and ourselves shot off, flat out, up the river. At the same time the captain of the flying-boat opened up his engines and the great craft lumbered with increasing speed over the surface of the water. For a while we raced along side by side, for all the world like a small dog yapping alongside a motor bus, but in a moment or two the race was over and we had turned home to our base. By the time we got back to the jetty the great boat whose wake was still foaming in the river had shrunk to a speck on the southern horizon.

Life on the Klong

Perhaps it was an early upbringing beside the turgid waters of the Great Ouse that made me see in Bangkok an attraction that is by no means universal. Some people cannot do with the place at any price, but to one brought up to a love of lazy waters and just messing about in boats, Bangkok has a strong appeal. The water lies only a few feet under the surface. Dig anywhere you like and you come to water. As a result the town is intersected by almost as many rivers, canals, and strips of static water, as roads. These waterways go by the delicious name of 'Klongs'. Alongside every road there runs the Klong. Thousands of people live permanently on the Klongs, in boats with thatched cabins—a homely, unsophisticated and perhaps insanitary existence, but of a pleasing simplicity beside our own. Others live in little wooden houses perched on stilts beside the Klong, using the water as their highway and their wash-basin, while the children spend the warm days splashing about in it and the family water buffalo just lies in it and contemplates. Everyone creates a private Klong in the garden, merely by digging, and in it he will grow the loveliest of water lilies; keep the geese, which do astonishingly well in this part of the world; and probably bathe. The Klong, in fact, is very much a part of the daily life of Bangkok. At one pleasant home, I remember, the son of the house was in trouble for having thrown the cat into the Klong. At the Embassy the solemnity of diplomatic life had just been relieved by a junior minister on a visit from England who borrowed some evening clothes from the Ambassador, went for a stroll in the garden after dinner, and inadvertently stepped into the Klong.

Siam is a country where no one is in a hurry—not that that is unique in the East—and if you have not the patience to take life at the same pace you will do well to stay at home, for no amount of ranting and raving will alter the tempo of a nation. Leaving out commerce and politics and speaking only of the essential qualities of life, I formed a great liking for the Siamese. Like most Asiatic people they have an abundance of charm and good manners, but what captivated me was their gracefulness, particularly that of the women. You never by any chance see an ugly movement or gesture. You never see people running or shouting or scolding—at any rate in public—as western people do. The women walk with some of the movements and none of the vulgarity of a Mae West, their hands and arms swinging beside them in a curiously relaxed way, and there is no such thing as the middle-aged spread. That lovely figure ahead of us, for instance, carrying the two pitchers from a yoke over her shoulders—what a poem of movement she is, swaying delicately at the hips, her head steady as though a glass of water were balanced on her crown. Glance discreetly as you pass and you find it to be a coolie woman of fifty or sixty. Even the letters of the alphabet are a series of graceful curves.

Higher class Siamese women do not appear a great deal in public, there being none of the 'Café Society' of the western world—but I remember one evening attending a party by a young Siamese to celebrate the birth of a son and heir. Many of his friends had brought their wives and with their gleaming black hair ornamented with flowers, their bronzed skin, delicate features and exquisite figures, these young girls were beautiful to a degree quite beyond my poor power to describe.

The Old Lancastrian

I came home in a B.O.A.C. Lancastrian returning from Karachi on a training flight and it was on this journey, fortified perhaps by the exhilaration of leaving so unholy a land as post-war Palestine, that I fell in love with the Lancastrian. I know it is narrow and uncomfortable and I know it makes an appalling noise, but I have an abiding affection for it and even if one day I lose my life in it I will still hear no word against it. I shall never forget standing in the cockpit beside Captain Copeland that night, admiring the silver sheen of the full moon on the wings and the four great engines behind, hauling us home at two hundred and fifty miles an hour high over the Mediterranean. Filled with the joy of one on the last leg towards the white cliffs of Dover, I sang aloud—though neither I nor anyone else could hear.

And on his next flight home from Lydda, Captain Copeland and all his crew were killed.

Splendid Transgressions

When the red earth of Mingladon had faded into the morning haze, and the golden pagodas of Rangoon slipped away behind, we settled down to the dull routine of flying across the ocean. I was idly studying the chart of our course, looking to see where we should strike land on the long peninsula leading down to Singapore, when my heart gave a jump.

Mergui!

It was true I had never been there, nor ever was likely to go, but you could not tell me anything about Mergui. The little town clustering round its ridge; the houses nestling on the hillside, some of them perched on stilts with the waters of the harbour running under them at high tide, the wooden jetties and the long thin boats with their thatched cabins; the boat-builders' yards; the cosmopolitan crowd of Burmese, Chinese, Siamese, Indians, Malayans and Europeans thronging the waterfront. Why, I knew it all by heart!

Actually, this was a picture of Mergui three hundred years ago—though the place had not altered much with the centuries—and it came from Maurice Collis's intriguing book *Siamese White*, which I must have read four or five times. Collis was for three years in charge of the administration in Mergui and in the course of it came on the trail of Samuel White, of Bristol. He even found the gravestone of White's wife, Mary. He followed the trail through the records in the India Office and elsewhere, and the result is a delicious blend of piracy, enterprise, blue waters, empire-building, and the incredible hardihood of our ancestors.

When White went out to Madras in 1675, it took eight months on a five hundred ton ship. Operating in the Bay of Bengal at that time were the great East India Company, still with its royal monopoly; the 'interlopers', whose views on monopolies in general coincided with ours today and to hell with the Company; and those who made, one might say, no crossbones about it and went in for straight piracy. In his day White did a bit of each. No doubt he was a great villain, but his were the kind of 'splendid transgressions', as Conrad has called them, on which England's prestige, and anyone else's in those days, was founded. Perhaps we could do with a few more of his ilk about the place today.

Anyway, it should not be long before we saw the first of the honey-comb of islands that make up the Mergui archipelago. Soon one appeared on our right, and this must surely be Tenassarim. Over on the distant left the one with the peak must be King Island, close on the entrance to Mergui; and beyond it the harbour itself. It was not long before we were passing over a maze of islands, some rising to surprising heights but all very much on a pattern. Dense, dark-green jungle, with great white-trunked trees sprouting from the undergrowth; a fringe of dazzling yellow-white sand; white surf, and deep blue sea. So long as we flew higher than their highest point they were nothing to us, but, as I gazed down enthralled, my mind went back to Samuel White. He, too, liked to know the altitude of the islands, and so did a lot of other customers in those waters; but they did not talk in thousands of feet. All they wanted to know was 'Will it hide the mast of a ship?' Said White, when things seemed to be closing in on him at Mergui and an English man-of-war was expected any moment, 'I will set fire to the town and immediately repair to my ship, where I will give them leave to find me out if they can, for they had as good look for a needle in a bottle of hay as for me, if I get but two days start of them.'

What a splendid rogue this fellow was, and what tales these islands could unfold! Somewhere down there, perhaps through the very channel I was gazing at, he had sailed in the *Derrea Dowlat*, with his loads of elephants for Hindustan, each with seventy banana trees as fodder for the twenty days' journey. Over in the distance there, he had risen to control Mergui for the King of Siam, paying with the royal funds hundreds of soldiers who never existed, selling to the King what was, in fact, his own property, and transmitting the proceeds home to Bristol. I thought of him crawling on all fours before the King of Kings to receive his brocaded robe of office and the conical hat with the gold rings; and of the Lord Phaulkon, the Greek adventurer who came to control Siam (until he was executed one early morning by being formally hacked into small pieces) offering White the equivalent of £30,000 a year of our money, plus what he could make out of it, to be virtually Prime Minister of Siam.

And, as the islands and Mergui receded all too soon into the distance, I thought of the night, towards the end, when he ran down on to the wharf 'without hat, slippers or anything but his nightgown and a pair of drawers' . . . raving, swearing, protesting, and 'pawning his soul'—till eventually they all went aboard the *Curtana* with Captain

Weltden, fell to drinking toasts, and decided that at each toast a gun should be fired; with the result that 'Accordingly that night sixty-four guns were fired shotted with bullets or stone, and that more were not fired was owing to the raininess of the weather.'

Those were the days!

A Person of Harmless Delight

They may indeed be all God's creatures, and those peoples of the East who on this account will not kill even a disease-bearing insect may well be right. I can only say that, with one exception, I do not share this view. The exception is the praying mantis, who sounds so sinister, but is, in fact, a person of harmless delight. The first I ever saw came and sat beside my soup one night in Rangoon. He was a beautiful shiny green and about three and a half inches tall. His grass-hopper wings were folded neatly down his back and he sat back on his haunches against the salt cellar, looking towards my plate in the most comical way, and rubbing his little hands together as though about to partake of the feast. Sometimes he would close them in the prayerful attitude that earned him his name and, if you prodded at him with a spoon, he went through the most laughable defensive antics. From that moment my heart belonged to the praying mantis, and if it were not so cold in England I would have them all over the house.

Coloured Cities

In my mind's eye places tend to associate themselves with certain colours. Hong Kong, for instance, is bright blue and yellow. Singapore is green and chocolate. Rangoon is red and grey, and Calcutta green and white. But clearest of all is Karachi. It is brown.

Jerusalem the Golden

I had formed no mental impression of Jerusalem. Nobody should. It is bound to be wrong. And the same goes for all the holy places, of which most of us carry to the day of our death the pictures we formed in the scripture classes of youth. Too often the reality is a disappointment; a challenge, even, to the beliefs of a lifetime. But Jerusalem is (or was, until they divided it into two armed camps of Jews and Jordanians), one of the wonders of the world.

Come and stand on the Mount of Olives in the spring sunshine and the crisp champagne air and gaze across the valley to the unbelievable loveliness of the Old City—the ancient square fortress-wall; the pinkish glow on the houses, many of them with the round bubble-shaped roofs, and no two just alike; the spires and minarets; and, presiding over it all, the Dome of the Rock, third holiest place in the Moslem world. On the day of judgment, they say, Mohammed will stand at one end of a long rope over this valley, and Our Lord at the other. Those who can walk across will find everlasting peace, and those who fall will perish.

As you stand there gazing, the mind too full for speech, from the top of the tall minaret behind you the voice of the priest calling the faithful to prayer breaks the stillness of the scene. The high chanting rises and fades as he calls from each side of the little balcony circling the tower. It floats across the valley and is answered by the chants of the muezzins calling from the towers in the Old City. One of those moments which you know, as you stand there, is imprinted for ever on your mind.

Jerusalem is full of such moments. Wander round the Old City—on foot, for mercifully no wheeled vehicle can penetrate its tiny streets—and time and again you stop short to register some fleeting impression on the memory. Sometimes you are walking between high stone walls broken by occasional archways into little courtyards. Maybe you are following the Via Dolorosa, or Path of the Cross. Or you may dive into a labyrinth of covered bazaars, where the shoe-makers and the grocers and the tailors and the cloth merchants and the rest have each their separate streets; their shops, very often, only a mere cutting in the rock scarcely big enough for them to squat behind their wares. Or again, turning up a tiny passage, you may find yourself in an open courtyard with two storeys of little stone cubicles—a caravanserai used by merchants since the days of the Crusaders. Another passage way is a cul-de-sac which culminates in the Wailing Wall, where ancient Jews, black-robed, bearded and with long cork-screw-curled hair, lean their heads against the wall, clutching the Sacred Book, wailing aloud, often weeping.

In the heart of the Old City is the Church of the Holy Sepulchre. True, it wears a certain 'tourist' aspect, now that travel involves none of the discomforts of pilgrimage. The passage ways are full of shops offering images, candles, crosses and souvenirs, and many a holy text is strewn before the visitor's eye. Inside, however, the thought that this pink rock may indeed conceivably be the sepulchre of Jesus is quite overwhelming. Here, within a few moments' walk must be the very ground over which He carried His cross to the appalling execution of those barbaric days, and the very spot on which He was crucified. He may actually have stood upon some of the pebbles on which one has trod on the Mount of Olives. His eyes, unquestionably, gazed upon the same shapes of the distant hills, the same sort of flowers and vineyards and terraces and villages that we see by the wayside in Palestine today.

Other moments stand out in the memory. Under the Church of the Holy Sepulchre is a tiny chapel, carved from the rock, cool, silent, away from this world. One evening I stood there alone, with the evening sun casting a diffused light down the spiral stone staircase. Overhead, a soft chanting of the evening service rose and fell. It was not of this world. . . .

Nor was the sight, one evening a couple of years later, of Jerusalem from the air. We were on our way back from the Far East. How we came to be flying over Jerusalem in a Lancastrian, one of the noisiest aircraft known to man, I do not know. Such a thing is a sacrilege of which only the present age could be capable. I reflected, however, that it was not my fault, and that to my generation was unaccountably afforded something not given to the previous centuries, to see Jerusalem as only the birds and the angels had seen it in the history of the world. We could take in the pattern of the city and its Seven Hills, and in the distance Bethlehem. The setting sun cast long black shadows from the minarets and from the huge yellow tower of the Y.M.C.A. building opposite the King David. The Old City, no more than a mile square, sprawled on its hill within the wall. I picked out the Dome of the Rock as through the wrong end of a telescope, and the Damascus Gate, and Mount Scopus and the Hebrew University and the Mount of

Olives. And then in a minute this pale, unreal, and lovely vision was gone.

Of Bethlehem and the Church of the Nativity I will say little. We all cherish some early childhood picture of the manger and the stall, Joseph and Mary and the wise men and the little Child—the simple story of our first picture-book, read to us, perhaps, in the lamplight at bedtime. If this story means anything in your life, my advice is: do not go to see the so-called reality. The Church of the Nativity is a grand enough church in the solid Crusader style, and when the followers of seven different branches of the Christian religion assemble there on Christmas Eve to sing carols, the scene must be impressive indeed, but somehow as I stood beside the railed-off grotto which is displayed as the probable site of the birthplace of Jesus and saw the names of the sightseers scrawled all over the walls, it struck no chord of reverence or solemnity in my mind. It did not occur to me that this *was* the birth-place of Jesus, though experts declare its authenticity to be at least as probable as that of the sepulchre and Via Dolorosa in Jerusalem. I can only say that it had none of the same effect upon me personally and that I prefer to carry in my mind the image placed therein by my mother when I was a child.

BORNEO AND SIAM

The Real Anna

By an extraordinary coincidence the two women who became the most celebrated royal governesses in history bore the same name—Anna Harriette Crawford, born in Caernarvon in 1834, and Marion Crawford, the 'Crawfie' of the nursery days of Princesses Elizabeth and Margaret.

Anna's father was killed on active service in India when she was six, and at the age of fifteen she went out there to join her mother. She fell in love at once with the dashing, if penurious, Major Thomas Louis Leonowens, and married him in Bombay in 1851. The love letters between the two when service life in India kept them apart are, to the writer at least, the most enchanting part in Miss Margaret Landon's book *Anna and the King of Siam*, which was to bring Mrs. Leonowens world-wide fame on stage and screen so many years after her death.

Their romance was tragically short-lived. Leonowens was ordered to Singapore and there they learned daily of the death of their friends and of Anna's relatives in the Indian Mutiny. Banks failed all over India and with them vanished Anna's small private fortune. Then, the crowning blow, Leonowens himself collapsed and died after a tiger hunt in Johore. His brother officers raffled his belongings and gave her the proceeds, but soon she and the two children, then six and five, were penniless. The girl was sent home to England, while Anna opened a school for officers' children and tried listlessly to resume normal life. It was soon after this, in 1862, that King Mongkut asked his agent in Singapore to find an English governess for the royal children. William Adamson, manager of the Borneo Company, suggested Anna.

Palace life in Bangkok, as readers of Miss Landon's book will vividly recall, was a mixture of beauty and barbarity. King Mongkut had one foot, as it were, in the despotic past, and the other in an almost scholarly future. He turned lightly from the whipping of slave girls to grappling with the English language, for much of which he relied directly upon the dictionary. It is true that he went into a tantrum for a week on seeing himself described in the *Bangkok Times* as a 'spare' man, taking it to mean 'superfluous', but considering the sparseness of English-speaking residents, his letters, many of which are preserved by the Borneo Company, are a delightful combination of quaintness and skill. The handwriting is beautiful and to have these letters in one's possession, to pore over them while imagining the scene as the King burned the midnight oil composing them in his palace and penning them on these very sheets of paper, has been, to the writer, a memorable and intriguing experience.

In 1862 the King wrote a long letter to Adamson. He inquires first about a small two-inch cannon that the Company had ordered for him in London, price not to exceed £300 sterling, and goes on about a breech-loading brass cannon and 1,000 rounds of ball ammunition that he understands Sir James Brooke to have put up for sale on his return to England. He has also, he says, run out of the excellent cough lozenges (correctly spelt), which the Company have been sending him and requests another half-dozen bottles—'I wish but those which are genuine'—to be sent up by the Chao Phya. The next paragraphs concern Anna and, since the day that Adamson introduced her to the King's attention was to have so profound an influence directly on the future of Siam, they shall be quoted in full.

My faithful agent Mr. Tan Kin Ching has told me in his letter to me that you and your lady has introduced Mrs. Leonowens to him with an application that she will be English School Mastriss here under the salary of $150 per month and her residence shall be near of Protestant Missionary here. For this we are hesitating on the subject considering that our English School will be just established and may be very small so the required salary seemed to be higher than what we proposed although proper because everything here cheaper than there at Singapore, also we wish the School Mastriss to be with us in this palace or nearest vicinity hereof to save us from trouble of conveying such the Lady to & fro, almost every day also it is not pleasant to us if the School Mastriss much more endeavour to convert the scholars to Christianity than teaching Language Literature, &c. &c. like American Missionaries here because our proposed expense is for knowledge of the important Language & literature which will be useful for affairs of country not for the religion which is yet disbelieved by Siamese Schoolars in general sense.

But now we have learnt that the said Lady agree to receive an only salary of $100 per month & accept to live in this palace or nearest place hereof, I am very glad to have her be our School Mastriss if the said information be true. I can give her a brick house in nearest vicinity of this palace if she would decide to live with her husband or maid-servant, but I will be glad if she would make written best arrangement with my faithful agent Mr. Tan Kim Ching before she would come up here.

When the said Lady came here & on being the Mastriss of our English School would do good & be so active as her Schoolar might become in facility of language literature quickly & the study of School might so increase as I would see her labour heavier than what we expected, myself will reward her some time or add her salary in suitable portion.

The King concluded his letter, 'Trusting you will see that my attention is in assistance to your firm always and will thank me for the same and beg to remain your good friend and well wisher, &c.'

The story of Anna is tolerably familiar. She must indeed have been a remarkable woman. An attractive girl in her twenties, she lived alone in Bangkok with her young son—standing up to the King's rages and to court intrigue in an atmosphere where to others a false move meant instant removal to the dungeon, or worse; teaching the royal children; comforting the slaves; acting as secretary; constantly called out in the middle of the night to dress and hurry over to the Palace, only to find that the King was stuck for a single English word. Her real impact on Siam, however, came when in 1868 the King died and was succeeded by the young Prince Chulalongkorn, whom she had taught all through his formative years. The gradual abolition of slavery is traceable directly to the influence of Anna on the young Prince and to her teaching that true greatness lay in those who endured suffering, not those who with a wave of the hand could inflict it on others. Though no one could have guessed it at the time, the day that Adamson of the Borneo Company said to Tan Kim Ching, 'What about Mrs. Leonowens?' was a turning point in the history of Siam.

The Wise Elephant

Despite the fantastic excavators, 'caterpillars', bulldozers, and such like, that were produced by the war, there is virtually only one 'machine' with which to extract teak from virgin hillsides, and that is our old friend the elephant. All mankind, irrespective of age or race, is fascinated by the elephant, and the more you work with them, so those with experience will tell you, the greater grows the fascination. Anywhere a man can go an elephant can go, through narrow jungle tracks or along precipitous mountain paths which no machine can reach. His life cycle, too, is the same as that of a man. He is broken in at the age of four, goes to school to learn his job till he is seventeen, and is at his muscular peak between thirty and forty. Thereafter his age and experience make him immensely valuable till, at the age of sixty, he retires. Sensibly enough, he starts work at dawn and stops at about two o'clock, declining to work through the heat of the day. He takes every third day off, and in the dry weather from January till May retires altogether to a rest camp higher up in the hills where there is green fodder.

Each working elephant is attended by a mahout and a footman, and the occasional savage one is also accompanied by a spearman whose job is to hold his spearpoint within a few inches of the beast's beady little eye. A spearman is also called upon when one of them goes 'musth', which means that he is seeking female company. This is reckoned somewhat bad management since it can generally be avoided, as in army camps during the war, by keeping the creatures fully occupied. While the herd must in the course of nature be maintained, 'musth', if not kept in check, can be a costly business, since nature in this case takes two years and a further female elephant inevitably downs tools and attaches itself to the mother and child as a kind of 'auntie'.

As a teak tree is knotty and has a varying heart liable to twists and turns inside the trunk, a long straight plank is a rarity and they will go to any lengths to get a sound thirty-foot log out whole. It is here that the elephant comes into his own, not merely for sheer strength but for his adaptability and the wisdom that comes from forty years in the forest. It is true that the mahout puts him into position, but if the elephant doesn't know that the teak is destined for a sawmill in Bangkok he certainly knows what is to be done with it now, and the best, possibly the only, way of doing it. The Borneo Company in the late 'nineties maintained a stud of six hundred—there are perhaps fifty or sixty now, with some hundreds hired from contractors during the season—and many are the tales of their sagacity. Sometimes whole stacks of logs, not yet assembled into rafts, get piled up in the river and the only thing—perhaps one should say the only person—who can untangle them is an experienced elephant. Logs are like trusses of hay on top of a stack, or matches in the 'match game'—there is always one which will come away without disturbing the rest. The elephant has to stand downstream of the log-stack, dislodging them one by one, and every time the right one. He knows as well as anyone else that if he disturbs the stack in the wrong way he will have several hundred tons of teak smashing down on him in mid-river.

Of the many stories they will tell you of elephants and their ways, and it is a subject to which the layman can sit up listening all night, perhaps the most appealing is of the one which tried to cross the river while hobbled by a chain on the forelegs and got the chain—which is designed to stop them roving too far in search of fodder—inextricably entangled in the branch of a sunken log. The river was rising fast and by the time help could be summoned he had disappeared under water. Mahouts dived frantically to release the chain, to no avail. Another elephant was brought along, also to no avail. Eventually they managed to attach a very long chain and wire ropes. In the meantime, twice every minute, up came the elephant's trunk like a periscope. Finally, with much heaving of other elephants from the bank, the branch of the log was broken and the beast was freed. He had been in the water for sixteen hours, for most of the time totally submerged and breathing through his 'snorkel'. And at no time during all the prodding and diving and heaving did he show the least sign of panic or interfere with the proceedings in any way.

Wild Men of Borneo

No man is alive today who can tell us what Borneo was like a hundred years ago. Maps bore no relation to fact, and it is fair to assume that throughout the first fifty years of the Borneo Company's existence the average Englishman's knowledge of that vast island was limited to a single expression—the Wild Men of Borneo.

Fortunately, however, there remains the evidence of one man who reveals not only what Borneo was like but what it was like to get there. As he reads it, the first-class traveller of today, wafted through the skies at several hundred miles per hour in his pressurized cabin, may lift his hat and be thankful.

Ludvig Verner Helms was a Dane. Long to be associated with the Borneo Company, though he did not know it at the time, he left his native land in September 1846, in the brig *Johanna Caesar*, bound for the island of Bali, amid whose primitive and exotic beauty a fellow countryman was said to be the only white man yet to establish himself. Forty years later, when his wanderings had taken him not only to Bali but to Borneo, Siam, China, Japan, Australia and California, he told his story in a book called *Pioneering in the Far East*. His voyage to Singapore will have been similar to that of the founders of the Borneo Company and some indeed may have sailed in the same convoy.

It took him seven days to reach the white cliffs of Dover. The *Johanna Caesar* found the convoy, eighty-five ships in all, lying in the Downs off Deal, within a mile or so of the present Royal Cinque Ports golf links, and together they beat down Channel, narrowly escaping collision during the night. Four days saw them off Bordeaux, when a gale drove them back on their course. The hatches were battened down and the man at the helm was lashed securely to the wheel, 'where, amidst the wildest tossings, he might comfortably assure himself that, if the ship went to the bottom, he would still be at his post'. The nine passengers were stowed away in the cabin below—'a pestiferous hole with nothing to cheer us except the reflection that, as no attempt was made to cook any food, it was perhaps fortunate that we were too ill to eat it, and with no excitement beyond the unpleasant one of hearing that a sailor had been washed overboard'.

On 4th December, more than two months later, they began to look out for the Cape, but the captain had miscalculated the position and they did not reach it till the 14th. After a short stop, during which a seventy-two-year-old Baptist minister with whom he had been sharing a cabin invited him to assist in smuggling ashore a vast quantity of jewellery and gold watches, Helms continued his journey, frequently becalmed, once landing on some uninhabited tropical paradise only to be eaten alive by mosquitoes and nearly by a crocodile, and on the last day of February—having started in September—he arrived at Singapore, an imposing town with esplanades, gardens, churches, public buildings and inviting-looking villas, 'one of the finest of the many watch-towers which Britain, for political or commercial reasons, has placed about the earth'.

If Rajah Brooke, the Borneo Company, and, as I am sure he would like it to be felt, Helms, 'made' Sarawak, the raw material from which they made it was raw indeed, even if at first sight it may at times have seemed very heaven. Helms could well understand, he said, how the first glimpse of Borneo may have inspired a romantic disposition, with picturesque mountains rising 5,000 feet from the sea and a succession of foothills and river valleys stretching down to a sea-shore bordered by casuarinas or mangrove trees. What is more, the climate, though the rainfall at Kuching is 160 inches a year, proved ideal for Europeans.

Closer experience, however, revealed a different picture. The lowlands were a jungle swamp full of snakes, crocodiles, and insects bearing diseases known and unknown. The primitive inhabitants were riddled with smallpox (James Brooke contracted it in 1853 and, though he recovered, was never the same man again). Tribal warfare and head-hunting were indiscrimate and incessant. A man never knew when within a few days all that would be left of him might be his head, baked, shrivelled, and suspended with others from a pole, like so many Spanish onions. Alternatively, if he put out to sea, he was liable to be intercepted and slaughtered by the piratical Sea Dyaks.

This was the scene over which James Brooke had been acclaimed Rajah in 1841. The progress he made, at first almost singlehanded, in reducing this barbarous outpost to some semblance of civilization is almost incredible. When Helms arrived ten years later in the steamship *Pluto* from Singapore, as agent of an unnamed commercial firm, 'to buy up the antimonial ore and generally to develop the trade of the country', he found a comfortable Government House in process of construction, half a dozen European bungalows and a pretty little church. The Rajah being on a visit to England, Helms was greeted by his nephew, Captain Brooke (who did not in fact, through an unhappy dispute, succeed him) and was made welcome to stay in Government House. Later in the day he was introduced to Mr. Arthur Crookshank, the magistrate; Mr. Ruppell, Treasurer; Mr. Spencer St. John, the Rajah's secretary; Mr. Crymble, in charge of the fort; the missionaries, Fox, Nicholls, and Chambers; and Mr. Hentig, a planter.

A month later he took possession of his own little mat-bungalow, a square box of palm leaves divided into bedroom and sitting room with a veranda overlooking the town and the river, his staff consisting of a Chinese cook and a Kling clerk and factotum, 'my faithful Abdullah who for twenty years served the Company and myself with unsurpassed devotion'. Abdullah was his only assistant then and their business transactions were trifling, but 'thousands of men,' he adds grandly, 'were to work for us, directly or indirectly, before I left.'

To reach the workings from Kuching took four hours by boat, and Helms waxed lyrical about the journey. The Malays improvised songs as he lay back in the boat, well screened from sun and rain, and admired a scene of tropical nature run riot, untouched by the hand of man. In places the river had worn through the limestone, leaving huge shelving masses over-hanging the water, from which trees of fantastic shape sprouted forth to form a cathedral-like vault. A wild tangle of vegetation—orchids, rhododendrons, lilacs, tree-ferns as tall as a house—lined the banks and above them all the stately tapang tree towering 150 feet to the first branch. Kingfishers, fireback pheasants, hornbills, doves of yellow, green, and pink, lent colour to the scene and, as night fell, the fireflies 'pulsated like electric sparks flashing from the leaves'.

You cannot, however, inspect antimony workings from a boat, and, when the party stepped ashore, life took on a less Utopian pattern. You had to hack your way through creepers and parasites till you chanced on a Dyak path, consisting of rounded slippery bamboos a few inches out of the mud. If you took your eye off the path, and often if you didn't, you slipped waist-deep into mud and were set upon instantly by leeches. Refreshing himself, as he thought, in a cooling stream at the end of a hard day, Helms emerged with twenty-seven. Nor were leeches the only hazard. To snare the game, the Dyaks set traps of a diabolical ingenuity, consisting of a concealed thread across the path and a strong bent-back sapling with a spearhead attached. As you touched the string, the sapling was released and drove the spear horizontally with great force, at an elevation from the ground calculated according to the intended victim. If set for pig, it would pass through a man's leg, but if set for deer, it would, as Helms observed.

pass through some more vital part. One could sympathize with his feeling that 'under such circumstances a tropical forest does not inspire the same sentimental enthusiasm as when one views it comfortably reclining in a boat and perchance reading the latest home news, while the Malays prepare a delicious curry on some pebbly bank in the river'.

To be a missionary in Borneo a hundred years ago needed faith indeed. When we learn that some of the more ardent propagators of the gospel issued a ration of tobacco to those attending church and provided, as Communion wine, 'gin slightly coloured red', and that one Dyak convert, on seeing a picture of the episode of David and Goliath, remarked that the former 'had secured a particularly fine head', most of us will smile with an indulgence tinged in no way with malice.

As the days passed, nothing could restrain either the Malays or the Sea Dyaks. The Malay chief took a party up the river and massacred a stockade-full of Chinese and a few nights later the Dyaks returned chanting in a fashion which indicated all too clearly the nature of their prize. Tidman in his diary described the scene on the morrow as the most disgusting part of the whole affair.

'The heads, after being cleaned, are hung over a slow fire and smoked; this effectually cures them and they are then ready for stacking. Perhaps thirty heads were hanging in different parts of the bazaar today. The Dyaks seem to take a particular pleasure in superintending the cooking in front of the Chinese in the bazaar and when any of these came up to recognize an acquaintance, maybe a friend, they looked as much as to say, "If it were not for the very great respect we entertain for the fire-ship's guns, we should feel the greatest pleasure in adding your head to this little collection".'

The White Elephant

The outside observer, surveying the Borneo Company's hundred years in Siam in a cheerfully detached sort of way, may be forgiven for concluding that the red-letter day in all this long and honourable record was founded upon an achievement not by any particularly gifted or hardworking member of the staff, but by the Company's elephant who gave birth, one day in 1926, to a white baby. Readers of 'Anna' may remember the sensation caused by the discovery of a white elephant in the annual round-up near Ayuthia, when seventy-five royal barges and a hundred boats were at once ordered to take the King and his suite to the scene. It is a tenet of the Buddhist religion, and one which we may respect since so many secretly subscribe to it in Christian countries, that the spirits of the departed return to earth in other forms—and indeed that the Great Buddha himself from time to time does so. Those especially worthy return as birds or animals of pure white, and of these the rarest and most distinguished is the white elephant.

It fell to D. F. Macfie, now forest manager in Siam, to do the honours regarding the new phenomenon. Pictures and accounts of it appeared in newspapers and magazines all over the world. To the sensation it caused in Siam his own accounts give graphic witness:

We have had a hectic week of it over this White Elephant Calf which has been born to one of the B.C.L. elephants. It was born last May, and rumours at once spread that it was a real white elephant and had all the proper points for a white elephant to have, light red skin, white hair on head and body, light blue eyes, and a very white roof to its mouth. The authorities heard of it and so, at the request of the Chief of Chiengmai and the Siamese commissioner here, I had it brought in, when they at once both went in off the deep end about it, and said it was a true white elephant, and an incarnation of Buddha, and very sacred and holy. Wherever it went it was followed about by hundreds of people who knelt to it and worshipped it, and fed the mother on cakes and sugar cane till she nearly got ill herself. It was escorted in by about seventeen big tuskers, and a band of gongs, across the bridge (where elephants are not allowed to cross as a rule, but this one was much too holy to be asked to ford the river), and so to the B.C.L. compound. The poor little animal was wonderfully good and stood by its mother scratching one hind leg with the other, looking very bored with the proceedings. I went out after dinner at about 10 p.m. to see how it was getting on and found it sleeping peacefully between its mother's forelegs, while she was still munching sugar-cane.

Macfie recorded that it proved to be an extraordinarily quiet, nice little animal, not a bit pugnacious or mischievous like other baby elephants. Everybody attributed this to the fact that it was a reincarnation of Buddha, and all sorts of stories were circulated, such as that when it was taken down to the river to bathe it always bathed upstream of its mother, and always chose slightly higher ground to sleep on. So great was the crowd that Macfie decided to bath it in the compound, for which purpose he produced a huge zinc footbath. The little beast promptly got right inside the bath and sat down—'the most comical sight you ever saw'—and this again was taken as proof of its human or god-like incarnation.

The whole thing was considered the most wonderfully lucky occurrence as, in the year that King Chulalongkorn acceded to the throne of Siam, this same Chief of Chiengmai's father had a white elephant calf born in Chiengmai which he presented to the King—and the King reigned for a record period of forty years. Now, in the first year of the new King's reign, this white calf was born in Chiengmai—an indisputable omen of prosperity. The King decided to come up to Chiengmai in January, the first time any King of Siam had ever been up there, and altogether the Borneo Company were reckoned to have acquired much merit. The visit was a tremendous success. The King and Queen were met at the station and escorted through the city by eighty-seven of the biggest elephants in Siam, and liked the place so much that they announced their intention of building a residence there and turning Chiengmai into a kind of Siamese Balmoral.

Macfie presented Their Majesties with an album of photographs and made a short address in which he said: 'It is a matter of the keenest gratification to the Borneo Company Limited, and especially to the staff employed in working the royal teak forests in northern Siam, that in the seventy-first year of the Company's career in Siam, and in the first year of Your Majesty's reign, it should have happened that an elephant portending prosperity both to Your Majesties and to your Kingdom, should so opportunely have been born.'

The King in turn said he was extremely pleased with the elephant, which he thought was a very good specimen of a true white elephant, and, in thanking the Company for it, he wished them many years of prosperity in Siam.

Eventually, the time came to take the now Sacred Elephant and its mother down to Bangkok, a journey of some six days, in a special truck with electric light, four water showers, and a telephone attachment through to the engine. The little creature, not unnaturally, declined at first to get in, so they sent for a big tusker who bundled it in willy-nilly seated on its posterior protesting violently. One of the mahouts who was shut up in the truck with it to ride on its neck and keep it calm, got his foot caught in one of the chains and nearly lost his leg, but eventually the journey was over, and it arrived amid unprecedented scenes in Bangkok. 'The Siamese,' reported Macfie, 'went absolutely mad over it and there have never been such scenes—people being crushed to death in the crowds, or pushed into the canals and drowned.'

An enclosure was erected for the elephant and its mother in front of the royal palace, and for days on end people flooded in from every quarter of Siam to witness a rite which had not been held within the last forty years. Macfie and senior officials of the Company attended at 9 a.m. in full evening dress—which is the ceremonial dress in Siam, as in the Vatican, though one difficult to bear in the full daytime heat of the tropics—and Macfie was presented by the King with the Order of the White Elephant and a gold bowl with a Siamese inscription giving the King's name in full as follows: 'Prabat Somdech Paramindra Maha Prajadhipok Phra Pok-Klao Chaoyuhua Siam.'

The feasting appears to have gone on all day and all night for the best part of a week. 'I hope,' wrote Macfie in closing his account, 'for the sake of my successors that no B.C.L. elephant so far forgets itself in future as to have a white baby.'

FARTHER EAST

Shambles in Shanghai

Our next field for research (in charter flying in the Far East immediately after the war) was Shanghai, so with hearts of lead and an equally heavy outward jocularity we booked ourselves a passage with one of the Chinese airlines.

However, our friends' constant inquiries as to the disposition of our effects, our next of kin, and suchlike, and further perusal of the 'other crash reports' section of the local paper eventually took the heart out of us, and, hearing that Jardine Matheson's had a ship going up to Shanghai at almost the same time, we fell to working out that after all there was very little difference between four days and one, and anyway the aircraft might be delayed by bad weather, and further that we needed the time to do a bit of the unhurried thinking that is so difficult in the confined bustle of Hong Kong or Shanghai, and anyway we could spend the time drafting our report. So we cancelled the air tickets and booked a couple of comfortable staterooms on the good ship *Wing Sang*.

She was a sturdy vessel, captained by a sturdy Lancastrian in the person of Captain Schofield, and she was lying up conveniently on the waterfront within walking distance of the hotel. It was said that for all her stolid build, there were times when she would stand up on her rudder and flap her wings like a duck. Still, better lose your dinner than your life, and we embarked more with relief than with apprehension.

In the state to which Chinese administration had reduced Shanghai the flow of traffic was away from the city rather than into it and, while previously we might have had to wait some time for a passage, now there were only half a dozen passengers in the upper-deck cabins—including the ship's doctor, who delivered two babies among the lower-deck passengers during the four days we were at sea. They ought, we thought, to be called Wing and Sang.

One evening Captain Schofield started on some of the yarns that you expect from a skipper who has been plying the China Seas for thirty years or more. I only venture upon one, not because the rest were unprintable, which was far from the case, but because these things often fall so flat on paper. The little anecdote that appealed to me so much that I take a chance of passing it on concerned a merchant skipper acquaintance of Schofield's with a gigantic voice. This man had finished his days as a pilot in one of the ports on the coast of China, where there was a tricky and narrow entry by way of the river. One day a ship tied up at the side had its boats out on the davits, and the old skipper, piloting another ship in, took it too fine. From beside and behind him there came the most fearful smashing and splintering as he ripped off the boats of the stationary vessel.

Standing squarely on the bridge and looking straight to his front, the old man spent the next two minutes bellowing to anyone who might be interested: 'Never touched it! Never anywhere near it! Never touched it. . . .'

As the *Wing Sang* ploughed along on her fourth afternoon the water turned a muddy brownish yellow and, although there was at the moment no land in sight, this was the efflux of the mighty Yangtze River which flows for 3,500 miles from west to east through China. I believe it is true that no fewer than a tenth of the whole world's population live in the valley of the Yangtze.

There can hardly be a more commonplace and uninspiring approach than that to Shanghai. Muddy river (the Whangpoo, an offshoot of the Yangtze), swampy mud flats, an assortment of dilapidated shacks and sheds. Nor can you see anything much of the city itself, except the upper half of a number of skyscrapers, till you free yourself from the customs sheds, docks, go-downs, and what-not on the riverside, and arrive on the celebrated Bund, or waterfront. Though we found the whole city in comparative chaos (nothing to what it became later, of course), it took no time at all to see what a fantastic achievement was the founding of modern Shanghai more than a century ago. Almost from the first moment regret began forming in my mind, and has been with me ever since, that I never saw Shanghai in the days of its splendour.

The British, the Americans, and the French all had their Concessions in Shanghai, where they were immune from the corruption and irregularities of Chinese courts—or, as I have seen it described, their 'medieval conception of jurisprudence'. The municipal council was probably the best of its kind in the world and the international settlement was generally reckoned a model. Shanghai did everything in a big way. It was a place where you could drink, gamble, or debauch yourself to death, or rise to fame and fortune.

Prices before the war enabled a man of reasonable means to live like a prince. A dollar (call it two shillings) bought a couple of hundred eggs.

Five dollars bought a bottle of gin and two bottles of vermouth, and left some change. There was no income tax and a youngish man could afford a house, servants, motor-car, rickshaws, golf, riding, shooting (pheasant, duck and snipe) and the rest of it. Those whose inclinations took them in that direction could visit a dozen different places of entertainment every night for a fortnight without entering the same one twice; while the best of music and the arts, so I am assured by the headmaster of my son's preparatory school, who spent twenty years in Shanghai, was available for those of a more serious turn of mind. But alas, all this has vanished now. Extraterritoriality, or 'extrality', in Shanghai and the other so-called treaty ports—Canton, Amoy, Foochow and Swatow—and more particularly the unbelievable success of Shanghai under foreign administration, had irked the Chinese for more than a hundred years, and in the recent war our position was sufficiently weakened to enable them to push us out. It happened in January 1943, and that is the date which marks the beginning of the decline and fall of Shanghai.

'Pedlars, hawkers, peepshowmen and loungers, cobblers, tailors, and sellers of tea and nuts, not to speak of men who just stared or begged loudly, packed the promenade, and though from time to time, when it became unbearable, the police would be sent for to clear them out, they filtered back again and continued as before to shout, beg, accost and stare.' Reading this description by Maurice Collis of Canton in the 1840's I was reminded of Shanghai a hundred years later. You could hardly pass along the pavement for hawkers and their wares, and if you stepped into the road you were run down by a rickshaw.

The fire brigade, once the pride of the city, had reverted in keeping with the rest and in a fully authenticated case had let a man's house burn down because they were unable to come to terms with his next-door neighbours as to what it was worth to them to have the fire put out.

Every good Englishman likes to read of a really first-rate swindle—perhaps because he knows he will never be able to pull one off himself. We all have a sneaking sympathy for the Bottomleys of this world. For sheer graft and corruption there can have been nothing in our time to beat Shanghai. Pilferage was up to eighty per cent and it was nothing for an importer to be offered his own goods for sale before he knew they had even arrived. But the finest racket was transport—and of course, U.N.R.R.A. (United Nations Relief and Rehabilitation Administration). A small ring of Chinese had got a stranglehold on all transport—which meant the river and coast shipping, for there was never more than 10,000 miles of railway in the whole of China (£12,000,000 worth of it British and not a penny paid since 1937) and much of that had either been destroyed or fallen into the hands of the Communists, and road traffic was in much the same state. Laws had been passed preventing foreigners engaging in river transport, so the ring had been able to secure a complete monopoly. The fact that they had practically no ships, nor men fit to run them, did not worry them in the least. Whatever there were, were theirs. You could use them and pay the price—or do the other thing.

So it cost more to ship a car across the river at Shanghai than to bring the car from San Francisco!

In an effort to test the market a British firm formed a Chinese company and sent a ship up the river, complete with a Chinese pilot. But, alas, he was soon stopped by one of Chiang Kai-shek's generals. One may so well imagine the conversation that ensued; the general regretting with the utmost politeness the inescapable necessity for him to requisition the ship; the protesting captain: the veiled bargaining, overlaid with a scrupulous veneer of courtesy; and the final settlement.

And what was that? Why, the general to take the full fares of half the passengers, plus ten per cent 'brokerage' on the other half!

Incidentally, most Chinese 'generals' are self-promoted to that rank. I dare say this applied to the one who was leaving Formosa by air, accompanied by his staff. When it was desired to weigh one rather insignificant member of the staff, he said: 'That is all right. This man is only my personal servant. He weighs nothing!'

U.N.R.R.A. was a splendid racket, too. U.N.R.R.A. goods were on open sale everywhere. From one ship alone 30,000 cases of milk were offered for sale in the city with the labels washed off. There was the case, which I heard from the skipper in question, of a ship taking 2,000 tons of fertilizer from Hong Kong to Shanghai, moving up the river, picking up 2,000 tons of exactly the same fertilizer, and taking it to Hong Kong. U.N.R.R.A. paid tens of thousands in freight and the brokers got the 'squeeze'. The best method, however, was to lose part of the ship's manifest. With it, of course, disappeared those goods that happened to be invoiced on the missing sheets.

Many British and American people worked hard in delivering U.N.R.R.A. supplies to China. Their job was to deliver the goods, which they did. It was after the goods got there that the fun and games began—unless, of course, the items happened to be something like the

2,000 cases of Worcester sauce which some bright spirit had sent for the rehabilitation of China and which now reposed in the go-down of one of the biggest British firms. Not a soul in China would touch it with the end of a barge pole.

But perhaps after all, while we are on the subject, the best racket of the lot was the Aid to China fund organized by Lady Cripps and other well-wishers in this country. Between them they raised £2,000,000. It was given by countless charitable folk out of the goodness of their hearts to relieve the distress among the poorer folk in China. But the trouble was that before it could reach them it had to pass (or, rather, the goods bought with it had to pass) through the hands of many not-so-poor Chinese, who did not subscribe to the view that either they or Lady Cripps were their brothers' keeper. Their view of the deserving poor was the old-fashioned one, namely that they are always with us. At any rate I asked several people in various eminent walks of Far East life how much of the £2,000,000 they thought to have reached its intended recipients. The highest estimate came from a senior R.A.F. officer. He said £10,000. And a man in a very high position in one of the senior British firms declared it to be within his certain knowledge that a large early instalment of the fund, when changed into Chinese currency to buy supplies for the poor, was changed at the official rate of 80 dollars to the pound—when the open rate was already 8,000. In other words the first squeeze was 7,920 dollars out of 8,000. The remaining 80 was, of course, milked further as it went down the line.

Not having been in Germany after the last war, I was experiencing for the first time in Shanghai a currency that had gone completely haywire. At the time in question Chinese national dollars stood at about 45,000 to the £. I well remember the childish delight with which we drew just over £20 apiece and became for the first time in our lives millionaires! Such innocent pleasure did we derive from the idea that we solemnly undid the vast bundle of notes (tightly compressed they came to about twelve inches), spread them in a great mass over the table and photographed each other in turn.

Still, 45,000 to the £ was bad enough. It meant forking out 25,000 dollars for a bottle of Eno's and, for those who had not a private source, 660,000 dollars for a bottle of whisky! You carried your money done up in lengths with string, and it was a comical sight to watch prosperous Chinese gentlemen bustling along with their hands stuffed up the opposite sleeves. You could be sure they had a million or two up each.

Though many have died in the process, no one has really lived till he has made a trip on a Chinese airline. An experience neither to be missed, nor, once you have got away with it, willingly repeated.

We were to assemble at the Cathay and make sure of being there before nine o'clock. Being model air travellers, we did so. There was, of course, no one in sight and for a moment there were ugly thoughts of having turned up at the wrong place and already the bus leaving from elsewhere without us. These were put at rest, however, by the arrival of a Chinese family, one of whom was evidently expecting to travel. And so, gradually, the place filled up. A small square in the middle of the hall, with a counter on three sides, was roped off for the customs, and at a quarter to ten two burly Chinese of particularly inscrutable and, as I thought, rather sinister countenance took up position therein and lit cigarettes. Meanwhile the hall was filling up nicely and there were now more than a hundred people.

The Chinese are not blasé like the Westerners, who think they lose face if they show excitement or emotion at such commonplace events as being hoisted into the firmament and deposited nine hundred miles away in a matter of hours. The Chinese are great travellers, but they still like to make an 'event' of it. The family turns up and a few friends, maybe, and the party being seen off is the centre of attraction. With him (or her) he probably has a vast roll of bedding, a suitcase or two, and half a dozen nets of assorted vegetables, fruit and fowls.

No directions were issued to the passengers, or to their admirers and hangers-on. They just milled to and fro, enjoying themselves. In the main channel of movement a huge suitcase blocked the fairway. Curtis and I spent about ten minutes fascinated at the attempts of people to get by. It was like watching ants who dash up to an obstacle, turn this way and that, retreat, come back again, and go through the process all over again. Anyone could have moved this particular obstacle in three or four seconds. I don't think it occurred to them to do so. A trivial affair, maybe, but it stuck in the mind—and seemed to explain a whole lot of things.

There was the usual set of scales, but it was only by insisting on it that we got ourselves and our baggage weighed. Very few others did, and if the trip had resulted, as seemed not unlikely, in an inquest, no one would ever have known the true weight of the load. The customs officials signified that they were now open for business and began methodically to unpack the miscellaneous bundles of the passengers. I need hardly describe the chaos involved. Nor were things improved by the fact that there is no such thing as queueing in China. You push. And no one pushes harder than the women, and the smaller they are the harder they push and the more likely they are to catch you where you don't like being pushed. But they all do it in a good, open, straightforward sort of way, clawing, elbowing, and shoving; not in the underhand manner by which Englishwomen push each other in a queue, each leaning heavily on the one in front and, when challenged with a glare, gazing blandly to the sky.

After an hour or so of this preparation for flight poor Curtis, who after all had been traffic manager of British European Airways, was pretty well beyond speech. Critical comment no longer flowed and he sat on his baggage, occasionally lifting his head to shake it wearily and then replacing it in his hands.

Soon after eleven, however, there was a good deal of confused shouting and it was clear that something was afoot. There was a scramble for a small door on the other side of the hall, the result calling to mind some vast egg-timer with human contents instead of sand, and a few minutes later we were all sitting packed in a couple of small buses with wooden forms, rattling our way out through the hordes of rickshaws towards the airfield at Lunghwan. And here at once occurred a splendid scene, in perfect harmony with the proceedings. Everyone got out of the buses and, there being nowhere for them to go, nor anyone to direct them, stood about in groups behind an adjacent Sky-master. I noticed one of the engines being 'run up' and, knowing what was probably coming, hopped quickly back into the bus. From the security of the driving seat I watched something reminiscent of films of the great dust bowl of the Middle West. As another engine joined in, a storm of hard-driven yellow dust obscured the passengers. As they faded from sight a hat or two flashed past the windscreen, twirling madly in its flight, but soon even the end of the bonnet was gone and I found myself in a clean, solitary, glass-contained little world of my own, cut off from human kind.

Eventually, the roaring subsided and then, very gradually, the dust. Minutes ago the passengers had worn the air appropriate to persons who have been seen off with full ceremony at the outset of a gallant and hazardous mission. They reappeared to human vision in sadly different guise, going through grotesque contortions as though attacked by a swarm of bees, bashing at hair, faces and clothes with newspapers, hats, or anything that came to hand, coughing, spitting and spluttering. Sand has no mean powers of penetration when driven by the full exhaust of four thousand horsepower.

This dusty baptism over, some traffic clerks appeared, dressed in the short fur-collared jacket and peaked service cap on the side of the back of the head which the Chinese knew from American films to be the hallmark of the intrepid aviator, and a number of customs men emerged from a tea-wagon. Another Skymaster was brought up and the usual free-for-all took place to see who could be first into the plane. A Chinese woman beside me, exquisitely turned out, as they always are, and wearing a mink coat, spat casually in the sand and turned back to her shoving. The rate of entry was slow, however, as a customs man stood at the top of the ladder examining the small baggage, from which his haul consisted of a gold ring and some trinkets.

At last we were settled, Curtis and I well in the tail, where survival rate is always highest, and the air hostess well in the front, where all the passengers could see her. She was a Chinese girl who had also come under the influence of Hollywood, with a much emphasized figure, huge scarlet mouth, and half-inch blood-red fingernails. Having struck a series of attitudes, she endeavoured to adjust her own seat and was unable to move it, this producing a satisfying rush of male passengers to the rescue and a running commentary from Curtis on the advantages of employing male stewards. At last the argument about the gold ring was concluded and the door slammed and locked. Now for it. . . .

And there we sat in dead silence, with not a movement of man or motor, for thirty-one minutes.

When at last we took off, it was more than four hours since we had assembled at the Cathay. Still, we did not figure in 'Other crash reports' and for that we were truly thankful.

A Day at the Races

There were many diversions in case our more serious purpose in Hong Kong looked like becoming monotonous, which it never did. A day at the races, perhaps, by kind invitation of Jardine's, whose private box was where you would expect it to be, plumb opposite the winning post, and who did the thing in the sort of style of which their pious founders would have well approved. The ponies had come up from Australia since the war but had been there long enough for their form to be known within half a length or so. As they were the only ponies on the island, there was no hope of pulling a fast one with an 'unknown' and there was therefore much working-out of placings and weights and what they did 'last time out but three', and such like, among the more serious punters. For myself, I bet neither on horses nor dogs, having known too many prosperous bookmakers in my younger days and having worked out that simple proposition, which evades the amateur punter to the end of his life—namely that he and the book-maker cannot both wax fat from a series of transactions between the two of them.

I did, however, wager a few dollars on a pony called Morning Express, which took my fancy. The jockey rode it flat out from the start and about three-quarters of the way round it was leading by more than I have ever seen a horse lead by before or since.

'Well,' I said, 'the only thing that can stop it now is if it falls down dead!'

It did. In front of the grandstand.

Gold Rush

I was at the country club at Shek-O one afternoon with Curtis. This is opposite to the Ly-mum Pass, through which ships and aircraft thread their way to Hong Kong. There was a sea mist down to a few hundred feet and squalls of rain. We watched a Dakota flying in low under the mist a mile or so from the shore and remarked to each other how gratifying it was to be standing on the solid earth of Shek-O. The plane disappeared into a rain squall and I fancy we were the last people to set eyes on it. A few minutes later it crashed into Mount Parker, killing its American pilot and crew, poor devils, within a few feet of the summit.

Mercifully there were no passengers to increase the tragedy. The cargo, however, was a remarkable one—no less than a million and a quarter pounds' worth of gold from the Philippines—and this was distributed over two or three hundred yards of the upper surface of Mount Parker as the plane tore its way to destruction. Such things can hardly be kept secret and it was not long before there was precipitated the biggest gold rush ever witnessed in the Far East. A great concourse resembling the Cup Final trek to Wembley approached the mountain from all sides at a steady jog-trot, the police well up with the field. As they wound their way towards the summit, it was 'fittest foremost' and the weaker contestants fell panting to the rear.

Chief prize was the 'Mexican eagles', gold coins which might with any luck be concealed about the person, though the flimsy pyjama-like clothing worn by many Chinese added difficulty to this manœuvre and one coolie soon got thirty days for having three in the turn-ups of his trousers. Gold bars, though ten a penny in the first few hectic minutes, were a tantalization but little more. So heavy that, when you try to lift one, it seems glued to the ground, they were not lightly to be secreted in the trouser leg or shirt front, and perhaps for this reason a large percentage of the gold was recovered.

Hope springs eternal, however, and no amount of press announcements to the effect that 'all the gold had now been accounted for' deterred the amateur prospectors. For weeks to come, Mount Parker was dotted with bowed figures, and even respectable citizens who would not normally move two hundred yards without a rickshaw were to be seen perspiring up the mountain on their Sunday stroll.

It was shortly after this unhappy business that our investigations led us to be discussing with the Hong Kong and Shanghai Bank the possible carriage of banknotes by air. Not only was there a very considerable note issue in Hong Kong but some millions of new notes must be needed every week in China to cope with the fantastic inflation. They would be excellent air freight for us and speed in delivery might make a big difference.

You may be quite sure that there is no British concern of any magnitude operating abroad which does not have in its employ at least one Scotsman named Morrison. In the Hong Kong and Shanghai Bank he was the chief cashier, the man who signed the Bank's notes. We had a congenial meeting with him and, interspersed with golfing reminiscences, he informed us that they had three months' reserve of notes and therefore a fast ship served the purpose perfectly well. He could not resist a dig at us to the effect that, anyway, they would not want to risk having all their notes distributed about the summit of Mount Parker. . . .

We had to admit this to be a point well taken and we retired with a feeling of having lost the first hole. Next morning, right across the front page of the local newspaper, was a headline announcing that thirty cases of banknotes sent by ship from Hong Kong to Shanghai had been found, when opened, to contain stones.

I remember with a childish satisfaction—and indeed, though quite alone, am smirking at the recollection as I write it down—taking out a sheet of notepaper, pinning the cutting to it, and writing to Morrison:

'We respectfully beg to draw your attention to the fact that, when Skyways carry banknotes, they deliver banknotes.

'We can, however, quote a special rate for stones.'

Flying Fish

Surfeited with the inevitable bacon and eggs, we decided one day in Hong Kong to order some fish for breakfast in our bedroom.

'Grilled fish,' we said.

The Chinese boy who had come to take the order seemed unusually dense. If we said it once, we said it half a dozen times. We spelled it out and made signs. No good. Eventually the boy produced a piece of paper and the stub of a pencil. We wrote it down, in large capital letters. The boy read it and, as the light of comprehension illuminated his features, his face broke into a vast, gold-toothed grin.

'Ah,' he said, 'glilled fish!'

I leave the reader to imagine the complications later involved when Curtis had a brainwave and started flying live fish fry from Hong Kong to restock the reservoirs at Singapore. It was successful enough in that ninety per cent arrived alive, instead of five per cent in the days when they went by ship in water tanks periodically stirred by coolies, but whether he was frying flying fish, or flying fried fish, or simply frying flied flish, the Chinese did not to the end discover.

Chinese Crackers

Anyone planning to make his first trip to any part of the Far East where Chinese predominate should be at pains to avoid arriving when they are celebrating their New Year. It is one of those useless bits of historical knowledge possessed by us all that the Chinese invented gunpowder. At the New Year they remind the world of the fact by letting off crackers—crackers beside which our own Guy Fawkes variety are as the shilling rocket is to the V2. Our bedroom in Hong Kong, overlooking the narrow street, was an ideal vantage point from which to appreciate the full significance of its being the Chinese New Year, since the celebrations tend to go on all through the night, or rather, several nights. Every urchin has a cracker. He may have only a ragged pair of pants, half a shirt and no shoes, but he has an inexhaustible supply of crackers. Only small ones, of course, lasting for perhaps ten seconds each. The echo, however, would bounce off the buildings on either side, dash in at the windows, and chase itself round the four walls of our bedroom; and by the time it had finished, another series would be in progress, this time lit perhaps by one of the better-off citizens, lasting a full half minute instead of ten seconds and ending not in one bang but two.

Sometimes several would be tied together, finishing with the father and mother of all explosions, perhaps forty yards, as the blast travels, from one's bed. To lie in the dark waiting for the final report was sheer agony. If this was the Chinese idea of fun, no wonder they were famous for their torture!

An Unforgettable Man

It is not often that you meet a truly singular character, singular in the sense that he is not merely rare but, you are pretty sure, unique. Such a man is Father Gherzi.

One of the innumerable problems that harass the life of the operator of air transport is 'Met.' In the Far East the violence of the weather in the shape of extreme heat, cyclones, and such-like (on a cyclone warning every aircraft at Hong Kong had to be flown off post-haste to Saigon, some six hundred miles away, or it would be whisked off the airfield at Kaitak and blown into the sea), to say nothing of the vast distances between landing grounds for the bigger aircraft, and the curious workings of the Oriental mind, all these make the forecasting of the weather more than usually essential and more than usually hazardous.

The tracks of anyone engaged seriously in the air business in China and the Far East must eventually lead to Father Gherzi, the greatest individual weather expert in the eastern hemisphere, and his observatory at Ki-wa-zei on the outskirts of Shanghai.

When we called to consult him, he was the more remarkable for the fact that he was quite alone in the observatory. As he took us from room to room in the big rambling building, most of them filled with fantastic Wellsian contraptions, we met not a soul in the place.

Father Gherzi, a man I should say in his fifties, is a Jesuit priest. He is more than six and a half feet tall, with a long narrow head and pointed beard, and wears undoubtedly the biggest pair of boots in Asia. They protrude like skis from under his long black cassock.

For some time we sat talking in his room, while he lit a procession of cigarettes which he burnt down till they nearly singed his beard. On the wall of his bare apartment I noticed a picture of one of the original Brothers, Von Bell, of whom the caption said: 'Arrivé en Chine 1522.' Father Gherzi himself had been in Shanghai twenty years. From the age of seven he had for some years pursued a calling which would have defied a thousand guesses—fishing off the banks of Newfoundland!

He escorted us round the building and showed us his work. For our benefit he spoke in what I am sure he thought to be the language of a children's meteorological primer, but I am afraid that the flow of information about air masses, lapse rates, isobars, and thermo-this, -that and the other was over the head of at least one of his two listeners. He showed us his library, with twenty-foot bookshelves and tall ladders, and laboratories with every kind of unintelligible instrument, including one with one of those vast aerials shaped like a spider's web, on which, if I remember, he said he had been measuring cloud levels by radar methods since 1936. Then there was his seismograph embedded in concrete, and five clocks sending out automatic time signals accurate to a five-hundred-thousandth of a second. Upstairs were hundreds of seismograph charts showing earthquakes of the last twenty years all over the world. I think he looked on them rather as a child looks upon, say, tame guinea pigs. Drawing one out he gazed at it almost with pride.

'Now there is a *very* fine earthquake,' he said.

Much of his research had been devoted to cyclones—or typhoons or tornadoes or hurricanes, according to locality, for they are all the same thing—and one discovery he had made, though of little satisfaction to ships, was of great interest to aircraft, namely that no cyclone had ever been higher than four kilometres, or about thirteen thousand feet. In other words, while ships had to run for their lives, aircraft could 'rise above it'. He showed us a picture, taken from a United States cruiser, of a seventy-foot wave in an otherwise dead calm in the exact centre of a cyclone, and a terrifying sight it was. The wave broke only sixty yards from the ship, he said.

Chinese National Airlines, to whom he was official adviser, and men like Captain Schofield in a less official way, all relied on Father Gherzi for their 'Met.' service, local facilities being somewhat less reliable—more, in fact, on a par with the Chinese lighthouse-keeper who, on being charged to record the passage of ships past his lighthouse, methodically passed away the time by recording the next two years' quota in advance!

We spent a good deal of time with Father Gherzi after our conducted tour of the observatory, and as I sat listening to this extraordinary man, puffing away at his chain of cigarettes and talking of the war, of the Chinese, of East and West, and their changing relationships, and the accumulated experience of his last twenty years, I knew that here was a man I should never forget.

THE HOUSE OF COMMONS

'Hon. and Gallant'

Standing for Parliament is one of those experiences upon which almost every one, at some period of his life, has allowed his imagination to dwell.

The usual procedure is that the local selection committee, from the numerous applications they will have received, choose a short list of, say, half a dozen or more, whom they wish to interview in person. In my own case, let me at once confess that I should have been gratified enough, first time of asking, to achieve a place on this short list. At Acton, I later learned, there were upwards of forty applicants, of whom the selection committee decided to interview nine. It was with no small delight therefore, that I received a notice from W. J. Twidell, agent to Norman Bower, M.P. for Harrow, who was to handle the by-election, requesting me to present myself before the selection committee, 'with your wife, if you are married,' at eight o'clock the following Thursday.

My wife and I duly presented ourselves at the headquarters of the Acton Conservative Party, a blacked-out shop in the High Street opposite the police station, and spent a few nervous minutes in conversation with Twidell (whose name rhymed with 'idle'), while the inquisition upon the previous candidate was concluded in the inner sanctum. He emerged at last—looking a little pale, I thought—and we found ourselves confronting a committee of four men and four women and, behind the desk, John Kent.

John Kent, as I soon came to learn, was a local 'character'. Every one knew John Kent. He was chairman of the Willesden bench of magistrates, and, the police told me, the best they ever had. He was short and bespectacled, and used to wear a black hat perched with a defiant air on the top of his head. Seventy-four summers, an early apprenticeship with Messrs. Whitbread, and years as a magistrate, had given him a tolerant, if cynical, understanding of the frailties of humankind. He had a ve-ry—er—de-liberate way of—er—speaking. I formed the opinion, and later had cause to confirm it, that there were very few flies on John Kent.

'Now,' he said, 'perhaps you will be so good as to tell us why it is that you wish to be the Member of Parli–a–ment for Acton.'

It is a formidable business to try to condense such a subject into one half-hour, including time for questions at the end; to make all the points you meant to make, yet not to say too much. I will not go into this significant half-hour in detail. Suffice to say that I was given—no doubt, like the others—a most friendly hearing, and answered to the best of my ability half a dozen questions or so. Had I any big industrial interests? Alas, no (the right answer, as it turned out). Why did I pick upon Acton? Had I any experience with hecklers ('You'll get plenty of them here!') and so on.

At last it was over, and the committee went off to their suppers, and my wife and I across to the 'King's Head' to bolster the morale and celebrate the fact that, come what might, we had achieved the short list and a number of eminent gentlemen had not. I felt that I had said what I had meant to say, had had a fair hearing, and no complaints. We could hardly expect to be at the top of the list. On the other hand, I did not see why we should be completely at the bottom. We went our respective ways, my wife back to the night shift at the B.B.C., and I to Anti-Aircraft Command to wrestle with the complexities of scientific research.

For two or three days nothing happened, and I scanned the newspapers for a small paragraph announcing that some vile fellow had been selected as Conservative candidate at Acton. No news was good news and I possessed my soul in patience. It was late on Saturday evening that I had just potted the last black in a game of snooker when one of the mess stewards put his head round the door and said: 'Captain Longhurst on the telephone, please.' I went across the passage to the little telephone box. It was Twidell.

'Congratulations,' he said. 'Unanimous!'

People talk of being 'struck dumb'—'unable to believe the evidence of their ears', etc. I now have more sympathy with them. There was a long pause.

'Why, didn't you expect it?' said Twidell.

'When can you start? Can you come over on Monday morning?' he went on.

The implications of what I had undertaken began to dawn on me and, as people do at points of crisis in their own little affairs, I wanted to be alone. I wandered out into the rose garden and gazed across the fields lying peaceful in the moonlight below. I thought of some words of Lord Woolton, who had just been appointed Minister of Reconstruction. 'I feel humbled by my responsibility,' he was quoted as saying. The words had struck me as curious at the time. Now, in my very small way, I knew what he meant.

I returned to the mess to reveal my strange secret and order drinks all round.

On Monday I duly reported for duty. The shop had been transformed into an office and a tremendous air of hustle and bustle—I will not say confusion—prevailed. Envelopes had appeared by the thousand and volunteers, mostly women, were busy at trestle tables addressing them from pages torn from the voting register. I was introduced to innumerable folk who wished me well and whose names I did my best to memorize. I was the object of much critical, though I am sure friendly, scrutiny, and felt rather like the 'condemned man'.

It does not take you long, when you are a parliamentary candidate for the first time, to realize that, though you may technically be the central figure in the picture, you are, in fact, small fry beside the agent. He is the real master of ceremonies. He alone knows the tricks of the trade, the organization, the cost, the procedure. There are many pitfalls into which the candidate may unwittingly fall, from casually buying a beer for a voter in the pub (which is sufficient to disqualify him) to failing to produce various documents at the right time at the town hall. The agent is not only the candidate's guide, philosopher and friend, but a combination of bodyguard, nursemaid and manager as well. When disaster seems to threaten, he encourages his man with tales of hideous things which occurred at previous elections within his experience—and yet his man got in. If his man appears to be verging on the over-confident, he applies the corresponding antidote. He stands between his man and a stream of visitors and deputations, advising him which to see and which are no good to him. It is impossible to conceive winning a hard election without the aid of a competent agent. A candidate can, I fancy, nominate himself as his own agent, but he needs a very safe seat to afford the economy—or luxury—of doing so.

It may be merely a sentimental gratitude that makes me feel that Twidell must have been one of the best election agents in the country, but I do not think so. It was his twenty-second election, and it was encouraging to think that he had only lost two. His comfortable figure and walrus moustache, surmounted by a villainous felt hat beside which the one I had dug up from the blitzed ruins of my civilian clothing resembled something out of a Lincoln and Bennett catalogue, gave him a welcome air of solidity and confidence. Whatever went wrong, he had always known worse.

There were at first ten candidates in the field. Though it was obvious that many of them would not eventually, in racing parlance, come under starter's orders, this fact, and the nearness of Acton to Fleet Street, was useful in attracting the notice of the press to the election. One candidate was a Mr. Owen. I forget what he stood for—I am not sure that he did not claim to represent the old-age pensioners—but he was a curious and entertaining figure and added much to the gaiety of the proceedings by walking about with a crate-like affair on his head, plastered with bills. With a faithful hound at his heels he marched rapidly about the streets, handing out tracts. In the local press he inserted odd advertisements advising the people of Acton to 'Store Potatoes Now. Under the Bed is a Good Place'. I ran across him in the market-place one day, and he complained that bills of mine had been plastered over his. Having made up my mind that there should be positively no dirty work on our side, I was a little concerned and promised to set things right. It turned out that they were our sites anyway. It was no surprise when Mr. Owen did not stand in the end, but I was glad not to have missed him.

Under the conditions of the party election truce, the constituency having previously been represented by a Conservative, the Labour Party, though they had a candidate-elect in Joe Sparks, a member of the local council and of the National Union of Railwaymen, did not enter the field. I did entertain the pious hope that since I supported the combined National Government of which the Socialists were a part (I called myself 'National Government and Conservative') they might lend their support, at the same time reserving the right to withdraw it the moment we returned to party politics, but I found that local differences on the council had reached such a point of acerbity as to rule out any possibility of co-operation. The Socialists recommended their followers to abstain from voting and 'keep their powder dry for the next election'.

In the end, the field resolved itself into four: Walter Padley, a twenty-seven-year-old 'political organizer' of the Independent Labour Party, those delightful citizens who held that we were fighting a 'capitalist–imperialist' war and that it was therefore no concern of theirs; Miss Dorothy Crisp, whose vigorous articles in the *Sunday Dispatch* had been attracting notice (though not, I fancy, so much as she had banked upon); Edward Godfrey, who proclaimed himself a 'British Nationalist'; and myself.

Padley had twice gone before conscientious objectors' tribunals and been turned down. Eventually he was hauled before a medical board, who decided that he was unfit anyway. He would obviously attract a great deal of the Socialist vote, and it may, perhaps, be chalked up to my credit that I never used these facts against him.

Miss Crisp, a lady with a ready pen and a lively intelligence, looked a more serious proposition—a 'vote splitter' if ever there was one. She had been one of the unsuccessful applicants for the honour that had eventually fallen to me, and it seemed to be accepting defeat with a rather ill grace when she decided to stand as an 'Independent Conservative'. We felt rather badly about this at the time, and I permitted myself to make the only personal 'crack' of the campaign at her expense. She lived in the May Fair Hotel and I referred to her, ungallantly but with a certain degree of wit, as 'the nightingale from Berkeley Square who wants to sing in Acton'. In the *Star* she had said: 'I have very definite ideas on how this country should be run, and I must put them over or burst'. We determined that it should be the latter. As to my wife, she could be galvanized into sheer frenzy at the very name of our female rival. (Let me add that we were all photographed shaking hands at the end and all was well!)

Of Edward Godfrey we knew practically nothing.

These were the four who turned up at the town hall on nomination day, accompanied by their agents and armed with their nomination papers and their £150 deposits. No cheques are accepted, and you have to bring the money in cash—though I noticed that it was returned by cheque! To get it back you have to poll one-eighth of the total votes cast.

By the time I arrived and set to work, much of the preliminary organization had been done by Twidell. Committee rooms had been arranged in various parts of the division, generally the front parlour in the house of some supporter, and halls had been booked for meetings. A by-election, hectic though it may be, can be conducted almost at ease by comparison with a general election, when it is 'every man for himself'. The resources of the party headquarters can be centred upon the one field of battle instead of being spread thinly over several hundred individual fights all over the country. The central office had sent down two or three regular agents, together with three more who were learning the business. Sir Robert Topping, director-general of the Conservative Party, came down and gave the benefit of his advice and encouragement. We were certainly not short of assistance—except that however hard the volunteers worked away at the envelopes, even taking them home to carry on in the evenings, the heaps of those yet to be addressed seemed as inexhaustible as the widow's cruse. One of the most assiduous of the volunteers was an old lady of eighty-seven.

She turned up every day without fail, handled a hundred envelopes or more, either addressing or, in the agents' jargon, 'stuffing' them—that is, inserting the election addresses—and used to ask punctually at five every day whether she 'could go now'. On being released, she made a point of kissing the candidate.

A wartime election lacked the more boisterous elements of the same affair in peacetime—for which the candidates, if not the public, might be grateful. There were none of the surging mobs, the hooliganism, the torchlight processions through the streets, which have characterized some elections in the past. Tomatoes and eggs were too precious to hurl at luckless fellows who had presumed to offer themselves for public service.

We held meetings, of course, but they were sparsely attended, and one could be excused for feeling that one was addressing the local reporter rather than the remainder of the audience. Our rivals fared, if anything, worse, and small audiences were no cause for alarm. It would have taken Churchill himself to fill a hall in the December black-out.

First in order of importance, in my own opinion, is the election address, of which a copy may be sent post-free to every citizen on the electoral register. With an out-of-date register and evacuations by the thousand, a great proportion of these election addresses were bound to miss the mark—the target having literally vanished—but, broadly speaking, everyone present in the division and entitled to vote ought to receive one. It is the only direct approach from the candidate to every citizen, and if it is made readable, not filled with long strings of political jargon, it must surely be the chief weapon in his armoury. My own did not take long to write. How many times, as I walked through the birch wood and across the fields from the headquarters to the mess each day, had my mind turned upon what I wanted to say in such a document if ever the chance arose! Now it had come, and the election address, at least, was ready made. We put photographs of myself on the front, and wife and children on the back—we all came out rather black and dingy on the cheap wartime paper—and the text, mercifully, met with the approval of the experts. Indeed, Beverley Baxter, M.P., was kind enough to inspire the *Evening Standard* to say that it was a 'brisk and vigorous Tory document'.

After the election address one's principal approach to the electorate is, or may be, through the press. In Acton we were lucky in having a truly local paper, the *Acton Gazette*. The paper gave a fair deal to every candidate, and for four successive issues carried almost exclusively news of the election, together with the advertisements of the candidates. We had a quarter-page each week, and, looking back on them, I think they were quite effective.

I had a mild apprehension lest, having achieved some small distinction in the parochial sphere of writing about the game of golf, I might in the national press be branded to my detriment as nothing but a 'golfer'. These fears did my colleagues in Fleet Street less than justice and, aided by the 'ten little nigger boys' aspect of the early stages of the election, we received a very fair notice indeed—even if the earliest notice of them all did confine itself to saying that, if elected, I should probably win the Parliamentary golf handicap!

The only jarring note came from a London paper whose editor appeared unable to believe that I could have achieved such prominence without influential 'backers'. Who were they? Favourite selections appeared to be General Critchley, Mr. Oliver Lyttelton (now Lord Chandos) and Lord Beaverbrook. Mercifully he telephoned to 'confirm' a paragraph suggesting the names of these gentlemen. I was able to assure him that General Critchley was abroad, and had not the remotest idea that I had even applied to be among those considered at Acton; Mr. Oliver Lyttelton I had not seen for three years, Lord Beaverbrook for the best part of five. The search went on, and the sleuths arrived next at the name of Lord Brabazon. This time they did not risk 'confirming' the story, since Lord Brabazon declared that he had never spoken to a soul in Acton. However, the paragraph appeared, headed 'Sponsor at Acton'. Lord Brabazon, it said, was not exactly my sponsor, but had often encouraged me to stand and 'thought I would be a very good candidate', which was nice. I had, the paragraph went on, 'made several applications to other constituencies, and had more than once been on the short list', which was, of course, wholly untrue.

Other weapons in one's electoral artillery are, thank heaven, more directly under one's control. Bills and posters, for instance. There are those who say that their chief use is to draw the attention of the citizens to the fact that there is an election at all, and that the mere repetition of 'Vote for ——', with no reasons given, is sufficient for this purpose. I took a rather higher view of the political intelligence of the citizens. I said that it was throwing opportunity away if we could think of nothing better to put on a bill than 'Vote for Longhurst'. So our bills, to take one or two at random, bore such legends as: 'Churchill has been to Persia for you. What will you do for him?' The answer, we suggested, was to vote for Longhurst. As a final shot, we issued fine double-sized bills: 'Churchill asks YOU to vote for Longhurst.' They hit people plumb in the eye and were very effective.

Many of the bills had the doubtful advantage of having a large reproduction of the candidate's photograph. We were pasting the first one up proudly outside the office when a lady passed by with a perambulator. She stopped and gazed.

' 'Bin all right if they'd left the face off!' she said, and passed on.

Then there were window cards and what the agents, in their hard-hearted way, call 'throw-away cards'. The former, as their name suggests, are hung in the front window by supporters, and a warming sight it is to see a road nicely 'hung' with your own cards. It is liable, however, to be a short-lived satisfaction, as the next road is almost certain to be festooned with those of your opponents. The 'throw-aways' are about the size of playing cards and carry the candidate's photograph, together with a simple exhortation to the recipient to vote for him. They are handed to all and sundry at all times.

A supporter was handing them out in the High Street one morning.

'Excuse me, madam,' he said to a lady passing by. 'Are you interested in the Acton by-election?'

'Certainly I am,' the lady replied. 'I am Mrs. John Kent.'

Children were particularly keen on these cards and crowded round to receive them. We were gratified at their early interest in the government of their country and used to tell them to take the cards home to Mum and Dad. One evening a most respectable citizen appeared and asked for me. He was flourishing a throw-away card.

'Are you aware, sir,' he said, 'that this card was brought by a boy to 44 —— Gardens this evening?'

I said that I was not, but that it was more than likely. He had taken the card, it seemed, and the following had ensued:

'Penny, please.'

The gentleman handed over the penny (they say there is one born every minute!)

'By the way where does the money go?'

'Oh, it goes to 'Enry Long'urst.'

'Oh, and what does he do with it?'

'Er . . . he takes it to the bank.'

That boy will go far!

Midway in the campaign there was handed to us by a telegraph boy what I hoped would prove to be an 'ace of spades'. Looking back, I think it probably did. It was a telegram from Mr. Churchill. The original hangs framed in the room in which I do my work, and I think it is my most treasured possession. It reads:

I am very glad that a young serving officer should offer himself as National Government candidate in the Acton division. As we approach the most crucial stage of the war in Europe our responsibilities do not diminish but increase. I have no hesitation therefore in asking the electors of the Acton division to give you their vote and thereby proclaim their unabated confidence in the Government which has seen the country through the most perilous years in its history. Britain stands high in the world's esteem today and the continued support of the nation united behind its National Government is vital, not only to ensure victory but to make it fruitful and lasting.

WINSTON S. CHURCHILL.

It was reprinted on bills; I showed it, with legitimate pride, I think, to all and sundry; and I read it several times a day by means of the next weapon in our armoury—the roving loudspeaker.

Here, having done a good deal of broadcasting, including not a few running commentaries, I ought to have been thoroughly at home. Strangely, I was not. I was extremely embarrassed, at least at first. I have a very strong respect for the rights of privacy. I hate public noises. I loathe aeroplanes trailing banners in the public sky—indeed, I have made a point of avoiding any article thus brought to my notice—and posters defiling the beauty of the countryside, and loudspeakers that blare over people's back gardens. It seemed at first that to stand in a crowded street and inflict politics upon people by means of a loud-speaker might be held to come in the same category. On reflection I am satisfied that it does not, and that it is the duty of a candidate to draw public attention to his views by whatever means may be available. Nevertheless, my first reaction was one of unwarranted intrusion and I shall not forget the feelings with which I stood at a roundabout on Western Avenue and delivered my first harangue. I still think of it whenever I pass the spot.

Spurred on, however, by Twidell who had no such squeamish sentiments regarding the electors, and encouraged by Mr. Boddy, of Fulham, who ran the loudspeaker car, I soon got into my stride, and in the end needed no prodding to induce me to 'give them a last shout before we go home'. The people upon whom this was inflicted will forgive me, I am sure, if I say that the position in which we liked to catch them was standing in a queue. There is something inexorable about a queue. The technique is to stop up-wind and deliver at a range of about fifty yards. They can't fail to hear. They can't answer back.

They can't move. They may shuffle a bit and pretend not to notice—and a very proper English reaction, too!—but there is nothing they can do about it. We came to know what time of day the most profitable queues were likely to form, and where; and shamelessly I am afraid we acted accordingly. Even to this day, when I see a nice long queue I am reluctant to pass by without giving it the benefit of a few well-chosen words!

On the whole, there was little dirty work. Padley got hold, from the library no doubt, of a copy of my inoffensive book, *It was Good while it Lasted*, and one morning we arrived to find the place festooned with posters shouting: 'Longhurst feasted with the Nazis! Millions of bottles of champagne . . . !' etc., etc. 'Good Lord!' I thought. 'When was that?' It was based, we found, on a chapter describing a visit to Germany before the war, including a call at Herr Henkell's champagne cellars at Wiesbaden. There is no doubt that this scurrilous attack did us harm, if only in the eyes of people who believe that most pernicious of all proverbs: 'There's no smoke without fire,' but, as Lord Vansittart has said, 'Everyone must expect his share of the knocks in controversy, and no one should resent being hit below the belt by those who can reach no higher.' William Barkley wrote a good lampoon in the *Daily Express* ridiculing this sort of electioneering, ending with the words: 'Oh, that mine enemy had written a book!'

(In the general election Sparks, the Communist-Socialist candidate, solemnly trotted this all out again, by leaflets and loud-speaker, the inference being that I was not a 'proved anti-Fascist'. Seeing that his own agent had been pleading for a negotiated peace in 1940, this struck me as a shade over the odds. Such, however, is politics.)

Then there were the kind folk who wrote to the Labour Party to inform them that they knew me, that I 'had Fascist tendencies' and 'had spoken disrespectfully of the Red Army', etc. What was in the mind of these gentlemen I honestly cannot say—but I should still like to meet them one day.

And then, of course, there was the little matter of our bills being pasted over with those of one of our rivals one night. Our bill-poster, a man with one arm and a wide vocabulary, was almost speechless. All he could do was to mutter: 'There won't be one there tomorrow. There won't be one there tomorrow!' Late that night, just as we were leaving, he reappeared.

'Come outside,' he said.

In the back of his little van was a heap of bills four feet high, still damp and sticky. When dawn came, our original bills held the field.

The election lasted only three weeks, but by that time both I and my wife, who had worked with great enthusiasm and been a tremendous asset, felt that another week would have finished us. Captain Harold Balfour, M.P., Under Secretary of State for Air, came down and spoke on the eve of the poll and next day Twidell and I made the traditional round of the polling stations. The poll, on account of the out-of-date register, was obviously going to be small, but so far as could be judged it was going fairly well and it warmed the heart to see so many of the polling cards we had sent out with the election addresses lying about the booths. At last, at nine o'clock, the last ballot paper was in, the ballot-boxes were sealed and carted away to the town hall and we retired for refreshment, knowing at least that no further efforts on anyone's part could alter our fate.

Next morning we all presented ourselves—candidates, wives, agents, supporters, officials, and hangers-on—at the Central Hall, Acton, to witness the counting of the votes. The black ballot boxes with their pink ribbons and seals were stacked on one side of the hall, and round the edges, horseshoe fashion, was a line of trestle tables. Admission is by ticket only, and once you are in, you are not allowed to leave. The counters of the votes sit on the inside of the horseshoe, and the 'scrutineers' to see fair play, watch them from the other side. Each group is supplied with a boxful of ballot papers which they sort into piles. The candidates, avoiding each other at first, peer over the shoulders of the counters with an air of disinterested confidence to see how their respective piles are growing. They come to know how the prisoner feels as he waits in his cell when the jury have retired to consider their verdict.

A really close count must be a nightmare: a recount sheer mental murder. For myself I missed a certain amount of thrill because I developed the symptoms of incipient 'flu—the dullness of mind, the general apathy, and what they call in the north a 'thrutched-up' feeling in the head. Even so, it was exciting enough. Peering over the shoulders of a counter as he sorts the papers, you see 'Longhurst, Longhurst, Longhurst, Longhurst', and make a mental note how satisfactory it is to stand in a constituency of such politically enlightened citizens. Wandering further, you see, 'Padley, Crisp, Padley, Padley, Godfrey, Padley', and wonder what can be the future of England under a democracy composed, it would appear, almost wholly of illiterates.

As the piles grow, they are sorted into bundles of fifty and placed on a table in the centre, and here is the real weather-gauge of the candidates' fortunes. You have the right to go through the piles searching for papers wrongly inserted, but the' chances are just as strong that you will find one of somebody else's in your pile as one of yours in somebody else's, and it is on the whole a profitless business. Both Twidell, however, and Padley's bearded agent appeared to think it worth while, and they spent much time in ferreting about among each other's piles, with ill-veiled sneers upon their faces. The only major success, let it be conceded, went to Padley's agent, but it was a two-edged triumph. He found a batch of fifty wrongly included in our quota. Unfortunately they were Crisp's.

I fell into conversation with Godfrey and spent much time with him. For myself I knew nothing about him, though much play had been made (not by me) of his alleged 'Fascist background'. To do him justice, I can only say that he expressed opinions of a strongly forthright English character and we got on well together, linked by a common dislike of Padley and all he stood for. Eventually the ice was broken with Miss Crisp, too, and even my wife was soon talking in an animated and amiable way with her. Godfrey, Crisp, and Longhurst, for all their political differences, at least had it in common that they believed it to be 'their' war. It was, in fact, Padley versus the rest, and I think we would gladly have pooled our votes to keep him out.

As the piles began to mass on the centre table, we gradually took the lead. There were checks and set-backs, but we kept ahead and with a furlong to go, so to speak, it was pretty clear that only some hideous disaster could keep us out. Twidell, bustling round and making extraordinary, and inaccurate, calculations on the backs of envelopes, reached the stage of forecasting not only the result but the majority, while I disappeared periodically behind a curtain to fortify myself with a swig from a bottle of influenza mixture. Padley was running a clear second, but Miss Crisp was upsetting the book of form by amassing a very small total beside what we, and indeed she herself, had had cause to forecast. Godfrey was clearly due to forfeit his deposit.

The instructions to voters in every polling booth were plain, one would have thought, beyond the powers of a lunatic to misunderstand. You put one cross on your paper, and only one. Yet a steady flow of spoiled or doubtful papers was trickling along to the Town Clerk's table at the foot of the platform. There must have been a hundred or more. Some had two crosses against one name. Some had crosses against different names. One or two had crosses against three names, while others had no mark whatever. One wondered what was the mentality of the individual who trapesed all the way to a polling station on a miserable December day to insert a blank paper in a ballot box.

Not all were disqualified. We assembled to watch the Town Clerk, as recording officer, adjudicate upon 'doubtfuls'. He allowed the ones with two crosses against one name, disqualified others. 'Good for Padley,' he would say. 'Bad. Good for Longhurst. Good for Crisp. Bad. . . .'

The result had become virtually a certainty, though the count was by no means over (I reckoned that we were 'dormy'), when a reporter from one of the news agencies came and asked for a 'message' on my victory. 'Not on your life!' I said, touching wood hastily. He argued and cajoled, and, knowing his problem from personal experience, I eventually agreed, pledging him under all manner of forefeits not only to hold the message till the result was announced, but, in the event of my losing, never to reveal to a soul that I had issued a message at all. I dictated in a quiet corner a message about 'this splendid majority being Acton's Christmas present to Mr. Churchill. . . .'

It was all over at last. I shook hands with the sheriff, Sir John Catlow, who was to announce the result.

'Delighted to come along,' he said. 'As a matter of fact, it has got me off a hanging!'

He mounted the platform, followed by the Town Clerk and the candidates, and rather as one in a dream I took the winner's traditional place, amid some friendly cheers, on his right hand. Padley, as runner-up, sat on his left, and beyond him Miss Crisp and Godfrey, each of whom had lost their £150. I recall the unworthy thought passing through my head that it was a pity these affairs were not run on the basis of 'winner take all'!

Sir John Catlow announced that there had been an election in the Acton Division of Middlesex and that the following was the result:

LONGHURST	5014
PADLEY	2336
CRISP	707
GODFREY	258
Majority	2678

I made a short speech, thanking the various folk who had done the work of organizing the election—not forgetting the police, who had stood guarding the polling booths with a finely impartial air in the perishing cold—and Padley said he was glad there was such a good minority in Acton in favour of 'international Socialism'. We came down from the platform, and there was much handshaking and patting on the back for my wife and myself from well-wishers, whose congratulations were all the more acceptable for the fact that they had only known us for three weeks. Twidell said he had 'never had a moment's doubt', and John Kent wore a suitably truculent air as though challenging any man to question the result. For myself, I felt I could sleep for twenty-four hours.

We were escorted away to the Conservative Club to celebrate. As we left the hall, Padley and a group of young gentlemen in macintoshes, long hair, and coloured scarves were engaged in singing 'The Red Flag'. Even in the hour of success, I fear that my heart did not warm to them. The *Evening News* took photographs of myself and Miss Crisp shaking hands, and all was over.

New Boy in the House

Every newspaper reader is familiar with the picture of the traffic in Westminster being held up to enable the new Member to cross the road and take his seat in the House of Commons for the first time. There can hardly be any one who has not, on seeing the picture, carried his thoughts along with this solitary figure and wondered exactly what happens to him when he gets inside. For myself, on the singular and unforgettable day when I experienced it, there was no traffic, and I don't think the war reserve policeman would have seen fit to hold it up if there had been. I presented myself, accompanied by my wife in her Sunday best, at the St. Stephen's entrance.

'Yes, sir?' said the policeman.

'I'm the new boy,' I said, or words to that effect.

He bowed kindly, and a photographer took pictures of us shaking hands.

'I suppose you're getting used to this sort of thing by now,' I remarked.

'Oh, yes,' said the policeman. 'Must have done it a couple of hundred times by now, sir.'

He ushered us in, got a temporary pass for my wife, and handed us over to a House of Commons messenger. We marched along St. Stephen's Hall, under which Guy Fawkes manipulated his unsuccessful gunpowder treason and plot. With a hasty glance at the statues of Charles James Fox, Pitt, and the rest, looking down from their pedestals on either side, I fortified myself with the thought that they, too, were new boys in their day. On the left was a boarded-up temporary office.

'Our Home Guard headquarters,' said the messenger. He was a corporal, he added, and some of the Members were privates in his section.

We came through to the Lobby, after introduction to the policeman at the door, and the messenger escorted me to the Members' cloak-room. This involves about half a day's journey down passages and cloisters, down the stairs, and round a few more corridors. I defy any man not to be lost at his first attempt. Indeed, as a fellow Member assured me, 'If you find your way about in a week, you will be doing uncommonly well.'

Next visit in the procedure of initiation is to the Whips' office (what you do if you are an Independent, I do not know). Here another kindly welcome was waiting—and heaven knows what a lot that means! They presented me with my Writ. The Writ to the new Member is what the ring is to the best man at a wedding. It was only a document showing that there had been a by-election at Acton, and that Henry Carpenter Longhurst had been elected—but it was impressed upon me by everyone I met in the next hour that I was as nothing without it. Like the best man with the ring, I put the Writ in a pocket that I do not habitually use, in order to make quite sure of its whereabouts—and then, every few minutes, clutched feverishly at the familiar pockets, found that it wasn't there, concluded that I had lost it, found it in the special pocket, transferred it to another one— and then repeated the process over again.

A new Member is presented to the House with a special drill. He is escorted, in the normal way, by the Chief Whip of the party he represents on his right, and a Member of his own choosing on his left. They assemble at the bar of the House—which is just a strip on the floor at the end opposite the Speaker—bow; take seven paces forward, starting with the left foot; bow; take seven more paces; halt; and bow again. It was not long, therefore, before three figures were to be seen rehearsing in an uninhabited corridor near the whips' office, solemnly bowing to no one in particular, advancing seven paces, bowing again, and so on. All very much like the 'prisoner and escort' who are to be seen in another sphere of life, marching into any regimental orderly room.

In my own case the sponsors were James Stuart, Chief Whip of the Conservative Party, and Peter Thorneycroft, who was then Member for Stafford. We duly assembled on the big red settee at the end of the Chamber, which is technically outside the House, and waited for our cue, my wife watching the proceedings from the Speaker's gallery. We were joined by Mr. James Maxton of the Independent Labour Party, whose candidate had run second in the by-election in which I had been elected. Like everyone else, he offered the 'new boy' a warm welcome—at the same time telling me of all the things he had been telling the electors of Acton to induce them to elect somebody else.

At last Question Time was over, but there was something to come, more important than the introduction of a new Member. The House was fairly full, and the press and public galleries were packed. (Incidentally they look so steep from down below that you can hardly see how people don't topple down on to the head of the Speaker underneath.) Anyway, Mr. Attlee, the Deputy Prime Minister, got up and said: 'I have a statement to make to the House',—and then read out the dramatic news of Mr. Churchill's illness.

Our turn came at last. The Speaker, a remote figure in a long grey wig, rose at the far end of the Chamber and said: 'Members wishing to take their seats will now come to the table.'

We advanced to the bar and formed ourselves up. 'Now,' whispered the Chief Whip out of the corner of his mouth. We bowed, and the ordeal was on. I like to think, in view of the mess that is sometimes made of it, that we got through the drill fairly well. At any rate, two sets of seven paces and three bows brought us duly to the table.

Here the sponsors fade away, and the new Member is left alone in the world, trying to take in all at once a series of pictures and emotions that can come to a man only once in a lifetime. The clerk at the table, taking the Writ, proffered a Testament and a rather frayed copy of the oath. I remember, holding the Testament in one hand and the oath in the other, reading: 'I, Henry Carpenter Longhurst, do swear, That I will be faithful and bear true Allegiance to His Majesty King George, His Heirs and Successors, according to the Law.'

Stepping over the distinguished ankles protruding from the Front Bench—among them Mr. Eden's—I recall, after a slight disagreement with the clerk as to the date, signing a vast vellum book at the top of a new page, amid cries of 'Hear, hear!' from both sides of the House. If there were also undertones of 'Who is it?' from one or two Members, well, what of it? Members who have sat in the House for many years may have forgotten how much that traditional 'Hear, hear!' of welcome means to the new boy. I shall never forget. I was to see many new Members introduced later, some of them to represent views which I abhor, but in gratitude I never failed to join in the chorus of welcome.

Having signed the book, I remember passing along beside the table to shake hands with the Speaker, leaning down from his high chair with another smile of welcome, and thence out of the House to make my way to the Strangers' Bar, a pleasant room overlooking the Thames, to celebrate with my wife and Peter Thorneycroft an occasion never to be repeated, never to be forgotten.

Later in the day there arrived an even newer Member than myself, and it made me feel quite an old hand to share with him the very limited knowledge I had accumulated. He was Captain Stanley Prescott, who had been elected, amid scenes of much excitement, for

Darwen. He told me how, at the first count, he was in by sixty. They counted again and he was out by five. Next time he was out by seven. When they added it up again, he was in by sixty odd. The fifth time he was in by seventy, so at last, as it was past two in the morning, they called it a day, and off he went to the House of Commons.

Prescott and I made further explorations together. We went to see the Serjeant-at-Arms, for instance. I rather felt that the bearer of such an impressive title ought to have a uniform rather like the Beefeaters' in the Tower of London, but in fact, he is represented by an ordinary person like the rest of us, sitting in a snug little office with a coal fire, right in the heart of the Palace of Westminster. He sold us some stationery and a copy of *Vacher's*, the *Who's Who* of Parliament, and allotted us each a locker, the particulars of which he wrote down in the sort of little notebook that you can see any day in any quartermaster's store. My locker was No. 22, handily next door to the tape machine and the Smoking Room.

House of Commons stationery was then of rather an 'austerity' character—which was as it should be—but I defy any man not to experience something of an inward thrill as he writes his first letter on it. My own went to an old-age pensioner in the constituency who had sent me a Christmas card.

Later in the day there came the question of going and taking one's seat in the House itself. To tell the truth, I was a good bit more nervous about this than about making the original bow to the Speaker. I don't know why, because there is nothing to it really—but that is what I found. People often ask me: 'Do you have a seat allotted to you?' The answer, of course, is: 'No, you don't.' For most of the day the majority of members are working elsewhere, on committees, in ministries, or merely earning their own living, and any Chamber that held the whole 615 would give an appalling feeling of emptiness except on the very rare occasions when it was full. The present Chamber, which, before the original was blitzed, was the House of Lords, held about 300, I should say. Apart from the Front Bench and one or two other special places with traditional occupants, you sit wherever you find a vacant seat.

There were plenty that afternoon when I slipped quietly into the far end of the House and sat myself down on a deserted red plush bench. It was the last day before the Christmas recess, when, I gathered, a certain spirit of levity and irrelevance was always allowed to colour the proceedings. Members will not accuse me of disrespect when I say that really it was very much like the last day of the Christmas term at school. People were taking the chance of holding forth on their pet subjects and the term was brought to a close by a lively, lower-form act in which Captain Cunningham Reid, the member for Marylebone, pressed for action in the distressing case of a young lady called Mary, and Miss Ellen Wilkinson pithily explained why it was that the Home Secretary proposed to take no further steps in the matter.

Many of the impressions of that day vanished with the increasing familiarity with the life into which it ushered me. Some remain. One was the vividness of the sensation of being back in one's schooldays as a new boy—fear of 'doing the wrong thing', fear of not paying appropriate respect to the 'upper school', fear of addressing the head-master by the wrong title, being given a locker and key, and so on; but, above all, the incredible friendliness of the place. Everyone anxious to help, irrespective of their political complexion. Every one saying: 'Now, if there is anything I can do, don't hesitate,' etc. I sensed in a moment that there was no place in the world like the House of Commons.

Maiden Speech

I defy any member of any parliament in living history to declare that he was completely confident and at ease as he sat in the House waiting to make his maiden speech. All the same it is a tremendous thrill. You know that, for what it is worth, it is a milestone in your own little history. In a few minutes you will have joined that select band of citizens who on their deathbeds can say: 'Well, at least I once addressed the House of Commons!'

I remember being told: 'The Speaker hopes he will be able to call you at about two o'clock.' Obviously, that meant no lunch. One can't risk the brain being dulled by the processes of digestion. A large pink gin seemed indicated instead. This was duly sent down, followed by another, engendering a well-known, if wholly illusory, feeling of confidence.

I think I knew my humble words pretty well by heart—most 'maiden' speakers would admit to that—but I took the precaution of getting them typed out and cut up into small sheets, to fall back upon in the event of that nightmare of orators and broadcasters, the total 'black-out'. Clutching them in moistened palm, I took my seat on the third bench below the gangway—and from that moment all trace of them vanished from the memory.

Not only could I not remember what I wanted to say: I could not even remember what it was about. Something to do with America— or something. Hastily re-reading the first paragraph, I essayed a desperate silent rehearsal, but concentration is impossible when some-one else is addressing the House. Three-quarters of your attention is lured away towards what he is saying. I confess that unworthy thoughts of another pink gin flashed across my mind; to be succeeded by the delicious idea of slipping out of the Chamber and postponing the whole ghastly business to a more favourable occasion.

The previous speaker sat down and, rather as the bather plunges into the pool after testing it with his toe and finding it even colder than he had dared to contemplate, I recall rising to my feet. Rarely in the history of Parliament would an Hon. Member have been happier not be catch the Speaker's eye. Memories came surging back of the old days on a more humble back bench, when one had not prepared the over-night translation and the baleful eye of the headmaster searched the class for the next victim. 'Captain Longhurst,' said the same kind of voice. This was it.

Perhaps the shock cleared the brain. At any rate, I will say no more of my own maiden speech than that I remembered what I wanted to say, and then, for what it was worth, said it. I don't think it altered the course of history, nor did our foreign affairs take a sudden upward turn as a result of it. If it had not the distinction of Lord Birkenhead's maiden oration, well, at least it was not as big a flop as Disraeli's. Perhaps the best thing about it was that it was over!

Acknowledgements and Sources

My publishers and I would like to thank the various copyright holders, publishers and companies who have readily given us permission to reprint extracts from my previously published work. The full list of sources is as follows:

From *Round in Sixty Eight*, and reprinted by permission of T. Werner Laurie Ltd.: Nightmare over Niagara; A Memorable Flight; 'Top of the Mark'; To Hell with Tennessee!; Where Every Prospect Pleases.

From *It Was Good While It Lasted*, and reprinted by permission of J. M. Dent & Sons Ltd.: Fisticuffs in Philadelphia; The Lotus Eater; Raucous Voice in Brooklyn; The Engine and the Fly; Nine Hours to Live (Donovan's account of his experiences in the condemned cell were first printed in the *Sunday Express*); Mutiny on the Moor; Pied Piper, 1940; Episode; Death in the Forest; Queen of them All; *Sic Transit Gloria . . .*; Pre-War Playground.

From the *Daily Sketch*, and reprinted by permission of Associated Newspapers Ltd.: 'Will I Give Ye the Daylight?'

From the *Sunday Times*, and reprinted by permission of Thomson Newspapers Ltd.; Baker Street Revisited; Done it at Last! (© The *Sunday Times* 1961); Much Grousing on the Moor; I Gotta Horse (© The *Sunday Times* 1962).

From *I Wouldn't Have Missed It*, and reprinted by permission of J. M. Dent & Sons Ltd.: All the pieces in SOMETHING OF A SOLDIER and THE HOUSE OF COMMONS.

From *Country Life*, and reprinted by permission of Country Life Ltd.: Foxhunt in Australia; Third Time Lucky; In Praise of Bull Terriers; Shooting Memories; Darkest Africa.

From *You Never Know Till You Get There*, and reprinted by permission of J. M. Dent & Sons Ltd.: 'Getting up' in Nassau; Few, Forgotten and Lonely; Prisoners at Play; Over the Sahara; The Ship that Flies; Life on the Klong; The Old Lancastrian; Splendid Transgressions; A Person of Harmless Delight; Coloured Cities; Jerusalem the Golden; Shambles in Shanghai; Intrepid Aviators; A Day at the Races; Gold Rush; Flying Fish; Chinese Crackers; An Unforgettable Man.